Fresh FROM THE Market

Fresh from the Market

SEASONAL COOKING WITH

LAURENT TOURONDEL

AND CHARLOTTE MARCH

PHOTOGRAPHY BY QUENTIN BACON

WILEY

John Wiley & Sons, Inc.

This book is printed on acid-free paper. ♾

Published by JOHN WILEY & SONS, INC., Hoboken, New Jersey
Published simultaneously in Canada

Designed by ERICA HEITMAN-FORD *for* MUCCA DESIGN
This book was set in Gardner, a serif font created and generously donated by Joshua Darden of Darden Studio.

Library of Congress Cataloging-in-Publication Data:
Tourondel, Laurent.
Fresh from the market / by Laurent Tourondel and Charlotte March.
p. cm.
ISBN 978-0-470-40242-9 (cloth)
1. Cookery, French. 2. Cookery—France—Montluçon. 3. Cookery, International. 4. BLT Market (Restaurant : New York, NY) I. March, Charlotte. II. Title.
TX719.T657 2010
641.5944—dc22
2009028790

Printed in China

10 9 8 7 6 5 4 3 2 1

CONTENTS

FOREWORD

Laurent and I met in the nineties, two Frenchmen living in New York City. We had so much in common: we had both worked in Michelin three-starred kitchens where we learned to cook with the freshest seasonal, local ingredients. We both followed our dreams to New York to cook in our mentors' new restaurants. We both worked to adapt our French techniques to the different ingredients and flavors that we were finding here.

Many years have passed since those early days of C.T. and Cello, but what Laurent has done since then has been remarkable. He opened his first trademark restaurant, BLT Steak, in 2004. Watching him turn one successful restaurant into an empire of starred BLT restaurants has been amazing. I still can't figure out how he managed to do it in less than 6 years.

But it wasn't until Laurent opened BLT Market that I knew he had come home, back to his roots, to make the food that he felt closest to. With this book, he is opening his world of seasonal cooking to all of us at home. His travels, his technique, and his unique way of adapting ideas and reinventing American classics—all of this can be found here.

To me, this is Laurent at his best—going to the market, talking to the farmers, using real, intensely flavorful local ingredients. With these recipes as your guide, you will want to dive headfirst into each season and all the delicious cooking it promises.

JEAN-GEORGES VONGERICHTEN
Executive Chef and Owner,
Jean-Georges Restaurants

Balsamic Radicchio, page 111

ACKNOWLEDGMENTS

I'd like to extend a heartfelt thank you to the chefs who collaborated with me on many of the recipes in this book. To Amy Eubanks, Shawn Glenn, Milena Molina, Reflection Israel, Chris Leahy, Chris Lim, Jaime Loja, David Malbequi, Liran Mezan, TJ Obias, Emilie Bousquet Walsh, and Steve Wambach, working daily with you all gives me renewed energy and inspiration.

The book would not be possible without ceaseless toil of my co-author Charlotte March and my assistant Lisa Tatelbaum, or the amazing team at John Wiley & Sons, especially Pam Chirls. And to my agent, Judith Weber, for her belief in this book and invaluable input.

Thank you to Fred Dexheimer for his thoughtful and inventive wine pairings and cocktails.

Many thanks to the very talented and spirited Quentin Bacon and his assistant Lauren Volo for helping me convey, through stunning photography, what American local cuisine is all about.

These amazing images, though, are only possible because I have been fortunate enough to work with a spectacular group of talented farmers and purveyors, like Mike Osinski of Widow's Hole Oyster Company, Art Ludlow of Mecox Bay Dairy, Paulette Satur of Satur Farms, the kind folks at Pellegrini Vineyards, Marc Sarrazin and George Faison of DeBragga and Spitler, John and Sukey Jamison of Jamison Farm, and Rob Kaufelt and Jason Donnelly at Murray's Cheese.

I would also like to thank my family for instilling in me a love and appreciation of the seasons and all that Mother Nature provides us. Fond memories of past meals and anticipation of future gatherings make it all worthwhile.

INTRODUCTION

In my life, the passing of the seasons has been marked not just by the change in temperature or the quality of light, but mostly by what can be found at the farmers' markets and around my table. Even my schooling placed an emphasis on the bounty of the seasons. Each week, we piled into a rickety old bus to visit the surrounding fields and orchards where we were shown budding trees, which in a few short months would produce ripe hazelnuts and chestnuts, or local berry brambles where we gorged on sweet, plump raspberries. My childhood was defined by these adventures in nature—spring conjures up memories of green buds peeking through the soil; summer brings memories of foraging for ripe wild fraises des bois; the vibrant changing leaves of the trees and weekend apple picking mark the fall; and winter offers visions of hunting of game in the Tronçais forests.

Eating seasonally and locally has always been my way of life. Even if I craved the delicate aroma of basil, it was not possible to get my hands on any in the dead of winter in Montluçon, my hometown in central France. Each meal my family shared together was based on what was available in our own backyard or at the neighborhood market. Our ritual was to harvest the ripest gems in the family garden—vibrant green and white leeks or ruby red stalks of rhubarb pulled fresh from the ground in the spring, while summer was a never-ending feast of tomatoes plucked from the vines, beans snapped right off the stalk, and an endless array of fresh and fragrant herbs sprouting here and there. We added to this bounty by visiting the local shopkeepers in town. Our first stop was at the fruit and vegetable market, where we consulted with the proprietor about the freshness of this or that, gently caressing the prize produce that would undoubtedly be the star of our meal. Next, we visited the local butcher where the freshest game caught in the nearby forests—wild boar, deer, pheasant, and partridge—hanging just outside the door, invited us to come in. Our local baker, an old widow, worked tirelessly from dawn to dusk, and we prized her miche loaves—giant, darkly crusted rounds baked in a wood-fired oven. The bread was something to savor on its own. The crunchy, almost charred crusts gave way to a soft, dense, and intensely moist interior, which I sampled as we strolled around town. My grandfather had to repeatedly remind me that the bread was for everyone to share, but followed that with a quick wink, which propelled me to take just one more bite.

While my grandfather, my father, and I made our stops in town, my grandmother would take a trip to a local farm where she would pick up a delicious raw-milk cheese tart or a wedge of tangy blue cheese. We would then return home and my grandmother, whose talent and ease in the kitchen inspired me to become a chef, would prepare a simple, yet completely satisfying meal. It was in this fashion that I learned to respect the seasons and understand that nature intended for us to enjoy the truly magical combinations of lamb and sweet green peas in the spring, tomatoes and cucumbers in the summer, sunchokes and mushrooms in the fall, and beets and citrus in the winter.

Inspired by the seasons, I wanted to open a restaurant that would pay homage to ingredients at their peak of freshness, flavor, and abundance. Drawing further on my traditional experience, I also wanted to highlight the great produce, cheese, fish, and meat produced by local artisans. The changing menus and daily blackboard specials in my restaurant would bring market to table by focusing on fresh seasonal ingredients. In the summer of 2007 at The Ritz-Carlton New York, Central Park, BLT Market was born.

This book is a collection of recipes from my childhood, my early career as a chef working all over the globe, and dishes that grace the table at BLT Market. There are suggested menus in each chapter for holiday feasts and family celebrations—use these as a guide but don't hesitate to personalize them. Throughout the book I mention specific cheeses and recommend certain purveyors; however, I urge you to search your own area for locally grown products at specialty shops and your farmers' market as well. I hope you enjoy the recipes and are inspired to enjoy ingredients at their peak of season and fresh from the market.

Spring

On the way home from school I always stopped by grandmother's to see what kind of afternoon treat she had prepared for me. I knew that spring had officially sprung when I began to find bowls of rhubarb compote cooling on the window ledge in the kitchen. While my simple snack of bread and cheese or a perfectly ripened piece of fruit awaited me inside, the steaming compote meant for our supper proved to be too much of a temptation. I surreptitiously enjoyed spoonful after spoonful not caring as it singed my tongue and stained the front of my crisp, blue school uniform. Afterwards, I would sneak off to a sun-dappled area hidden behind the garden to bask in the newly warm spring air and ride out my grandmother's irritation.

Spring is the season when the earth is reborn. Budding blossoms alight on tree branches while tender shoots burrow up through the soil and warmer temperatures start to prevail. This freshness and newness translate to the table as well. Bright greens dominate the color spectrum of spring produce. Ramps, asparagus, fava beans, and artichokes flood the market. Don't be mistaken though, spring is a somewhat temperamental season as well, with conditions that can still be quite bone chilling. For that reason, heavier meals like braised veal or rabbit, still grace the table, with the welcome addition of spring vegetables. Alternatively, the warmer days during this season beg for lighter dishes like salads laden with sugar snap peas and mâche or seared fish and gently braised artichokes.

Another rite of spring is the appearance of new and seasonally limited cheeses at the marketplace. The sweet spring grasses blanketing the diary pastures add a great amount of flavor and nuance. Some of my favorites, like Lively Run's Cayuga Blue or the fresh sheep's-milk ricotta from Dancing Ewe, become available at this time of year. Seek out these artisanal farmstead products with limited accessibility and you will be amazed by their distinct flavors and pungent aromas.

April

Vegetables
Artichoke
Baby Lettuce
Black Kale
Chive Blossom
English Pea
Fava Bean
Fiddlehead Fern
Fingerling Potato
Green Almond
Green Garlic
Nettle
Pea Pod
Pea Shoot
Radish
Ramp
Red Orac
Snow Pea
Spinach
Spring Onion
Sprouting Broccoli
White Asparagus

Seafood
Mackerel
Maine Sea Scallop
Maine Sweet Shrimp
Skate
Trout

Meat
Spring Lamb

Fungi
Hedgehog
Morel
Porcini
Yellow–Foot

Fruit
Kiwi
Mexican Mango
Rhubarb

May

Vegetables
Artichoke
Baby Lettuce
Black Kale
Chive Blossom
Fava Bean
Fiddlehead Fern
Nettle
Pea Pod
Pea Shoot
Ramp
Red Orac
Sorrel
Spinach
Spring Garlic
Spring Onion
Sprouting Broccoli
Wild Asparagus
Wild Roquette
Zucchini Flower

Seafood
Black Bass
Mackerel
Mussel
Rock Shrimp
Soft-Shell Crab
Trout

Fungi
Black Trumpet
Hedgehog
Morel
Porcini
Summer Truffle
Yellow-Foot

Meat
Spring Lamb

Fruit
Kiwi
Mexican Mango
Rhubarb

June

Vegetables
Chive Blossom
Dandelion Green
Pea Pod
Pea Shoot
Red and Green Chard
Sugar Snap Pea
Summer Squash
Vidalia Onion
Zucchini
Zucchini Flower

Seafood
Black Bass
Cod
Flounder
Fluke
Lobster
Mussel
Rock Shrimp
Soft-Shell Crab

Fungi
Black Trumpet
Morel
Mousseron
Porcini
Summer Truffle

Fruit
Key Lime
Lime
Rhubarb
Sour Cherry
Sweet Cherry

Jack Rabbit

Jack Rabbit

I love this brightly colored cocktail. It has a nice kick from the ginger but is mellowed out by the sweetness of the carrot juice.

SERVES 1

3 ounces freshly squeezed carrot juice
1½ ounces Crop organic vodka or other premium vodka
1 ounce Ginger Syrup (page 314)
½ ounce freshly squeezed lemon juice
1 thin carrot shaving, for garnish
1 sprig fresh carrot top, for garnish

Combine the carrot juice, vodka, ginger syrup, and lemon juice in a cocktail shaker. Add ice, shake, pour into a highball glass, and garnish with the carrot shaving and carrot top.

Rhubarb Mule

This cocktail is a jazzed up version of the classic Moscow Mule, which combines vodka, ginger beer, and fresh lime juice. The rhubarb purée adds a great tang and a brilliant reddish pink color.

SERVES 1

2 ounces Level vodka or other premium vodka
2 ounces Rhubarb Purée
½ ounce freshly squeezed lime juice
Ginger beer
1 thin slice candied ginger

Combine the vodka, purée, and juice in a cocktail shaker. Add ice, shake, and pour into a highball glass. Top with a splash of ginger beer and garnish with the candied ginger on the rim of the glass.

Rhubarb Purée

8 ounces rhubarb, roughly chopped
½ cup sugar
¼ cup water

Combine the rhubarb, sugar, and water in a heavy small saucepan and simmer until the rhubarb softens, about 30 minutes. Bring to a rapid boil for 5 minutes and remove from the heat. Pass through a fine-mesh strainer into a clean bowl. The purée will last for 1 week stored in an airtight container in the refrigerator.

Kiwi Collins

Kiwi fruit is not generally associated with cocktails, but once you try it you'll be hooked. The bright, sweet flavor of the fruit is well matched with many spirits—particularly vodka.

SERVES 1

1 kiwi, peeled
1 ounce Simple Syrup (page 314)
2 ounces Ketel One vodka or other premium vodka
1 ounce freshly squeezed lemon juice
Club soda

Cut a ¼-inch-thick slice of kiwi and reserve it for the garnish. Cut the remaining kiwi into large cubes; muddle the cubes with simple syrup in a cocktail shaker. Add the vodka, juice, and fresh ice. Shake and strain into a highball glass with ice. Top with a splash of soda and garnish with the kiwi slice on the rim of the glass.

Mango Rum Punch

Rum punch is a classic Caribbean cocktail. The addition of mango adds another hint of the exotic.

SERVES 1

2 ounces Bacardi light rum or other premium light rum
1½ ounces store-bought mango purée
1 ounce apple juice
1 ounce freshly squeezed lemon juice
1 slice dried mango

Combine the rum, mango purée, apple juice, lemon juice, and ice in a cocktail shaker. Shake and pour into a highball glass. Garnish with the dried mango slice on the rim of the glass.

Spring Blossom

The elderflower liqueur adds not only sweetness but a floral essence that brings to mind spring's first blossoms.

SERVES 1

2 ounces Plymouth gin or other premium gin
1 ounce cranberry juice
1 ounce freshly squeezed ruby red grapefruit juice
1 ounce St-Germain elderflower liqueur
Splash of freshly squeezed lemon juice
Thin wedge of grapefruit

Combine the gin, cranberry juice, grapefruit juice, elderflower liqueur, lemon juice, and ice in a cocktail shaker. Shake and strain into a martini glass. Garnish with the grapefruit wedge on the rim of the glass.

904

Green Garlic Bread

This vibrant green garlic butter is good on just about everything. I love to stuff it under the skin of a chicken before roasting, dollop it on top of grilled steak, or fold it into a bowl of perfectly blanched peas. You can also add other herbs depending upon your tastes. At my restaurant we like to serve this on a Sullivan Street Bakery's striato loaf, which is similar to a small baguette.

SERVES 6

¼ cup parsley leaves, chopped
4 tablespoons unsalted butter, softened
½ small shallot
1 garlic clove
Sea salt and freshly ground black pepper
1 Sullivan Street Bakery striato or small baguette

Preheat the oven to 500°F. Place the parsley, butter, shallot, and garlic in a food processor fitted with a metal blade. Pulse on and off until all the ingredients are incorporated and the color of the butter is bright green. Season to taste with salt and pepper.

Without cutting completely through the bottom of the loaf, cut the bread diagonally with a serrated knife into 1½-inch-thick slices. Spread the butter between each slice. Place the bread on a baking sheet and heat uncovered in the oven until the butter has completely melted and the bread is piping hot, about 5 minutes. Serve immediately.

Poached White Asparagus with Ramp Béarnaise

White asparagus are grown in complete darkness, under loose mounds of soil, which prevents the plant from producing chlorophyll and having a green color. Due to the lack of chlorophyll, its flavor is remarkably different from green asparagus and is much nuttier with hints of hearts of palm and sunchoke.

SERVES 6

Béarnaise Reduction
¼ cup dry white wine
¼ cup finely diced ramp bulbs
¼ cup white wine vinegar
2½ teaspoons chopped fresh tarragon stems
2 teaspoons finely chopped garlic
¾ teaspoon freshly ground black pepper

Ramp Purée
1 pound fresh ramps, leaves separated from the stems
2 tablespoons extra virgin olive oil

Béarnaise Sauce
5 large egg yolks
½ teaspoon (or more) sea salt
½ teaspoon (or more) freshly ground black pepper
1 cup clarified butter, melted (see page 305)
¼ cup fresh tarragon leaves, coarsely chopped

White Asparagus
24 large white asparagus
1 cup dry white wine
2 garlic heads, halved crosswise
½ bunch fresh thyme
¼ cup kosher salt

Make the béarnaise reduction ➤ Combine the wine, ramps, vinegar, tarragon stems, garlic, and pepper in a small saucepan over medium heat. Simmer until the mixture reduces to 1 generous tablespoon, about 5 minutes. Scrape the reduction into a large metal bowl and set it over a bowl of ice water to cool completely.

Make the ramp purée ➤ Bring a large saucepan of salted water to a boil. Add the ramp leaves and blanch for 2 minutes. Using a slotted spoon, remove the ramp leaves and immediately transfer them to a bowl of ice water. Once cool, pat the ramp leaves dry.

Place the blanched leaves in a blender and add the olive oil. Blend until smooth, but not too loose, about 1 minute. Transfer the purée to a small bowl and press plastic wrap onto the surface of the purée to ensure the purée keeps its bright green color. Refrigerate until ready to use.

Finish the béarnaise sauce ➤ Add the egg yolks and ½ teaspoon each of salt and pepper to the béarnaise reduction. Place the metal bowl over a saucepan of simmering water and whisk vigorously until the eggs are light and fluffy, about 2 minutes. Once the eggs have doubled in size, remove the bowl from the heat and whisk in the clarified butter, adding it very slowly in a thin, steady stream. Fold in ½ cup of the ramp purée and the chopped tarragon; reserve any remaining ramp purée for another use. Season the sauce to taste with more salt and pepper.

Cook the white asparagus ➤ Grip each asparagus spear with three fingers just below the tip and drape it over a small bowl to prevent it from breaking. Peel the thick outer layer of the spear, starting just below the tip and turning the spear as you peel.

Combine 2 gallons of water with the wine, garlic, thyme, and kosher salt in a large pot and bring to a rolling boil. Add the asparagus and cover the pot; make sure all the asparagus are submerged in the water. Cook until tender, about 7 minutes. Using a slotted spoon, transfer the asparagus to a serving platter.

To serve ➤ Set the bowl of béarnaise sauce over a saucepan of gently simmering water and whisk until the sauce is warm, if necessary. Place the platter of warm asparagus in the middle of the table with the béarnaise sauce on the side.

Wine suggestion ➤ Serve this dish with a clean and crisp Sauvignon Blanc that offers aromas of grapefruit, fresh-cut grass, and minerals, such as Sauvignon Blanc, "River Road Ranch," Geyser Peak, 2006, Russian River Valley, California.

La Quercia Prosciutto & Blue Ledge Farm Crottina Salad with Creamy Lardon Vinaigrette

How I love this creamy, tart, and decadent dish. The aged Blue Ledge Farm crottina goat cheese from western Vermont has a velvety texture while the La Quercia prosciutto adds the perfect amount of bite. This might truly be my favorite appetizer, but don't tell the others.

SERVES 6

Vinaigrette

¼ pound sliced bacon, cut crosswise into ¼-inch-thick pieces
½ cup red wine vinegar
1 cup heavy cream
Freshly ground black pepper

Croutons

1 small baguette
1 tablespoon extra virgin olive oil
1 garlic clove, halved
2 Blue Ledge Farm crottina, 4 ounces each (or another soft-ripened goat's-milk cheese)
1 garlic clove, thinly sliced

Salad

1 head frisée, light green and yellow leaves only
2 cups baby arugula
3 tablespoons extra virgin olive oil
1 tablespoon red wine vinegar
Sea salt and freshly ground black pepper
4 ounces La Quercia prosciutto, very thinly sliced
2 tablespoons chopped fresh chives
Shaved black truffles (optional)

Make the vinaigrette ➤ Cook the bacon in a medium sauté pan over medium heat until the fat has rendered and the bacon is crispy, stirring often, about 5 minutes. Deglaze with the vinegar and continue to simmer until the vinegar is reduced to 2 teaspoons, about 3 minutes. Add the cream and bring to a boil. Simmer the vinaigrette until it thickens slightly and coats the back of a spoon, about 2 minutes. Season the vinaigrette to taste with pepper.

Make the croutons ➤ Adjust the top rack of the broiler 4 inches from the heat source and preheat the broiler. Slice the baguette into twelve ½-inch-thick slices. Arrange the baguette slices on a baking sheet, brush them with olive oil, and rub each slice with the cut side of the halved garlic. Slice each crottina into 6 thin slices and place 1 slice atop each crouton. Press a slice of raw garlic into the cheese. Broil until the cheese begins to melt and the edge of the bread is toasted, about 1 minute.

To assemble and serve the salad ➤ In a medium bowl, toss the frisée and arugula with the olive oil and red wine vinegar and season to taste with salt and pepper. Divide the salad among 6 serving plates and arrange the prosciutto over the salad. Place 2 croutons on top of each salad and drizzle the bacon vinaigrette over the croutons. Garnish with chopped chives and black truffle, if using.

Wine suggestion ➤ Serve this dish with a Chardonnay that offers flavors of rich lemon, minerals, and a touch of toasty oak, such as Chardonnay, "Scherrer Vineyard," Scherrer, 2005, Alexander Valley, California.

THE LA QUERCIA PROSCIUTTO GREEN LABEL is the first and only organic prosciutto commercially available in the United States and is made with a Berkshire cross pig raised by Becker Lane Organic Farms. Herb and Kathy Eckhouse, the founders of La Quercia, are involved in all aspects of the business—selecting and buying pork, salting, trimming, and handling the hams.

Their appreciation for prosciutto grew out of the three and a half years they lived in Parma, Italy, prosciutto's area of origin. Their desire to produce a product that is organic, healthful, and incredibly satisfying is wildly evident. They take immense pride in using pigs that are raised humanely, with access to the outdoors and an opportunity to socialize, and fed an all vegetarian grain-based diet. Their prosciutto is created with a traditional dry-curing method, without any nitrates. It is by far one of the most superior prosciuttos I have ever tried.

Pea Pod & Mint Risotto with Steamed Maine Red Shrimp

Maine red shrimp, small but prized for their sweet and tender meat, thrive in the cold, deep coastal waters off of Maine. Their season is brief because they can only be caught during the short period when the females venture closer to shore from deeper waters to release their eggs. The season generally begins in late February and lasts only a few weeks.

SERVES 6

Pea Purée
- 3 pounds fresh English peas
- 2 tablespoons unsalted butter
- 4 small shallots, finely diced
- 2 cups Chicken Stock (page 303) or Vegetable Stock (page 304)

Risotto
- 5 cups Chicken Stock (page 303) or Vegetable Stock (page 304)
- 3 tablespoons extra virgin olive oil
- 1 small onion, diced
- 2 garlic cloves, finely chopped
- 2 cups Arborio rice
- 1 cup dry white wine
- 1 pound Maine red shrimp, peeled and deveined
- 3 tablespoons mascarpone cheese
- 2 tablespoons chopped fresh mint
- Sea salt and freshly ground black pepper
- 6 fresh mint sprigs, for garnish

Make the pea purée ➤ Shell the peas, leaving 6 pods intact (you should have about 2¼ cups of shelled peas). Bring a large pot of salted water to a boil and add the fresh peas and the 6 reserved pea pods. Cook until the peas are tender, about 3 minutes. Using a slotted spoon, immediately transfer the peas to a bowl of ice water. Once cool, strain the peas from the water.

Melt the butter in a small sauté pan over medium heat. When the butter begins to foam, add the shallots and sauté until tender, about 5 minutes. Combine the shallots and the stock with 1¼ cups of peas in a blender and purée until smooth.

Make the risotto ➤ Warm the stock in a small saucepan. Heat the olive oil in a medium saucepan over medium heat. Add the onion and garlic and sauté until the onion is translucent, about 5 minutes. Add the rice and stir to coat with the oil. Add the wine, reduce the heat to medium-low, and simmer until most of the wine has evaporated, about 5 minutes. Add 1 cup of the warm stock to the rice mixture and continue to cook, stirring constantly, until most of the stock is absorbed. Repeat this process with the remaining 4 cups of stock, making sure each addition of stock is fully absorbed before adding more.

Bring 2 cups of salted water to a simmer in a large saucepan. Arrange the shrimp in a steamer basket or in a metal colander. Set the basket over the simmering water and cover with a tight fitting lid. Steam until the shrimp are firm and pink, about 3 minutes.

To serve ➤ Fold the steamed shrimp, mascarpone, chopped mint, and the remaining 1 cup of peas into the risotto. Season to taste with salt and pepper. Divide the risotto among 6 bowls and garnish each with 1 pea pod and 1 mint sprig. Serve immediately.

Wine suggestion ➤ Serve this dish with a fresh and lively Sauvignon Blanc that offers flavors of grapefruit, lemon, and a touch of fresh herbs, such as Sauvignon Blanc, Honig, 2007, Napa Valley, California.

Spring Onion Gratinée with Hooligan Cheese & Crispy Bacon

The origin of this soup is firmly planted in France, though the exact era it came about and who created it is up for debate. Hooligan cheese, from artisan cheesemaker Cato Corner Farm in central Connecticut, is a delicious washed-rind raw cow's-milk cheese that is perfect for melting and has a pungent aroma and flavor.

SERVES 6

Onion Soup

4 tablespoons unsalted butter
2 ounces thick-cut bacon, cut crosswise into ¼-inch-thick pieces
2 pounds spring onions, thinly sliced
2 fresh thyme sprigs
1 bay leaf
2 tablespoons sugar
1 cup dry sherry
1 cup dry white wine
5¼ cups Chicken Stock (page 303)
5¼ cups Veal Stock (page 304) or beef stock
Sea salt and freshly ground black pepper
6 slices thin-cut bacon

Croutons

6 slices country bread, ½ inch thick
1 garlic clove, halved
1¼ pounds Hooligan cheese, grated

Make the onion soup ➤ Melt the butter in a large saucepan over medium heat. Add the bacon pieces and sauté until the fat has rendered, about 4 minutes. Add the spring onions, thyme, and bay leaf and sauté until tender, about 5 minutes. Sprinkle the onions with the sugar and continue to sauté until well combined. Reduce the heat to low. Cover and cook the spring onions, stirring regularly, until completely caramelized, about 45 minutes. Deglaze the onions with the sherry and simmer until the sherry is almost completely evaporated, about 5 minutes. Add the white wine and simmer until the wine is almost completely evaporated, about 10 minutes. Add the chicken stock and veal stock and simmer uncovered over low heat to reduce the liquids slightly and to concentrate and blend the flavors, about 20 minutes. Season to taste with salt and pepper.

While the soup is simmering, cook the 6 slices of bacon in a medium sauté pan over medium heat until the fat has rendered and the bacon is crispy, about 5 minutes. Transfer the bacon from the pan to a plate lined with paper towels.

Make the croutons ➤ Position the top rack of the broiler 4 inches from the heat source and preheat the broiler. Preheat the oven to 350°F. Arrange the bread slices on a baking sheet and broil until the bread is golden brown, about 2 minutes. Turn the bread slices over and continue to broil for another 2 to 3 minutes. Transfer the bread to the oven and continue to toast until the croutons are completely dry, about 8 minutes. Remove the croutons from the oven and rub both sides of the croutons with the halved garlic.

To assemble and serve ➤ Move the broiler rack down 1 notch. Remove the bay leaf and thyme sprigs from the soup. Divide the soup evenly among 6 ovenproof soup bowls and place 1 crouton in the center of each bowl. Sprinkle the cheese over the croutons. Place the bowls on a rimmed baking sheet and broil until the cheese is completely melted and caramelized, about 10 minutes. Top the crouton with a slice of crispy bacon and serve immediately.

Wine suggestion ➤ Serve this dish with a crisp Pinot Gris that offers flavors of Asian pear, citrus, and a touch of spice, such as Pinot Gris, Maysara, 2007, Willamette Valley, Oregon.

Grilled Marinated Salmon Salad with Sugar Snap Peas, Pea Shoots, Cucumber, Watercress, & Radishes

When I feel like I have been overindulging and want something light but also really flavorful, this is my go-to dish. The abundance of greens and grilled salmon make me feel rather virtuous; however, the spicy Asian flavors will satisfy any appetite. You can serve this as a main course with steamed white rice on the side.

SERVES 6

Salmon Marinade

½ cup hoisin sauce
1½ tablespoons rice vinegar
2 teaspoons sambal oelek (Asian chili-garlic paste)
1 teaspoon grated peeled fresh ginger
Zest and juice of ½ orange
4 skinless center-cut salmon fillets, 4 ounces each

Salad

1 cup sugar snap peas, trimmed
1 small head Boston lettuce, cored and quartered
2 cups bean sprouts
2 cups pea shoots
1 cup mâche
1 cup roughly chopped fresh cilantro
1 cup watercress, large stems removed
¾ cup roughly chopped fresh Thai basil
½ cup roughly chopped fresh mint
½ English cucumber, halved lengthwise then thinly sliced into half-moons
2 small spring onions, thinly sliced
2 small radishes, halved lengthwise then thinly sliced into half-moons
2 scallions, thinly sliced diagonally
Sea salt and freshly ground black pepper

Dressing

½ cup rice vinegar
¼ cup light sesame oil (not toasted)
3 tablespoons soy sauce
2 tablespoons honey
2 tablespoons peanut oil
2 teaspoons dry Chinese mustard
1½ teaspoons fish sauce

Marinate the salmon ➤ Mix the hoisin sauce, vinegar, sambal oelek, ginger, orange zest and juice in a medium bowl. Transfer half of the marinade to a shallow baking dish and arrange the salmon in a single layer in the marinade. Cover and refrigerate the salmon for 2 hours, turning the salmon over after the first hour. Reserve the remaining marinade at room temperature.

Make the salad ➤ Bring a large pot of salted water to a boil over high heat. Add the sugar snap peas and cook for 3 minutes. Using a slotted spoon, immediately transfer the peas to a bowl of ice water. Once cool, remove the peas from the ice water and pat them dry on a kitchen towel. Combine the sugar snap peas in a large bowl with the Boston lettuce, bean sprouts, pea shoots, mâche, cilantro, watercress, basil, mint, cucumber, onions, radishes, and scallions. Cover and refrigerate until ready to serve.

Make the dressing ➤ Whisk the vinegar, sesame oil, soy sauce, honey, peanut oil, mustard, and fish sauce in a medium bowl to blend.

Grill the salmon ➤ Preheat the grill to high heat. Remove the salmon from the marinade; discard the marinade. Grill the salmon to medium-rare doneness, about 3 minutes on each side. Remove the salmon from the grill and brush with the reserved unused marinade. Allow to rest for 10 minutes.

To assemble and serve ➤ Toss the salad with the dressing and season to taste with salt and pepper. Divide the salad among 6 plates. Break the salmon into smaller pieces and scatter them over the salads. Serve immediately.

Wine suggestion ➤ Serve this dish with a clean and refreshing Pinot Blanc that offers aromas of melon, lemon meringue, and crisp acidity, such as Pinot Blanc, Erath, 2007, Willamette Valley, Oregon.

Mâche & Chive Blossom Salad with Deviled Quail Eggs

Diminutive and dappled quail eggs used to be quite exotic but are increasingly available at gourmet markets. The flavor is very similar to regular chicken eggs but their yolk is larger in proportion to the white. I make this salad in late winter or early spring when black truffles are still in season. Add a few truffle shavings on the top of the salad to make it truly divine.

SERVES 6

Deviled Quail Eggs
16 quail eggs
1 teaspoon white wine vinegar
2 tablespoons mayonnaise
1 tablespoon finely chopped fresh chives
¼ teaspoon truffle oil
Sea salt and freshly ground black pepper

Lemon Garlic Vinaigrette
⅔ cup extra virgin olive oil
⅓ cup freshly squeezed lemon juice
½ teaspoon finely chopped garlic

Salad
1 pound mâche, large stems removed
2 ounces shaved Sartori Stravecchio (or another domestic Parmesan cheese)
3 white mushrooms, thinly shaved on a mandoline
¼ cup chive blossoms
1 watermelon radish, thinly shaved on a mandoline

Make the deviled quail eggs ➤ Place the eggs and vinegar in a medium pot, cover with cold water, and bring to a boil over high heat. Boil the eggs for 4 minutes. Using a slotted spoon, remove the eggs from the pot and immediately place them in a bowl of ice water. Once the eggs have cooled, peel them and slice lengthwise in half. Carefully remove the yolks and place them in a medium bowl; set the whites aside. Mash the yolks with a fork until smooth. Stir in the mayonnaise, chives, and truffle oil until well combined. Season to taste with salt and pepper. Transfer the yolk mixture to a pastry bag fitted with a small star tip and pipe the yolk mixture into the egg white halves.

Make the vinaigrette ➤ Whisk the olive oil, lemon juice, and garlic in a medium bowl to blend. Season to taste with salt and pepper.

To assemble and serve the salad ➤ Place the mâche in a large wooden salad bowl and top with the cheese. Arrange the deviled eggs over the mâche and scatter the sliced mushrooms around the eggs. Sprinkle the chive blossoms and watermelon radish slices over the salad, then drizzle the vinaigrette over and serve immediately.

Wine suggestion ➤ Serve this dish with a crisp, unoaked Chardonnay that offers flavors of lemon, butter, tangerine, and exotic fruits, such as Chardonnay, Diatom, 2006, Santa Rita Hills, California.

Green Papaya & Mango Salad with Dungeness Crab & Spicy Thai Basil–Mint Dressing

Found in the Pacific Ocean from Mexico to Alaska, Dungeness crabs are one of the most flavorful crabs. They have a distinct large, heart-shaped shell and provide a plentiful amount of crabmeat compared to many other crab varieties.

SERVES 6

Pickled Carrots and Daikon

2 cups rice vinegar
½ cup sugar
1 small daikon radish, peeled and cut into matchstick-size strips
2 small carrots, peeled and cut into matchstick-size strips
1 garlic clove, finely chopped
1 red Thai chile, finely chopped

Spicy Thai Basil–Mint Dressing

½ cup lemon-lime soda (such as Sprite or 7-Up)
¼ cup freshly squeezed lime juice
¼ cup freshly squeezed tangerine juice
1 shallot, finely chopped
1 garlic clove, finely chopped
1 red Thai chile, finely chopped
2 tablespoons chopped fresh mint
2 tablespoons fish sauce
1½ teaspoons sambal oelek (Asian chili-garlic paste)

Green Papaya and Mango Salad

4 cups matchstick-size strips peeled pitted green mango
4 cups matchstick-size strips peeled seeded green papaya
2 English cucumbers, peeled and cut into matchstick-size strips
2 bunches watercress, large stems removed
½ cup fresh cilantro leaves
½ cup fresh Thai basil leaves
¼ cup fresh mint leaves
3 scallions (green parts only), thinly sliced
1 pound Dungeness crabmeat or peekytoe or blue crabmeat

Pickle the carrots and daikon ➤ Stir the vinegar and sugar in a large bowl until the sugar has completely dissolved. Stir in the daikon, carrots, garlic, and chile. Cover and refrigerate for a minimum of 1 hour.

Make the dressing ➤ Whisk all the ingredients together in a small bowl until well blended.

To assemble and serve the salad ➤ Strain the pickled carrots and daikon, discarding the pickling liquid, and place them in a large bowl. Add the mango, papaya, cucumbers, watercress, and half of each of the cilantro, basil, mint, and scallions. Pour the dressing over the salad and toss until well combined.

Transfer the salad to a large serving bowl and garnish with the remaining cilantro, basil, mint, and scallions. Scatter the Dungeness crabmeat over the salad and serve.

Wine suggestion ➤ Serve this dish with an exotic Gewurztraminer that has flavors of honeysuckle, lychee, and jasmine, such as Gewurztraminer, Red Newt, 2006, Finger Lakes, New York.

Shrimp Chowder with Fennel Pollen

Chowder is the perfect way to ward off spring's deceptively chilly temperatures. I like to serve this with saltine crackers or oyster crackers and a healthy dash of Old Bay seasoning. You may substitute lobster, clams, or crab for the shrimp in this recipe, depending upon what looks best at your fishmonger's. The fennel pollen used to garnish this dish is simply the pollen gathered off wild fennel when the plant is in bloom. It imparts a subtle fennel fragrance and flavor.

SERVES 6

Shrimp Stock

2 tablespoons extra virgin olive oil
2 pounds large shrimp (26 to 30 per pound), peeled and deveined, shells reserved
1 fennel bulb with fronds, roughly chopped
½ cup roughly chopped Spanish onion
1 cup dry white wine
1 cup Pernod
1 bouquet garni (1 dark green leek leaf, 3 fresh tarragon stems, 3 star anise; see page 305)

Chowder

3 large russet potatoes (1 potato, peeled and roughly chopped; 2 potatoes, peeled and cut into ½-inch dice)
1 cup heavy cream
1 tablespoon extra virgin olive oil
1 tablespoon unsalted butter
4 ounces applewood-smoked bacon, cut into ½-inch dice
3 celery stalks, cut into ½-inch dice
2 fennel bulbs, cut into ½-inch dice, fronds discarded or reserved for other use
½ Spanish onion, cut into ½-inch dice
2 tablespoons finely chopped garlic
Sea salt and freshly ground black pepper
1 teaspoon (about) ground star anise
8 tarragon sprigs, leaves julienned (stems reserved for the bouquet garni)
⅛ teaspoon fennel pollen

Make the shrimp stock ➤ Heat the olive oil in large pot over medium heat. Add the shrimp shells and sauté until the shells turn bright pink, about 4 minutes. Add the chopped fennel and onion and sauté until the vegetables become translucent, about 4 minutes. Deglaze the pot with the wine and the Pernod and continue to cook until the liquid reduces by half, about 4 minutes. Add 4 quarts of water and the bouquet garni and bring to a boil. Reduce the heat and simmer until the liquid has reduced by half, about 30 minutes. Remove and discard the bouquet garni.

Using a slotted spoon, transfer the solids and 3 cups of the liquid shrimp stock to a blender. Purée until the shells begin to breakdown, about 3 minutes. Return the purée to the stock and then strain the stock through a fine-mesh strainer into a large container.

Make the chowder ➤ Combine the roughly chopped potato, cream, and 2 cups of the shrimp stock in a large saucepan. Simmer over medium heat until the potatoes are fork tender, about 4 minutes. Transfer to a blender and purée until smooth.

Heat the olive oil and butter in a medium saucepan over medium heat. Add the bacon and cook for 3 minutes. Add the celery, fennel bulbs, onion, and garlic and cook until the vegetables become translucent, about 3 minutes. Add the remaining shrimp stock and bring the mixture to a boil. Add the remaining diced potatoes and reduce the heat to low. Cook until the potatoes are tender, about 8 minutes. Strain the chowder through a fine-mesh strainer set over a large clean saucepan; reserve the vegetables to use later.

Place the saucepan of chowder over medium heat and whisk in the blended potato mixture. Season to taste with salt, pepper, and star anise. Add the shrimp and cook until they turn pink, about 3 minutes. Finally, add the reserved vegetables and simmer for 1 minute.

To serve ➤ Divide the chowder evenly among 6 soup bowls. Garnish with the tarragon leaves and dust with the fennel pollen. Serve immediately.

Wine suggestion ➤ Serve this dish with a crémant-style rosé sparkling wine that offers flavors of ripe raspberries, fresh-picked strawberries, and cherries, such as Chateau Frank, "Célèbre Rosé," NV, Finger Lakes, New York.

Warm Poached Globe Artichoke with Tarragon Caper-Anchovy Vinaigrette

The best way to enjoy a whole artichoke is by first pulling the leaf through your teeth to remove the yielding, pulpy, delicious portion of the leaf. Continue with the remaining leaves until you reach the soft, luscious heart. Cut the heart into pieces and eat it with any remaining vinaigrette.

SERVES 6

Vinaigrette
½ cup mayonnaise
1 tablespoon Dijon mustard
1 tablespoon red wine vinegar
1 tablespoon sherry vinegar
½ cup canola oil
¼ cup extra virgin olive oil
⅓ cup finely chopped sun-dried tomatoes
2 tablespoons finely chopped red onion
2 tablespoons finely chopped white anchovies
1 tablespoon finely chopped capers
1 tablespoon finely chopped fresh chervil
1 tablespoon finely chopped fresh parsley
1 tablespoon finely chopped fresh tarragon
1 tablespoon finely chopped preserved lemon rind
½ teaspoon freshly ground black pepper
½ teaspoon garlic powder
½ teaspoon sea salt

Artichokes
1 cup all-purpose flour
1 cup dry white wine
6 globe artichokes, dark leaves removed
3 lemons, thinly sliced
3 hard-cooked eggs (see page 306), peeled and finely chopped

Make the vinaigrette ➤ Whisk the mayonnaise, mustard, red wine vinegar, and sherry vinegar in a medium bowl to blend. Slowly whisk in the canola oil and olive oil. Add the remaining vinaigrette ingredients and stir until well combined.

Cook the artichokes ➤ Bring a large pot of salted water to a boil. Whisk in the flour and wine until well blended. Lay an artichoke on its side and cut ¾ inch off the top. Cut off the stem at the base of the artichoke so that it will sit flat. Repeat with the remaining artichokes. Place a slice of lemon on top each artichoke and secure them together by tying the artichoke like a package with kitchen string. Place the artichokes in the pot and simmer until the base is tender when pierced with a sharp knife, about 45 minutes. To ensure the artichokes are submerged in the water, place a small lid or plate over the artichokes to weigh them down while they are simmering. Once tender, remove the artichokes and turn them upside down to drain and cool slightly.

To serve ➤ Spread the leaves of the artichokes open slightly and gently pull out the choke, or the inedible inner leaves, from the center of the artichokes. Using a small spoon, scoop out the fuzzy fibers covering the heart. Transfer the artichokes to a large platter. Spoon 3 tablespoons of the vinaigrette inside each artichoke. Sprinkle with the chopped eggs and serve immediately with some additional vinaigrette on the side.

Wine suggestion ➤ Serve this dish with an earthy sparkling wine that offers flavors of lemon, baked apple, and a touch of yeast, such as Shady Lane Brut, 2000, Leelanau Peninsula, Michigan.

Crispy Maryland Soft-Shell Crabs with Chili-Garlic Dressing

This simple and classic Asian method of frying and seasoning crab is fairly easy and the result is incredibly flavorful. While I like to serve these crabs with the chili-garlic dressing and pea shoots, I also enjoy pairing them with the Green Papaya & Mango Salad and Spicy Thai Basil–Mint Dressing (page 22).

SERVES 6

Chili-Garlic Dressing

¼ cup hoisin sauce
3 tablespoons freshly squeezed orange juice
1 tablespoon sambal oelek (Asian chili-garlic paste)
1 teaspoon fish sauce
1 teaspoon freshly squeezed lime juice
Zest of 1 orange

Crabs

Vegetable oil for frying
½ cup unsweetened coconut milk
1 large egg
1 cup rice flour
12 soft-shell crabs, cleaned (see Chef's note)
1½ cups pea shoots
1 teaspoon extra virgin olive oil
Sea salt and freshly ground black pepper

Make the dressing ➤ Whisk the hoisin sauce, orange juice, sambal oelek, fish sauce, lime juice, and orange zest in a medium bowl to blend and set aside.

Fry the crabs ➤ Fill a deep heavy pot or deep fryer with 4 inches of vegetable oil and heat to 375°F. Whisk the coconut milk and egg in a small bowl to blend. Scatter the rice flour on a plate. Dip 1 crab into the egg mixture to coat it completely. Remove the crab from the egg mixture and allow any excess egg mixture to drip off. Transfer the crab to the rice flour and coat evenly on all sides. Shake the crab gently to remove any excess flour. Continue the process with the remaining crabs. Working in batches, fry the crabs until golden and crispy, about 2 minutes on each side. Transfer to a plate lined with paper towels and allow the excess oil to drain.

To assemble and serve ➤ Place the fried crabs in a large mixing bowl. Spoon the dressing over the crabs and toss gently to coat.

Toss the pea shoots in a large bowl with the olive oil and season to taste with salt and pepper. Scatter the pea shoots over a large platter. Arrange the fried crabs over the pea shoots and serve immediately.

Chef's note ➤ Cleaning soft-shell crabs is not for the faint of heart, so if possible, ask your fishmonger to clean them for you. Using kitchen shears, snip off the eyes of the crab. Turn the crab over and remove the gills or lungs from the underside of the crab and any soft tissue from the tail end. Keep the crabs on ice until ready to cook. Once cleaned the crabs need to be cooked soon thereafter.

Wine suggestion ➤ Serve this dish with a slightly off-dry Riesling that offers flavors of apricots, ripe peaches, and a touch of white flowers, such as Riesling, "Semi-Dry," Heron Hill, 2006, Finger Lakes, New York.

Creamy Zucchini & Squash Blossoms with Fresh Almonds

The creamy zucchini and chanterelle purée is finished with cheese and chopped almonds, creating a chunky pesto-like sauce. This sauce can also be used to lightly dress pasta or as a dip for crudités. If possible, seek out fresh green garlic, which lends a softer and more nuanced garlic flavor, at your farmers' market to use in this recipe.

SERVES 6

Creamy Zucchini
2 tablespoons extra virgin olive oil
2 cups chanterelle mushrooms, cleaned and cut into ¼-inch pieces
2 tablespoons unsalted butter
2 teaspoons finely chopped garlic
2 teaspoons finely chopped shallot
2 medium zucchini, cut into ¼-inch dice (about 3 cups)
6 tablespoons heavy cream
¼ cup fresh ricotta
¼ cup grated Sartori Stravecchio (or another domestic Parmesan cheese)
2 tablespoons chopped fresh basil
2 teaspoons chopped fresh mint
Sea salt and freshly ground black pepper

Squash Blossoms
Vegetable oil for frying
¾ cup cornstarch
½ cup all-purpose flour
½ teaspoon fine sea salt more for seasoning
¾ cup chilled club soda
6 squash blossoms

30 green almonds, shelled and roughly chopped
2 tablespoons fresh ricotta

Make the creamy zucchini ➤ Heat the olive oil in a large sauté pan over medium-high heat. Add the mushrooms and sauté until lightly browned and all of the water has been released, about 4 minutes. Add the butter, garlic, and shallot and cook until fragrant, about 1 minute. Add the zucchini and cook for 2 minutes. Add the cream and bring to a boil. Remove from the heat and transfer the mixture to a food processor fitted with a metal blade. Pulse until coarsely chopped. Stir in the cheeses and herbs and season to taste with salt and pepper.

Fry the squash blossoms ➤ Fill a deep heavy pot or deep fryer with 2 inches of vegetable oil. Heat the oil to 375°F or until a small drop of the batter browns quickly in the oil. Whisk the cornstarch, flour, and ½ teaspoon of fine sea salt in a medium bowl. Whisk in the club soda until well combined. The batter should have the consistency of heavy cream. Working in batches, dip the squash blossoms into the batter and fry until golden brown, about 2 minutes. Using a slotted spoon, remove the blossoms from the oil and transfer to a plate lined with paper towels. Season to taste with the sea salt.

To serve ➤ Fold the fresh almonds into the creamy zucchini and divide the mixture among 6 shallow bowls. Top with a dollop of ricotta cheese and a fried squash blossom. Serve immediately.

Wine suggestion ➤ Serve this dish with a white Rhône-inspired blend that offers flavors of crisp apples, roasted nuts, and a touch of white flowers, such as Core, White Blend, 2006, Santa Barbara County, California.

FRESH ALMONDS are grown abundantly in the Central Valley of California. Fresh or green almonds are sold in their fuzzy green pods and have to be gently pried from the pods and then tenderly peeled. Like walnuts, almonds harden after you pick them and the green fuzzy pod surrounding the nut turns to the pointy, brittle, hole-ridden shell you recognize. Once harvested, both the outer shell and almond within change in character and taste in a matter of days. The outer portion of the nut becomes more bitter and inedible and the inner almond goes from a sweet, grassy vitreous gel to a milky solid. The season for fresh almonds lasts just 3 to 4 weeks, so get them when you can.

Seasonal Crudités with Homemade Boursin

This classic crudités of raw vegetables and dip is very simple to make and to serve but still has an air of sophistication. Feel free to add different vegetables depending upon what looks fresh and in season at the market. Make sure to include a variety of colors and shapes to create a beautiful presentation.

SERVES 6

Boursin

8 ounces fresh Coach Farm goat cheese
2 tablespoons chopped fresh chives
2 tablespoons chopped fresh parsley
2 tablespoons heavy cream
1½ tablespoons extra virgin olive oil
1 tablespoon chopped shallots
1 tablespoon granulated garlic
½ teaspoon onion powder
Sea salt and freshly ground black pepper

Crudités

½ cup broccoli florets
6 white mushrooms, cleaned and halved
12 pencil-thin asparagus stalks
½ cup green cauliflower florets
½ cup purple cauliflower florets
½ cup white cauliflower florets
10 baby carrots, trimmed and peeled
½ cup radishes, halved
½ cup haricots verts, trimmed
½ cup baby turnips, peeled and halved

Make the Boursin ➤ Combine the first 8 ingredients in the bowl of a stand mixer fitted with the paddle attachment. Mix on low speed until well combined. Season to taste with salt and pepper.

To serve ➤ Arrange the crudités vegetables on a large platter and serve with the homemade Boursin.

Wine suggestion ➤ Serve this dish with a refreshing Sauvignon Blanc that offers flavors of grapefruit, key limes, and fresh cut herbs, such as Sauvignon Blanc, Handley, 2007, Dry Creek Valley, California.

Grilled Skirt Steak with Mustard, Caramelized Spring Onions, & Pleasant Ridge Reserve Cheese

This grilled favorite is great accompanied by a salad of spicy wild arugula dressed with lemon juice and extra virgin olive oil. If possible, burn a piece or two of fruit wood along with the charcoal in your grill. The smoky flavor complements both the sweetness of the onions and the fruity and herbaceous Pleasant Ridge Reserve cheese.

SERVES 6

3 tablespoons extra virgin olive oil
3 medium spring onions, thinly sliced
2 tablespoons sugar
6 skirt steaks, preferably Kobe, 6 ounces each
Sea salt and freshly ground black pepper
6 teaspoons Dijon mustard
3 tablespoons chopped fresh tarragon
8 ounces thinly sliced Pleasant Ridge Reserve cheese (or another washed-rind, semi-aged cow's-milk cheese)

Heat the olive oil in a large nonstick sauté pan over medium heat. Add the onions and sauté until they are tender and translucent, about 8 minutes. Add the sugar and sauté until the onions are caramelized and golden brown, about 5 minutes.

Lay the steaks on a work surface and season both sides with salt and pepper. Spread 1 side of each steak with the mustard. Sprinkle the tarragon over the mustard and top with the caramelized onions and cheese. Beginning at the thinner end of the steak, tightly roll up the steak, jelly-roll style, and secure with a toothpick.

Heat the grill or a grill pan over medium-high heat. Grill the steaks to medium-rare doneness, about 7 minutes per side. Remove the steaks from the heat and rest, tented with aluminum foil, for 5 minutes.

Slice the steaks crosswise in half and gently remove the toothpicks so that the filling stays rolled in the meat. Serve immediately.

Wine suggestion ➤ Serve a spicy red wine made from Grenache that offers flavors of ripe raspberries, baking spices, and Mediterranean herbs, such as Grenache, Herman Story, 2006, Santa Barbara County, California.

Pan-Seared Sweetbreads with Madeira-Braised Morels & Calabro Ricotta Gnocchi

Preparing sweetbreads involves many steps so give yourself a few days to make this dish. However, you will want to begin the process the very day you purchase the sweetbreads as they spoil quite easily.

SERVES 6

Sweetbreads

1 pound milk-fed veal sweetbreads
4 cups whole milk
1 tablespoon kosher salt
2 fresh thyme sprigs
1 bay leaf
1 cup Wondra flour
3 tablespoons unsalted butter
2 garlic cloves, peeled and smashed
1 fresh thyme sprig

Ricotta Gnocchi

1½ pounds Calabro ricotta (or other fresh cow's-milk ricotta)
All-purpose flour for dusting + 1 cup (or more)
2 large eggs
2 tablespoons chopped fresh parsley
1 tablespoon kosher salt
1 tablespoon truffle oil
Freshly ground black pepper

Gnocchi Sauce

1 tablespoon unsalted butter
3 shallots, finely chopped
2 garlic cloves, thinly sliced
2 fresh thyme sprigs
Sea salt and freshly ground black pepper
1 cup dry vermouth
2 cups heavy cream
1 cup Chicken Stock (page 303)

Morels

2 tablespoons unsalted butter
1 shallot, finely diced
1 fresh thyme sprig
2 garlic cloves, peeled and smashed
1 pound fresh morel mushrooms, cleaned and halved lengthwise
1 cup Madeira

2 tablespoons chopped fresh tarragon, for garnish

Prepare the sweetbreads ➤ Two days before you plan to serve this dish place the sweetbreads in a bowl with the milk, making sure they are completely submerged. Cover and refrigerate overnight.

Set a wire rack on a rimmed baking sheet and line the rack with paper towels; set aside. Remove the sweetbreads from the milk and rinse them under cold water. Place the sweetbreads in a large saucepan and add just enough water to cover them. Add the salt, thyme, and bay leaf. Bring to a boil over high heat. Reduce the heat to medium-low and simmer for 5 minutes. Using a slotted spoon, immediately remove the sweetbreads from the simmering liquid and transfer them to a bowl of ice water. Once cool, remove the sweetbreads from the water and place them on the wire rack. Place another baking sheet on top of the sweetbreads and then place several large canned goods on top to press down the sweetbreads. Allow the sweetbreads to drain overnight in the refrigerator.

Make the gnocchi ➤ Place the ricotta in a fine-mesh strainer set over a bowl. Cover and refrigerate overnight to drain.

Line a rimmed baking sheet with parchment paper and then lightly dust with some all-purpose flour. Using a pastry knife or 2 forks, mix the ricotta, the 1 cup of all-purpose flour, the eggs, parsley, kosher salt, and truffle oil in a medium bowl until it comes together to form a dough. Season the mixture to taste with pepper. Add more all-purpose flour if the dough is too sticky, then transfer the dough to a pastry bag. Pipe the dough into a ½-inch-thick rope onto a lightly floured surface. Dust the dough rope with flour. Using a paring knife, cut the rope into 1-inch pieces. Transfer the gnocchi to the prepared baking sheet, making sure they do not touch or they will stick together.

Bring a large pot of salted water to a boil. Cook the gnocchi in 2 batches, stirring with a wooden spoon, until the gnocchi rise to the surface, about 7 minutes. Using a slotted spoon, remove the gnocchi and transfer to a bowl of ice water.

Make the gnocchi sauce ➤ Melt the butter in a small saucepan over medium heat. Add the shallots, garlic, and thyme and season to taste with salt and pepper. Sauté until the shallots are translucent, about 4 minutes. Deglaze with the vermouth and continue to cook until the alcohol has evaporated, about 3 minutes. Reduce the heat. Add the cream and chicken stock and simmer until the mixture is thick and creamy, about 8 minutes. Strain the sauce through a fine-mesh strainer into a medium saucepan, pressing against the solids to release as much of the liquids as possible. Discard the solids.

continued

Cook the morels ➤ Melt the butter in a large sauté pan over medium heat until the butter begins to foam. Add the shallot, thyme, and garlic and sauté until fragrant, about 1 minute. Add the morels and season to taste with salt and pepper. Deglaze with the Madeira and simmer until the liquid has mostly evaporated, about 5 minutes. Discard the garlic.

Sauté the sweetbreads ➤ Remove the sweetbreads from the refrigerator and peel off the outer layer of skin. Cut the sweetbreads into 1-inch pieces. Evenly coat each piece with Wondra flour. Melt the butter in a large sauté pan over medium heat. Once the butter begins foam, sauté the sweetbreads until they are lightly golden on all sides, about 4 minutes. Reduce the heat and add the garlic and thyme. Continue to cook until the sweetbreads are cooked through and light brown, about 2 minutes. Remove the sweetbreads with a slotted spoon and transfer them to a plate lined with paper towels to drain.

To assemble and serve ➤ Heat the sauce over low heat. Transfer the gnocchi to the sauce and warm them through. Arrange the gnocchi around the exterior of 6 shallow serving bowls. Place the sweetbreads in the middle of the bowl and top with the morel mushrooms. Garnish with the chopped tarragon and serve immediately.

Wine suggestion ➤ Serve this dish with an earthy Chardonnay that offers flavors of apple skins, citrus, and a touch of smoke, such as Chardonnay, Brick House, 2006, Willamette Valley, Oregon.

MORELS are the quintessential springtime mushroom. These small dark brown mushrooms have a distinct nutty and meaty flavor, making them one of the most sought after mushrooms. They grow throughout the United States and Europe in moist areas, around dying or dead elm, sycamore, and ash trees, old apple orchards, and maybe even in your own backyard. The conical honeycombed caps exude the essence of spring in their heady and earthy aroma. Due to the texture of the cap, sandy sediment often gets trapped on the surface of the mushrooms. The best way to clean overly gritty morels is to submerge them in a large container of cool water and gently agitate the mushrooms to dislodge the sand and grit. Lift the mushrooms from the water and lay on kitchen towels to drain the excess water.

Spicy Crispy Chicken

The secret to this chicken's crispy golden skin and juicy meat is twofold: leaving the chicken uncovered in the refrigerator overnight to get the skin dry enough and adding baking powder to the spice rub. The baking powder acts as a drying agent and tenderizes the meat. If by chance there are any leftovers, I love to enjoy it as a sandwich on white bread with spicy mayonnaise and watercress.

SERVES 6

1 whole organic chicken, 4½ to 5 pounds
2 teaspoons baking powder
2 teaspoons celery salt
2 teaspoons coarsely ground black pepper
2 teaspoons ground ginger
2 teaspoons lemongrass powder (see Sources, page 317)
1½ teaspoons sea salt
1 teaspoon garlic powder
1 teaspoon ground allspice
½ teaspoon chili powder

Place the chicken, breast side down, on a work surface. Make a 2-inch incision in the skin along the back between the legs. Insert the handle of a wooden spoon through the incision to loosen the skin between the thighs and breast. Turn the chicken breast side up. Using a metal skewer, poke about 20 holes into the skin of the breast and thighs.

Whisk the remaining ingredients in a small bowl to blend. Using your hands, season the chicken with the spice blend, making sure to evenly coat the entire chicken. Place the chicken on a wire rack set atop a rimmed baking sheet and refrigerate uncovered for 24 hours.

Position the oven rack in the lower third of the oven and preheat the oven to 425°F. Remove the chicken from the refrigerator and set it aside at room temperature for 15 minutes. Roast the chicken on the lower rack until the skin is golden brown and crisp and the juices run clear when the chicken is pierced with a knife at the joint of the leg, about 40 minutes. To check for doneness, insert an instant-read thermometer in the thickest part of the thigh, making sure not to touch the bone. The temperature reading should be 165° to 175°F.

Carve the chicken into 8 pieces by gently pulling the legs away from the body and cutting the leg and the thigh off in 1 piece. Cut the leg and the thigh apart at the joint and repeat the process for the other leg. Cut the breasts away the main breast bone, scraping the breast meat away from the bone with the knife. Cut each breast in half. Serve immediately.

Wine suggestion ➤ Serve this dish with a Pinot Noir that offers flavors of roasted cherries, plums, and Asian spices, such as Pinot Noir, "Chamisal Vineyard," Domaine Alfred, 2005, Edna Valley, California.

Veal Cheeks Blanquette with Fingerling Potatoes & Black Trumpet Mushrooms

A blanquette is a French "white" stew, meaning the meat is not seared in the beginning and no dark wine or stock is added. The veal cheeks in this recipe are braised in the oven, though the dish is classically made by simmering the veal in water at length to tenderize it. I think braising allows you to concentrate and collect even more of all the exquisite flavors.

SERVES 6

Blanquette

2 tablespoons extra virgin olive oil
2 leeks (white and pale green parts only), halved and rinsed
2 onions, halved
3 celery stalks, halved crosswise
1 garlic head, cut in half crosswise
1 teaspoon whole black peppercorns
3 tablespoons unsalted butter
3 tablespoons all-purpose flour
3 cups dry white wine
5 fresh thyme sprigs
1 bay leaf
18 pieces veal cheeks, cleaned
Sea salt and freshly ground black pepper
1 cup heavy cream
1 tablespoon unsalted butter
Juice of ½ lemon
1 tablespoon fresh tarragon leaves

Potatoes

18 medium fingerling potatoes
1 garlic head, cut in half crosswise
2 tablespoons kosher salt
4 fresh thyme sprigs
1 bay leaf

Black Trumpet Mushrooms

2 tablespoons extra virgin olive oil
½ pound black trumpet mushrooms, trimmed
1 small shallot, finely diced
1 garlic clove, smashed
2 fresh thyme sprigs

Prepare the blanquette ➤ Preheat the oven to 350°F. Heat the olive oil in a large Dutch oven over medium heat. Add the leeks, onions, celery, garlic, and peppercorns and sauté until the leeks and onions just begin to soften but have no color at all, about 3 minutes. Add the butter. When the butter begins to foam, scatter the flour over the vegetables. Cook the flour for 2 minutes, stirring constantly with a wooden spoon so that the flour does not brown. Deglaze with the wine and simmer until the alcohol cooks off, about 1 minute. Add 8 cups of water, the thyme and bay leaf and bring to a boil. Season the veal cheeks with salt and pepper and carefully slide them into the simmering liquid. Cover the pot with a lid or aluminum foil and transfer to the oven. Braise until the veal cheeks are very tender, about 3 hours.

Transfer the veal cheeks to a large plate. Strain the braising liquid through a fine-mesh strainer into a large saucepan over medium heat. Simmer the liquid until thickened to the consistency of heavy cream, about 10 minutes. Season the sauce to taste salt and pepper. Return the sauce and the veal cheeks to the Dutch oven. (The recipe can be made up to this point 2 days in advance. Cool, then cover and refrigerate.)

Prepare the potatoes ➤ Place all the ingredients for the potatoes in a medium saucepan and add just enough water to cover. Bring to a boil and gently simmer until the potatoes are tender, about 15 minutes. Drain the potatoes. While the potatoes are still warm, peel the skins off with a paring knife.

Sauté the mushrooms ➤ Heat the olive oil in a large sauté pan over high heat. Add the mushrooms and sauté for 1 minute. Add the shallot, garlic, and thyme and sauté until all the liquid has evaporated, about 2 minutes. Remove the garlic and thyme, then add the mushroom mixture to the veal cheeks.

To assemble and serve ➤ Warm the veal cheeks over medium heat. Add the cream and potatoes and simmer until the liquid coats the back of a wooden spoon, about 5 minutes. Stir in the butter and lemon juice.

Transfer the blanquette to a large serving dish, garnish with the tarragon and serve immediately.

Wine suggestion ➤ Serve this dish with a rustic Pinot Noir that offers flavors of wild strawberries, blueberries, and fresh herbs, such as Pinot Noir, Mount Eden Vineyards, 2006, Santa Cruz Mountains, California.

Pan-Seared Skate with Crunchy Fava Bean Tabbouleh

Skate fish are very flat like a manta ray. Due to this shape the meat from the fish is referred to as wings rather than fillets. This dish came about after my travels throughout the Middle East where I enjoyed a multitude of tabbouleh. I wanted to add a bit of crunch and additional color so I decided to substitute uncooked fava beans for the traditionally used cracked wheat.

SERVES 6

Tabbouleh

1 cup peeled shelled fresh fava beans
1 small red onion, finely chopped
1½ cups chopped fresh parsley
½ cup extra virgin olive oil
¼ cup + 2 tablespoons freshly squeezed lemon juice
2 tablespoons chopped fresh mint
Sea salt and freshly ground black pepper

Skate

6 skate wings, 6 ounces each
3 tablespoons Wondra flour
3 tablespoons (about) extra virgin olive oil

Lemon Brown Butter

3 tablespoons unsalted butter
3 tablespoons freshly squeezed lemon juice

½ cup wild roquette, for garnish

Make the tabbouleh ➤ Coarsely chop the fava beans in a food processor. Transfer the beans to a medium bowl and stir in the onion, parsley, oil, lemon juice, and mint until well combined. Season to taste with salt and pepper.

Prepare the skate ➤ Season the skate with salt and pepper. Sprinkle the Wondra flour evenly over 1 side of each skate wing, shaking off any excess flour. Heat 1 tablespoon of the olive oil in a large sauté pan over medium-high heat. Once the pan begins to smoke, place 2 pieces of the skate, flour side down, in the pan. Sear until golden brown, about 4 minutes. Turn the skate over and cook 1 minute more. Transfer the skate to a large platter and repeat the process 2 more times with the remaining 4 skate wings, adding more oil as needed.

Make the lemon brown butter ➤ Once you have seared all the skate wings, add the butter to the same sauté pan. Cook the butter over medium heat, swirling the pan, and allow it to brown. Add the lemon juice to the brown butter and bring to a boil for 1 minute. Remove from the heat.

To serve ➤ Spoon the tabbouleh into the center of 6 serving plates and arrange the skate wings around the tabbouleh on each plate. Drizzle the warm lemon brown butter over the skate, scatter a few leaves of wild roquette on top, and serve immediately.

Wine suggestion ➤ Serve this dish with a crisp Albariño that offers flavors of white peach, lime zest, and a touch white flowers, such as Albariño, Havens Wine Cellars, 2006, Napa Valley, California.

Braised Rabbit Legs in Chablis with Tarragon Tagliatelle & Mousseron Mushrooms

In America, many people associate Chablis with those insipid, sweet wines that were sold in massive jugs in the 1970s and 1980s. Real Chablis is clean, lean, and mildly acidic. Mousseron are delicious, small, wild mushrooms and can be found abundantly in the United States. If necessary, substitute oyster mushrooms.

SERVES 6

Rabbit Legs

5 tablespoons unsalted butter
3 tablespoons extra virgin olive oil
6 hind (rear) rabbit legs
Sea salt and freshly ground black pepper
½ cup Wondra flour
7 shallots, thinly sliced
1 garlic head, top ¼ inch trimmed off
1 bottle (750 ml) Chablis
3 cups Chicken Stock (page 303)
1 bouquet garni (1 dark green leek leaf, 4 fresh sage leaves, 4 fresh thyme sprigs, 1 bay leaf; see page 305)
2½ tablespoons Dijon mustard
2 tablespoons whole grain mustard
½ cup heavy cream

Mushrooms and Pasta

2 tablespoons extra virgin olive oil
1 shallot, finely chopped
1 garlic clove, finely chopped
2 fresh thyme sprigs
4 cups mousseron mushrooms, cleaned
1 pound dried tagliatelle pasta

3 tablespoons fresh tarragon leaves, for garnish

Braise the rabbit legs ➤ Preheat the oven to 350°F. Melt 3 tablespoons of the butter with the olive oil in a large Dutch oven over medium heat. Season the rabbit legs with salt and pepper and dust with flour. Once the butter begins to foam, sear the rabbit legs until golden brown, about 3 minutes on each side. Remove the rabbit legs from the pot. Discard the fat from the pot. Place the pot back over medium heat and add the remaining 2 tablespoons of butter. Add the shallots and garlic and sauté until softened, about 2 minutes. Deglaze with the Chablis and simmer to reduce by half, about 10 minutes. Add the chicken stock and bouquet garni and bring to a simmer. Stir in the Dijon mustard and the whole grain mustard. Return the rabbit legs to the pot. Press a piece parchment paper over the surface of the stew and cover with a lid. Transfer the pot to the oven and braise until the meat is fork-tender, about 1½ hours.

Sauté the mushrooms ➤ Heat the olive oil in a sauté pan over medium heat. Add the shallot, garlic, and thyme and sauté until just softened, about 1 minute. Add the mushrooms and increase the heat to high. Sauté until all the liquid has evaporated, about 4 minutes.

Cook the tagliatelle ➤ When the rabbit is fork-tender and ready to be removed from the oven, bring a large pot of salted water to a boil. Cook the tagliatelle until al dente. Drain and then transfer the tagliatelle to a large bowl.

Finish the sauce ➤ Transfer the rabbit legs to a large platter. Remove and discard the bouquet garni and head of garlic. Place the pot on the stovetop over medium-high heat and whisk in the cream. Cook until the liquid begins to thicken, about 5 minutes. Spoon half of the sauce over the rabbit legs and the remaining half over the tagliatelle. Toss the pasta to coat evenly with the sauce.

To serve ➤ Divide the tagliatelle evenly among 6 serving plates. Arrange 1 rabbit leg atop each bowl of pasta and garnish with the mushrooms and tarragon leaves.

Wine suggestion ➤ Serve this dish with a Chablis-inspired Chardonnay that offers flavors of green apple, citrus, and minerals, such as Chardonnay, "Unoaked," Iron Horse, 2006, Green Valley, California.

Grilled Jamison Farm Double Lamb Chop with Vegetable au Vert & Gorgonzola Polenta

Spring vegetables are so vibrantly green and look even lovelier when bathed in a creamy herb and pea purée. The parsley in the purée adds a lot of color and the blanching removes any overt bitterness. I love to serve this at festive occasions because most of the preparations can be done a couple of hours beforehand.

SERVES 6

Lamb

3 Jamison Farm racks of lamb, 8 ribs each, frenched
2 tablespoons fennel seeds
2 teaspoons coriander seeds
1 teaspoon dried lavender
½ teaspoon whole black peppercorns
3 tablespoons plain whole-milk yogurt
1 tablespoon chopped fresh parsley
2 teaspoons fresh thyme leaves
Zest of 1 orange
¼ teaspoon Espelette pepper

Vegetables

1 cup sugar snap peas
1 cup shelled fresh English peas
6 asparagus stalks, trimmed and peeled
1 cup haricots verts, trimmed

Sauce

2 cups fresh parsley leaves
2 cups fresh chervil
½ garlic head, roasted (see page 306)
1 cup heavy cream
Sea salt and freshly ground black pepper
8 fresh mint leaves
1 tablespoon unsalted butter

Gorgonzola Polenta

Marinate the lamb ➤ Cut the lamb racks in quarters and place them in a nonreactive pan just large enough to hold them. Grind the fennel seeds, coriander seeds, lavender, and black peppercorns together in a spice grinder until they are medium-coarse. Transfer to a mixing bowl and stir in the yogurt, parsley, thyme, orange zest, and Espelette pepper until well combined. Generously coat the lamb with the marinade. Cover and refrigerate for at least 3 hours or overnight.

Blanch the vegetables ➤ Bring a large pot of salted water to a boil. Add the snap peas and cook until tender, about 2 minutes. Remove the snap peas with a slotted spoon and immediately transfer them to a bowl of ice water. Repeat the process with the English peas, asparagus, and haricots verts. Once the haricots verts have cooled, cut them in half crosswise.

Prepare the sauce ➤ Bring a medium saucepan of salted water to a boil. Add the parsley and simmer for 3 minutes. Using a slotted spoon, immediately transfer the parsley to a bowl of ice water. Repeat the process with the chervil but reduce the cooking time to 1 minute.

Once all the herbs have cooled, remove them from the ice water and pat dry. Gently squeeze the herbs to remove any excess water.

Squeeze the cloves from the roasted garlic into a small saucepan over medium-high heat. Add the cream and cook until the cream has reduced by a third, about 5 minutes. Season the sauce to taste with salt and pepper.

Combine the warm sauce, the blanched parsley, chervil, mint, and half of the blanched English peas in a blender and process until smooth.

Cook the lamb ➤ Preheat an outdoor grill or broiler for high heat. Wipe the lamb chops with paper towels to remove the marinade. Wrap the bones with aluminum foil to keep them from burning and place the lamb chops, bone side up, on the grill or on a pan under the broiler.

Grill or broil the lamb chops on all 4 sides until charred and cooked to medium-rare doneness, about 3 minutes on each side. To check for doneness, make a small cut near the bone and insert an instant-read thermometer into the thickest part of the meat. The temperature should be 140° to 150°F.

Remove the aluminum foil from around the bones and allow the meat to rest for 4 to 5 minutes.

To serve ➤ Gently rewarm the blanched vegetables, sauce, and butter in a small pot over medium heat. Once the vegetables and sauce are warm, spoon them onto a large shallow platter. Cut each lamb chop in half. Interlock the lamb bones and place over the vegetables. Serve with the Gorgonzola Polenta on the side.

Wine suggestion ➤ Serve this dish with a Bordeaux-inspired red blend that offers flavors of black cherries, cigar box, and spicy oak notes, such as Robert Craig, "Affinity," 2005, Napa Valley, California.

Gorgonzola Polenta

SERVES 6

4 cups whole milk
1 teaspoon sea salt + more for seasoning
2 cups white polenta
Freshly ground black pepper
2 tablespoons unsalted butter
½ cup crumbled Gorgonzola dolce
3 tablespoons grated Sartori Stravecchio (or another domestic Parmesan cheese)

Preheat the broiler. Bring 4 cups of water, the milk, and 1 teaspoon of salt to a boil in a large saucepan over medium heat.

Whisk in the polenta, stirring constantly to make sure it does not clump. Bring to a simmer, cover, and reduce the heat to the lowest possible flame or setting. Cook until softened, stirring every 5 minutes, about 30 minutes. Season to taste with salt and pepper and stir in the butter.

Evenly divide the polenta among six 10-ounce ramekins. Scatter the Gorgonzola over the polenta and then sprinkle the Sartori Stravecchio over the Gorgonzola.

Place the ramekins on a rimmed baking sheet and broil until the cheeses begin to brown, about 1 minute. Serve immediately.

Roasted Lamb Shoulder Stuffed with Merguez & Swiss Chard

Merguez, a red, spicy sausage that originated in North Africa, is made most commonly with lamb, and sometimes beef. The red tint is due to the cayenne, paprika, and harissa that's used to flavor the sausage. It is mostly sold as a fresh sausage but can also be found cured in oil.

SERVES 6

Lamb

1 boneless lamb shoulder, about 4 pounds
2 tablespoons dried oregano
2 tablespoons coarsely ground black pepper
3 tablespoons extra virgin olive oil
Kosher salt
5 tablespoons canola oil
2 lemons, halved crosswise
6 shallots, halved
1 garlic head, halved crosswise
8 fresh thyme sprigs
3 fresh rosemary stems
Juice of ½ lemon

Merguez Stuffing

1 bunch Swiss chard, leaves and stems separated
4 tablespoons extra virgin olive oil
1 small onion, cut into ¼-inch dice
2 garlic cloves, finely chopped
½ pound merguez sausage, casings removed
1 teaspoon finely chopped fresh rosemary
2 teaspoons chopped fresh thyme
½ cup panko (Japanese breadcrumbs)
Zest of 1 lemon
2 tablespoons chopped fresh mint
2 tablespoons chopped fresh parsley
Sea salt and freshly ground black pepper

Season the lamb ➤ Spread the lamb open on a work surface. When unrolled, the meat should be a rectangle of sorts. Score the inside of the meat with a paring knife, making incisions every ¾-inch and being careful not to cut all the way through the meat. Rub the inside of the lamb with 1 tablespoon each of the oregano and black pepper. Turn the lamb over and rub the outside with the remaining oregano and black pepper. Drizzle the outside with the olive oil. Transfer to a rimmed baking sheet, cover with plastic wrap and refrigerate for 1 hour.

Make the merguez stuffing ➤ Bring a large pot of salted water to a boil. Add the Swiss chard leaves and cook for 1 minute. Using a slotted spoon, immediately transfer the chard to a bowl of ice water. Once cool, drain and squeeze out the excess water and then coarsely chop the chard leaves. Thinly slice the chard stems until you have 1 cup; discard any remaining stems.

Heat 2 tablespoons of the olive oil in a large sauté pan over medium heat. Add the onion and sauté for 1 minute. Add the garlic and chard stems and continue to cook until the onions are translucent and the garlic is fragrant, about 3 minutes. Transfer the onion mixture to a bowl. Add the remaining 2 tablespoons of olive oil to the pan and increase the heat to high; crumble the sausage into the pan. Cook until the sausage is brown, 2 to 3 minutes. Add the blanched chard leaves, reserved onion mixture, rosemary, and thyme and stir until well combined. Add the panko, lemon zest, mint, and parsley and remove the pan from the heat. Season to taste with salt and pepper. Spread the stuffing on a rimmed baking sheet and allow to cool.

Roast the lamb ➤ Preheat the oven to 350°F. Remove the lamb from the refrigerator and season both sides with kosher salt. Set the lamb aside to reach room temperature. Spread the cooled merguez stuffing over the scored side of the lamb and loosely roll up, jelly-roll style. Tie 5 pieces of kitchen string in intervals to secure the rolled lamb shoulder.

Heat the canola oil in a roasting pan over high heat. Sear the lamb on all sides until brown, about 2 minutes on each side. Place the lamb, seam side down, in the roasting pan. Scatter the lemons, shallots, garlic, thyme sprigs, and rosemary stems around the lamb and transfer to the oven. Roast for 20 minutes. Gently turn the lamb over and cook for about 10 minutes longer for medium doneness. Transfer the meat to a cutting board and reserve the pan to make the jus. Loosley cover the meat with aluminum foil and set aside to rest for 10 minutes.

continued

Make the jus ➤ Place the roasting pan on the stove over medium heat. Deglaze with ½ cup of water and the lemon juice and cook, scraping up any browned bits with a wooden spoon, about 2 minutes.

To serve ➤ Remove the kitchen twine from around the lamb. Using a sharp carving knife, cut the lamb into 12 slices. Arrange the sliced lamb on a large platter and scatter the roasted lemon, shallots, garlic, and herbs around the meat. Spoon the pan jus over the lamb and serve immediately.

Wine suggestion ➤ Serve this dish with a spicy Syrah that offers flavors of blackberry jam, Asian spices, and a touch of earthiness, such as Syrah, "Hudson Vineyard," Lewis Cellars, 2005, Carneros, California.

Spicy Roasted Maine Lobster with Ramps & Ginger

Maine lobsters, one of the most delicious ocean delicacies, live in the wild, rocky ocean habitat off the coast of Maine. They roam the seafloor and dine on a diet of crabs, mussels, sea urchins, and clams. Lobsters are harvested year-round, however their peak season begins in mid-June. I like to serve this meal with Lemongrass Sticky Rice (page 256).

SERVES 6

- 3 Maine lobsters, 2 pounds each
- 1 cup Chicken Stock (page 303)
- 3 tablespoons hoisin sauce
- 2 tablespoons vegetable oil
- 5 ramps, thinly sliced
- 5 garlic cloves, thinly sliced
- 1 piece (3 inches) fresh ginger, peeled and cut into matchstick-size strips
- 1 cup snow peas, cut into matchstick-size strips
- 1 red Thai chile, thinly sliced
- 2 tablespoons roughly chopped fresh cilantro
- 2 tablespoons roughly chopped fresh Thai basil
- Sea salt and freshly ground black pepper

Bring a large pot of salted water to a boil. Using a lobster cracker or the back of the blade of a large heavy chef's knife, crack off the claws of the lobsters. Twist the tails off of the body. Add the claws to the boiling water and cook for 6 minutes. Add the tails to the boiling water and cook for an additional 2 minutes. Transfer the lobster claws and tails to a large bowl of ice water. Once cool, crack open the claws and remove the meat; discard the claw shells. Cut the tails in half lengthwise with a large heavy chef's knife or kitchen shears but do not remove the meat from the shell.

Whisk the chicken stock and hoisin sauce in a small bowl to blend. Heat the vegetable oil in a large sauté pan over medium heat. Add the ramps, garlic, and ginger and sauté until soft and very fragrant, about 2 minutes. Add the lobster tails, flesh side down, and cover the pan with a lid. Cook until the lobster meat is fully cooked through, about 5 minutes. Remove the lobster tails from the pan. Add the snow peas and Thai chile and cook until the snow peas are crisp-tender, about 1 minute. Deglaze the pan with the hoisin sauce mixture and bring to a boil over medium-high heat. Simmer the sauce until thickened, about 1 minute. Season to taste with salt and pepper. Return the lobster tails and claw meat to the pan. Add the cilantro and Thai basil. Cover and cook for 2 minutes.

Transfer the lobster mixture to a large platter and serve immediately.

Wine suggestion ➤ Serve this dish with a tropical Viognier that offers flavors of pineapple, peach, and grapefruit, such as Viognier, Pearmund Cellars, 2006, Virginia.

RAMPS, a type of wild onion sometimes referred to as wild leeks, possess a powerfully pungent, spicy aroma and flavor very similar to that of garlic or shallots. They have broad, smooth, green leaves, often with deep purple or burgundy tints on the lower stems, and scallion-like bulbs. Ramps and wild leeks are distinguished primarily by growing in different regions of the United States. Where they are found growing in the Appalachian range they are known as ramps. Harvest in this region typically begins around the middle of April. A few weeks later they are harvested in the Great Lakes region where they are called wild leeks.

Pan-Seared Arctic Char with Braised Artichokes, Fava Beans, & Lemon-Basil Pesto

Arctic char is a close relative to both salmon and trout but has a finer texture and milder flavor. Char are primarily a freshwater fish but are also fished in the waters off of Canada. The brightly colored flesh of the fish looks sensational against the vivid green of the pesto broth studded with favas and artichokes.

SERVES 6

Artichokes and Fava Beans

6 large globe artichokes
2 lemons, juiced; peel of 1 lemon thinly sliced
3 tablespoons extra virgin olive oil
12 cipolline onions, peeled
1 carrot, thinly sliced
½ fennel bulb, core removed, thinly sliced
1 garlic clove, thinly sliced
Sea salt and freshly ground black pepper
2 cups dry white wine
1 bouquet garni (1 dark green leek leaf, 3 fresh basil sprigs, 2 fresh thyme sprigs, 1 bay leaf; see page 305)
1 cup shelled fava beans

Lemon-Basil Pesto

4 cups fresh basil leaves
½ head roasted garlic (see page 306)
5 tablespoons extra virgin olive oil
3 tablespoons toasted pine nuts
Zest of 1 lemon
1 cup coarsely grated Sartori Stravecchio cheese (or another domestic Parmesan cheese)

Arctic Char

4 tablespoons vegetable oil
6 arctic char fillets with skin, 7 ounces each

Prepare the artichokes ➤ Trim 1½ to 2 inches off the top of the artichokes. Using a very sharp paring knife, trim off the outer dark green leaves of the artichokes, leaving only the very tender light green leaves. Using a peeler or a sharp paring knife, peel the green tough outer layer off the stem. Cut the artichokes into quarters and scoop out the purple leaves and hairs that cover the artichoke heart. Soak the artichokes in a bowl of cold water with the juice of 1 lemon until ready to use.

Heat the olive oil in a large high-sided sauté pan over medium heat. Add the onions, carrot, fennel, garlic, and lemon peel. Season to taste with salt and pepper. Sauté until tender, about 3 minutes. Add the wine and bouquet garni and simmer until the alcohol has mostly cooked off, about 4 minutes. Drain the artichokes and add them to the sauté pan with 1 cup of fresh water and the remaining juice of 1 lemon. Simmer until the artichokes are tender when pierced with a knife, about 10 minutes. Remove the pan from the heat.

Prepare the fava beans ➤ Bring a small saucepan of salted water to a boil. Add the fava beans and cook until tender, about 1 minute. Immediately remove the beans from the boiling water and place them in a bowl of ice water. Once cool, remove the fava beans from the ice water and slip the outer skin off each bean by puncturing 1 end with your fingernail or a knife and gently squeezing the green bean out. Discard the skin and rinse the beans under gently running cold water.

Make the lemon-basil pesto ➤ Bring a small saucepan of salted water to a boil. Add the basil and simmer for 1 minute. Drain and immediately place the basil in a bowl of ice water. Once cool, remove the basil from the ice water and squeeze out the excess water. Place the basil in a blender. Peel the roasted garlic and add it to the basil. Add the olive oil, pine nuts, and lemon zest. Blend until smooth and bright green. Transfer to a mixing bowl, stir in the grated cheese, and season to taste with salt and pepper. Press a sheet of plastic onto the surface of the pesto to prevent it from turning brown.

Cook the arctic char ➤ Place the artichokes and their broth over medium-low heat. Divide the vegetable oil between 2 nonstick sauté pans over medium heat. Season the arctic char with salt and pepper and place them, skin side down, in the nonstick pans. Cook until the skin is crisp, about 3 minutes. Turn the fish over and cook for an additional 10 seconds. Immediately transfer the fish, flesh side down, to the artichoke broth and cook until the fish is just cooked through, about 2 minutes. Remove the fish and arrange on a large platter.

To serve ➤ Stir the pesto and fava beans into the artichoke broth and continue to cook until warmed through, about 2 minutes. Spoon the vegetables and broth around the fish and serve immediately.

Wine suggestion ➤ Serve a Bordeaux-inspired white blend that offers flavors of honeydew melon, citrus zest, and a touch of honey, such as Semillon/Sauvignon Blanc/Muscadelle, Buty, 2007, Columbia Valley, Washington.

Breaded Maine Sea Scallops with Old Bay–Caper Butter & Spring Onion Purée

Breading scallops with thinly sliced or finely diced bread adds a pronounced texture that contrasts well with the creamy onion purée. However, if you want to simplify this recipe, just omit the breading and carry on. Old Bay seasoning, created by a German immigrant in Maryland, has been around for nearly sixty years. The distinct flavors of celery salt, bay, and mustard seed are perfectly suited for most seafood.

SERVES 6

Scallops

18 dry-packed jumbo scallops, about 2 pounds total
1½ teaspoons Old Bay seasoning
1 teaspoon sea salt
10 slices brioche bread, ¼-inch thick
1 large egg
½ cup all-purpose flour
4 tablespoons clarified butter (see page 305)
4 tablespoons unsalted butter
1 spring onion, thinly sliced (optional)

Spring Onion Purée

2 tablespoons unsalted butter
1 pound spring onions, bulbs halved and thinly sliced
Sea salt and freshly ground black pepper
¾ cup heavy cream
1 fresh thyme sprig
1 bay leaf

Old Bay–Caper Butter

3 tablespoons salt-packed capers, soaked in water for 1 hour and drained
Juice of 1 lemon
2 tablespoons chopped fresh parsley

Dry the scallops ➤ Remove any muscles that may still be attached to the scallops. Arrange the scallops on a baking sheet lined with paper towels and refrigerate for 1 hour to dry before cooking.

Make the spring onion purée ➤ Melt the butter in a medium sauté pan over medium heat. Add the onions and season to taste with salt and pepper. Add the cream, thyme, and bay leaf. Simmer over low heat until the onions are tender, about 10 minutes. Remove the thyme sprig and bay leaf and discard. Transfer the mixture to a blender and purée until smooth. Season to taste with salt and pepper.

Prepare the scallops ➤ Season both sides of the scallops with the Old Bay seasoning and salt. Using a 1-inch round cookie cutter, cut out 18 disks from the brioche slices. Whisk the egg and 2 tablespoons of water in a small bowl to blend. Place the flour on a plate. Coat 1 side of a scallop with the flour, shaking off any excess, and then dip the floured side of the scallop into the egg wash. Gently press the scallop onto a brioche disk making sure it is fully adhered. Repeat the process with the remaining scallops.

Cook the scallops and make the Old Bay–caper butter ➤ Heat 2 tablespoons of the clarified butter in a large sauté pan over medium-high heat. Once the butter is hot, add half of the scallops, brioche side down, and cook until the bread is golden brown, about 2 minutes. Turn the scallops over and add 2 tablespoons of the unsalted butter. Continue to cook until the scallops are golden brown on the bottom, about 2 minutes. Transfer the scallops to a clean plate and repeat the process with the remaining scallops, clarified butter, and unsalted butter.

Add the capers to the sauté pan and deglaze with the lemon juice, scraping up any browned bits from the bottom of the pan with a wooden spoon. Remove the sauté pan from the heat and stir in the parsley.

To serve ➤ Spoon the spring onion purée in the center of 6 plates. Arrange 3 scallops, brioche side up, over the purée on each plate and drizzle with the caper butter. Garnish with thinly sliced spring onion, if desired, and serve.

Wine suggestion ➤ Serve this dish with a rich and creamy Chardonnay that offers flavors of tropical fruits, citrus, and Tahitian vanilla, such as Chardonnay "Reserve," ZD Wines, 2006, Napa Valley, California.

Halibut en Papillote with Fava Beans & Green Garlic

The clean Asian flavors in this dish are terrific and uncomplicated, just like the cooking method. The halibut and the vegetables are simply steamed in the paper by the heat from the oven and the moisture from the wine. You can make these packets a few hours in advance and place them in the oven when you are ready to eat, which makes this ideal for entertaining. There is a bit of a wow factor when these parcels are presented at the table.

SERVES 6

½ cup shelled fresh fava beans
3 lemongrass stalks
1 tablespoon + ½ cup extra virgin olive oil
6 center-cut halibut fillets, 6 ounces each
Sea salt and freshly ground black pepper
5 medium shiitake mushrooms or yellow-foot mushrooms, stemmed and thinly sliced
3 tablespoons roughly chopped fresh cilantro
2 Thai chile peppers, thinly sliced
4 green garlic cloves, thinly sliced
½ cup + 1 tablespoon dry white wine
1 large egg white
1 lime, cut into 6 wedges

Bring a small pot of salted water to a boil. Add the fava beans and cook for 1 minute. Immediately drain the beans and transfer them to a bowl of ice water. Once cool, remove the fava beans from the ice water and slip the outer skin off each bean by puncturing 1 end of the skin with your fingernail or a knife and gently squeezing the green bean out. Discard the skins and rinse the beans under gently running cold water.

Cut off the bottom 4 inches of the lemongrass stalks and discard the rest. Peel the tough outer leaves off until you reach the soft inner core. Grate the lemongrass on a Microplane grater or chop it very finely.

Preheat the oven to 375°F. Cut six 20 × 12-inch pieces of parchment paper. Lay them out before you. Pour ½ teaspoon of the olive oil in the center of each parchment paper. Season the halibut on both sides with salt and pepper and place 1 fillet on top of the oil on each parchment paper. Divide the mushrooms, cilantro, peppers, garlic, lemongrass, and fava beans on top and around the fish. Drizzle the fish with the white wine and the remaining ½ cup of olive oil. Brush the edges of the paper with the egg white, which will act as glue. Bring the top edge of the parchment down over the fish to the bottom edge to create a little package. Fold and crimp the edges of the paper together and brush again with the egg wash to seal the packets. Arrange the packets on 2 baking sheets. At this point, the papillotes can be refrigerated, up to 4 hours, until ready to bake.

Bake the papillotes in the oven until they begin to puff up, 12 to 15 minutes.

To serve ➤ Remove the papillotes and place 1 on each of 6 serving plates. Serve the parcels tableside along with a wedge of lime. Have each person open their parcel with a knife or 2 forks and squeeze the lime juice over the top.

Wine suggestion ➤ Serve this dish with a Sauvignon Blanc that has been aged in oak and offers flavors of key limes, tropical fruit, and a rich finish, such as Sauvignon Blanc, Hartwell Vineyards, 2006, Napa Valley, California.

Chocolate-Amaretto Icebox Pie with Milk Chocolate Ice Cream

Icebox pies are an old Southern tradition that consisted of a no-bake filling that set up while the pie was stored in the icebox, a precursor to the modern-day refrigerator. One of my pastry chefs created this version, which has become my favorite of all his desserts.

SERVES 10

Special Equipment
10-inch springform pan

Feuilletine
1 cup hazelnut praline paste
4 ounces bittersweet chocolate (66% cocoa), chopped
2 tablespoons unsalted butter
2½ cups feuilletine
½ cup almonds, toasted and roughly chopped

Dark Chocolate Mousse
10 ounces bittersweet chocolate (66% cocoa), chopped
5 large egg yolks
¼ cup + 2 tablespoons sugar
1¼ cups heavy cream

White Chocolate Mousse
10 ounces white chocolate, chopped
4 large egg yolks
¼ cup sugar
2 gelatin sheets
1¼ cups chilled heavy cream

Amaretto Crème Anglaise
1 cup heavy cream
1 cup whole milk
½ cup sugar
5 large egg yolks
⅓ cup amaretto or other almond liqueur
½ teaspoon almond extract

Milk Chocolate Ice Cream (page 309)

Make the feuilletine ➤ Line 2 large baking sheets with parchment paper and line a 10-inch springform pan with parchment paper. Melt the hazelnut praline paste, chocolate, and butter in the top of a double boiler over simmering water, stirring until smooth. Pour the mixture into a small bowl and fold in the feuilletine. Spoon half of the mixture onto 1 sheet of parchment paper and spread evenly with an offset spatula to form a 10-inch disk. While the chocolate is still warm, sprinkle with half of the almonds. Repeat the process with the remaining feuilletine and almonds to create a second disk. Chill the feuilletine sheets in the freezer until firm, about 10 minutes. Remove 1 of the feuilletine disks from the parchment paper and place it in the prepared springform pan. Place the springform pan and the second sheet of feuilletine in the refrigerator until ready to use.

Make the dark chocolate mousse ➤ Melt the chocolate in the top of a double boiler over simmering water, stirring until the chocolate is completely melted. Remove from the heat and set aside until cool but still fluid. Once cool, beat the egg yolks with the sugar in a large bowl until pale and fluffy, about 2 minutes. Using a rubber spatula, fold the egg and sugar mixture into the melted chocolate until well combined.

Using an electric mixer with chilled beaters, whip the cream in a chilled large bowl until it forms medium-firm peaks. Using a rubber spatula, fold the whipped cream into the chocolate and egg mixture until well combined. Spread the mousse evenly over the feuilletine in the cake pan. Remove the remaining disk of feuilletine from the parchment paper and place it over the chocolate mousse. Return the pan to the refrigerator.

Make the white chocolate mousse ➤ Melt the white chocolate in the top of a double boiler over simmering water, stirring until the chocolate is completely melted. Remove from the heat and set aside until cool but still fluid. Once cool, beat the egg yolks with the sugar in a large mixing bowl until pale and fluffy, about 2 minutes. Using a rubber spatula, fold the egg mixture into the melted chocolate until well combined.

Soak the gelatin sheets in 2 cups of cold water until soft, about 5 minutes. Remove the gelatin from the water and squeeze out any excess water. Place the gelatin in a medium metal bowl and whisk over simmering water until completely melted. Fold the gelatin into the white chocolate mixture.

Using an electric mixer with chilled beaters, whip the cream in a chilled medium bowl until it forms medium-firm peaks. Using a rubber spatula, fold the whipped cream into the white chocolate mixture until well combined. Spread the white chocolate mousse over the feuilletine. Cover the cake pan with plastic wrap and place in the refrigerator overnight.

Make the amaretto crème anglaise ➤ Bring the cream, milk, and sugar to a simmer in a medium saucepan over medium-low heat, stirring to dissolve the sugar.

Whisk the egg yolks in a medium bowl until thick and well blended. Slowly pour the warm cream mixture over the yolks, whisking constantly so the eggs do not cook. Transfer the mixture to a clean saucepan and add the amaretto and almond extract. Cook over medium-low heat, stirring constantly, until thick enough to coat the back of a wooden spoon, about 2 minutes (do not allow the mixture to boil). Pour the crème anglaise into a clean bowl set over a bowl of ice water. Stir frequently to cool.

To serve ➤ Remove the cake from the springform pan and slice it into wedges. Arrange the slices on serving plates. Place a scoop of ice cream alongside each slice and top with a drizzle of crème anglaise. Serve immediately.

Wine suggestion ➤ Serve this dish with a late harvest Zinfandel that offers flavors of dried plums, wild blackberries, and vanilla, such as Zinfandel, "Late Night Harvest," Venge, 2007, Napa Valley, California.

Mammy Louisette's Ginger-Rhubarb Tart with Vermont Double Cream Ice Cream

My grandmother Louisette, an amazing cook, used to make this sweet delight with rhubarb freshly cut from her garden. While I knew the tart was intended to enjoy after our family dinner, I would inevitably find the compote cooling in the window and sneak a few bites before my grandmother would catch me, literally red-handed, with the compote dripping down my hands and chin.

SERVES 6

Special Equipment

10-inch round fluted tart pan with removable bottom

¼ cup sugar
1½ tablespoons cornstarch
1 teaspoon grated peeled fresh ginger
1 vanilla bean, split lengthwise and seeds scraped
4 rhubarb stalks, cut into ½-inch-thick pieces (about 2 cups)
1 sheet store-bought frozen puff pastry, preferably Dufour brand, thawed
2 tablespoons confectioners' sugar
Vermont Double Cream Ice Cream (page 311)

Make the filling ➤ Preheat the oven to 375°F. Combine the sugar, cornstarch, ginger, and vanilla bean seeds in a large bowl and mix well. Fold in the rhubarb.

Prepare the crust ➤ Using a floured rolling pin, roll out the puff pasty on a lightly floured surface to a ⅛-inch thickness. Trim the dough to a 13-inch disk and carefully fit it into a 10-inch round fluted tart pan with a removable bottom. Gently press the dough into the pan and allow the dough to hang over the edge by 1½ inches. Place the tart pan in the freezer for 30 minutes.

Bake the tart ➤ Spoon the filling into the tart shell and fold the excess dough over the filling. Bake until the rhubarb is tender and the pastry is cooked through, about 25 minutes. Remove the tart from the oven and sprinkle with the confectioners' sugar.

To serve ➤ Allow the tart to cool for several minutes and then remove it from the pan. Serve each slice of the tart with a scoop of ice cream.

Wine suggestion ➤ Serve this dish with a late harvest Gewurztraminer that offers flavors of crystallized ginger, lychees, and a touch a rose petals, such as Gewurztraminer Late Harvest, Torii Mor Winery, 2006, Willamette Valley, Oregon.

Sour Cherry Pie with Pistachio Chantilly

Look for fresh sour cherries at your local farmers' market in mid to late June. Their smaller size, more pronounced tartness, and firm texture make them an ideal fruit for baking. If you are unable to find fresh sour cherries, use sweet cherries and decrease the amount of sugar in the filling.

SERVES 8

Special Equipment
9-inch-round, 2-inch-deep tart pan with removable bottom

Pistachio Chantilly
1½ cups heavy cream
3 tablespoons pistachio paste

Dough
2¾ cups all-purpose flour
4 teaspoons sugar
½ teaspoon salt
8 tablespoons chilled unsalted butter
7 tablespoons chilled vegetable shortening
3 tablespoons ice water
¾ teaspoon white vinegar

Filling
6 cups fresh sour cherries, pitted
⅔ cup sugar
¼ cup cornstarch
Pinch of salt
1 tablespoon ground cinnamon
Zest and juice of 1 lemon

1½ tablespoons heavy cream
4 tablespoons turbinado sugar
Cherry Sorbet (page 313)

Make the pistachio chantilly ➤ In the chilled bowl of an electric mixer fitted with the whisk attachment, whisk the cream at medium speed until medium peaks form, about 2 minutes. Add the pistachio paste and mix until well combined, about 1 minute. The mixture will begin to lose some of its volume due to the oil in the pistachio paste. Transfer to a mixing bowl, cover, and refrigerate for at least 5 hours.

Make the dough ➤ Combine the flour, sugar, and salt in the bowl of a stand mixer fitted with the paddle attachment and mix until well combined. Add the butter and vegetable shortening and continue to mix until crumbly, about 1 minute. Add the water and vinegar and mix until the dough just comes together, about 2 minutes. Wrap in plastic wrap and refrigerate for 1 hour.

Line a baking sheet with parchment paper. Divide the dough into 2 equal pieces. Using a floured rolling pin, roll out 1 piece of dough on a lightly floured surface to a ⅛-inch-thick round. Trim the dough into a 14-inch disk then fit it into a 9-inch pie pan, allowing the dough to hang over the edge by 1 inch. Roll out the remaining dough into a ¼-inch thickness and trim it into a 9-inch disk to place on the top of the pie. Place the top crust on the lined baking sheet. Refrigerate both the pie shell and the top crust for 1 hour.

Make the filling ➤ Cook 2 cups of the cherries with the sugar, cornstarch, and salt in a medium sauté pan over medium heat, stirring regularly with a silicone spatula, until the mixture begins to thicken, about 5 minutes. Remove from the heat and stir in the remaining 4 cups of cherries, the cinnamon, and lemon zest and juice. Allow the filling to cool to room temperature.

Bake the pie ➤ Preheat the oven to 350°F. Pour the cherry filling into the prepared pie shell. Place the top crust over the cherry filling. Using your fingers, firmly press the top and bottom pie crusts together so that they adhere. Using a paring knife, trim any excess dough off the sides. Cut a small round hole in the middle of the top crust for steam to escape. Make 4 additional decorative slits around the hole in the top crust. Brush with the heavy cream and sprinkle with the turbinado sugar. Bake until the dough is golden brown and cooked through, about 45 minutes.

To serve ➤ Remove the pie from the oven and allow to rest on a cooling rack for 30 minutes before cutting. You may either serve the pie warm or refrigerate it so that it is easier to cut. Serve with a dollop of pistachio chantilly and a scoop of sorbet.

Wine suggestion ➤ Serve this dish with a sweet port wine made from cherries and offers flavors of cherry pie, vanilla, and violets, such as Cherry Port, Longview Vineyards, 2007, Leelanau Peninsula, Michigan.

Key Lime Pavlova

There is an ongoing debate about whether New Zealand or Australia invented this dessert. It is known that the name pavlova was chosen in honor of the Russian ballerina, Anna Pavlova, who toured both New Zealand and Australia in 1926. A pavlova is a meringue cake with a light, delicate, crisp crust and a soft sweet marshmallow center that is produced by folding a little vinegar and cornstarch into stiffly beaten egg whites and sugar. I have updated this classic by replacing the soft inner part of the meringue with a sweet and tart creamy filling.

SERVES 6

Meringue
3 large egg whites
½ teaspoon vanilla extract
Pinch of cream of tartar
¾ cup sugar
1 tablespoon + 1½ teaspoons cornstarch
1 teaspoon white vinegar

Key Lime–Mascarpone Cream
½ cup heavy cream
1 cup mascarpone
3 tablespoons sugar
Zest of 3 Key limes

Key Lime Sauce
½ cup sugar
½ cup + 1 tablespoon freshly squeezed Key lime juice
3 tablespoons unsalted butter, room temperature

Zest of 3 Key limes, for garnish

Make the meringue ➤ Preheat the oven to 200°F. Line a baking sheet with parchment paper. Using a stand mixer fitted with the whisk attachment, whisk the egg whites, vanilla, and cream of tartar in the mixer bowl at medium speed until soft peaks begin to form, about 3 minutes. With the stand mixer running, gradually add the sugar and continue to mix for several minutes until the egg whites become stiff and glossy. Remove the bowl from the mixer. Using a silicone spatula, fold in the cornstarch and the vinegar.

Transfer the meringue to a piping bag. Pipe 6 peaked rounds onto the prepared baking sheet. Bake until the meringues begin to crisp, about 2 hours. Remove from the oven and place the meringues on a large plate to cool slightly.

Line the baking sheet with a clean sheet of parchment paper. Using a small spoon, gently tap the bottom of each meringue so that a hole is formed. Carefully scoop out the inside of the meringue and discard. Transfer the hollow meringues back to the baking sheet and bake until the inside of the meringues begins to dry out and becomes crispy, about 20 minutes. Remove from the oven and allow to cool uncovered on a wire rack.

Make the Key lime–mascarpone cream ➤ In a stand mixer fitted with the whisk attachment, whisk the cream in the mixer bowl at medium speed until it is thick but does not hold any peaks, about 1 minute. Transfer the cream to another mixing bowl. Combine the mascarpone and sugar in the bowl of the stand mixer and whisk at medium speed until the sugar is dissolved and the mixture is smooth, about 2 minutes. Using a silicone spatula, fold the beaten cream into the mascarpone mixture. Add the lime zest and fold until well incorporated.

KEY LIMES are small, somewhat larger than a walnut, and oval in shape with a thin yellow-tinted rind prone to splotchy brown spots. They are aromatic and very juicy, with a stronger and more complex acidic flavor than more common Persian limes. Key limes, like most citrus, originated in Asia and made their way to other parts of the world via the traders and explorers in centuries past. Until the mid-1920s, Key limes were grown throughout Florida and the Florida Keys. In 1926, when a hurricane wiped out the groves, growers replaced the Key lime trees with Persian lime trees because they were more resistant to disease and easier to harvest. Key limes are now grown in limited quantities in Florida, Texas, and California.

Transfer the mixture to a piping bag and refrigerate for a minimum of 1 hour or until ready to serve.

Make the Key lime sauce ➤ Combine the sugar and 3 tablespoons of water in a small saucepan. Cook over medium-high heat, swirling the pan occasionally, until the mixture forms a light caramel, about 4 to 5 minutes. Reduce the heat to medium-low and whisk in the lime juice. Continue to cook, whisking constantly, until thick and smooth, about 2 minutes. Remove from the heat and whisk in the butter until smooth.

To serve ➤ Spoon 3 tablespoons of the warm sauce onto each of 6 plates. Remove the mascarpone cream from the refrigerator and pipe the cream into the meringues through the hole at the bottom. Arrange the meringue on top of the sauce and garnish with the lime zest.

Wine suggestion ➤ Serve this dish with a late harvest Riesling that offers flavors of tangerine, dried apricots, and lime sorbet, such as White Riesling Late Harvest, Hogue, 2006, Columbia Valley, Washington.

Caramelized Mango–Coconut Cream Tart

Mangoes have a sweetness and perfume that is undeniably appealing, so it's not suprising they are purportedly the most widely consumed fresh fruit in the world. Mangoes come in over fifty varieties and are native to Southeast Asia.

SERVES 6

Special Equipment
13¾ × 4½-inch rectangular tart pan; kitchen torch

1¼ cups unsweetened coconut milk
1 vanilla bean, split lengthwise and seeds scraped
3 large egg yolks
¼ cup sugar
2½ tablespoons cornstarch
1 tablespoon + 2 teaspoons unsalted butter, softened
Tart Dough (page 141)
2 cups heavy cream
2 large ripe mangoes, peeled, halved, and sliced ⅛ inch thick
¼ cup turbinado sugar

Make the coconut cream ➤ Combine the coconut milk and the scraped vanilla bean seeds in a medium saucepan over medium heat and bring to a boil. Whisk the egg yolks, sugar, and cornstarch in a large bowl until the mixture is pale and fluffy. Slowly pour the hot coconut milk into the egg mixture, whisking constantly so that the eggs do not cook.

Strain the mixture through a fine-mesh strainer set over a clean saucepan. Bring the mixture to a boil over medium-low heat, whisking constantly until it begins to thicken, 1 to 2 minutes. Once the mixture is thick and bubbling, whisk for 3 to 4 minutes so that the starch is cooked through and the mixture is smooth. Transfer the hot mixture to the bowl of a stand mixer fitted with the paddle attachment and mix over medium speed. Slowly add the butter a little bit at a time. Continue to mix until smooth and fully blended, about 5 minutes. Transfer the coconut cream to a bowl. Press a sheet of plastic wrap onto the surface of the coconut cream so that a skin does not form, and refrigerate overnight. The coconut cream will begin to firm up as it cools.

Prepare the crust ➤ Make the tart dough according to the recipe. Form the dough into a square, wrap it in plastic wrap, and refrigerate for a minimum of 1 hour.

Preheat the oven to 325°F. Using a floured rolling pin, roll out the dough on a lightly floured surface to a ⅛-inch-thick rectangle that is about 16 × 7 inches. Fit the dough into a 13¾ × 4½-inch rectangular tart pan. Roll the rolling pin over the top of the tart to trim any excess dough from the edges. Line with parchment paper and fill with dried beans. Bake until golden brown and cooked through, about 20 minutes. Remove from the oven and cool on a wire rack. Gently remove the dried beans and parchment paper from the crust.

Assemble the tart ➤ Using a stand mixer fitted with a whisk attachment, whisk the heavy cream in the mixer bowl at medium speed until it forms medium peaks, about 1 minute. Remove the bowl from the mixer and, using a rubber spatula, fold the cold coconut cream, one-third at a time, into the whipped cream. Make sure the cream is uniformly combined and transfer it to a pastry bag. Pipe the coconut cream inside the prepared crust.

Layer the sliced mangoes over the coconut cream, making sure the top is completely covered and that no coconut cream is visible. Refrigerate the tart until ready to serve.

To serve ➤ Sprinkle the turbinado sugar over the mango slices. Using a kitchen torch, caramelize the sugar. Serve immediately.

Wine suggestion ➤ Serve this dish with a late harvest Viognier that offers flavors of dried apricots, ripe tropical fruits, and honey, such as Viognier Late Harvest, "Saralee's Vineyard," 2006, Sonoma County, California.

Baked Cacao Gratins

For those of you who love soufflés, here is another way to create a similarly airy and rich custard dessert. This recipe, however, can be made without the dread that it may implode at a moment's notice. Gelatin is added to the custard and the egg whites are whipped with hot sugar to make an Italian meringue, providing extra structure as well as peace of mind. You can make the mousse and freeze it a day in advance. Just bake the gratins in the oven and caramelize the tops before serving.

SERVES 6

Special Equipment

Six 3½-inch ring molds (½ inch high); kitchen torch

Cocoa Cream

4 gelatin sheets
¼ cup unsweetened cocoa powder
⅓ cup sugar
1½ tablespoons cornstarch
4 large egg yolks
1 cup whole milk

Meringue

2 tablespoons + 6 teaspoons sugar
2 tablespoons light corn syrup
4 large egg whites
Nonstick cooking spray

Confectioners' sugar for dusting
Chocolate Sauce (page 283)

Make the cocoa cream ➤ Soak the gelatin sheets in 2 cups of cold water to soften. Whisk the cocoa powder, sugar, cornstarch, and egg yolks in a medium bowl until fully incorporated. Bring the milk to a boil in a small saucepan over medium heat. Slowly pour the hot milk into the egg yolk mixture, whisking constantly so the yolks do not cook. Strain the mixture through a fine-mesh strainer set over a clean saucepan. Place the saucepan over medium heat, whisking constantly, until the mixture thickens, about 3 minutes. Remove the pan from the heat.

Remove the gelatin sheets from the water and squeeze out any excess water. Whisk the gelatin sheets into the cocoa cream until they dissolve. Transfer the cocoa cream to a clean mixing bowl and press a sheet of plastic wrap onto the surface to prevent a skin from forming. Allow the cocoa cream to cool to room temperature.

Make the meringue ➤ Combine the 2 tablespoons of sugar and 3 tablespoons of water in a small saucepan. Add the corn syrup and bring to a boil over medium-high heat until it reaches 240°F, about 4 minutes. While the sugar is heating, whisk the egg whites in the bowl of a stand mixer fitted with the whisk attachment until they are frothy. With the mixer running, pour the boiling sugar syrup into the egg whites and increase the speed to high. Beat until the whites triple in volume and become very glossy, about 5 minutes. Continue to whip until the meringue begins to cool, about 4 minutes. Allow the meringue to cool to room temperature.

Assemble the gratins ➤ Line a rimmed baking sheet with parchment paper. Place six 3½-inch ring molds (½ inch high) on the paper. Spray the inside of each ring mold lightly with nonstick cooking spray. Fold the meringue into the cocoa cream and mix until uniform. Spoon into the prepared ring molds and freeze for at least 5 hours.

Bake the gratins ➤ Preheat the oven to 325°F. Gently remove the ring molds from around the mousse. Bake until the gratins have puffed and resemble a soufflé, about 15 minutes.

To serve ➤ Sprinkle 1 teaspoon of the remaining sugar over each gratin. Using a kitchen torch, caramelize the sugar until golden brown. Dust with confectioners' sugar. Serve immediately with the chocolate sauce on the side.

Wine suggestion ➤ Serve this dish with a port-inspired blend that offers flavors of dark fruits, chocolate, and toasted nuts, such as Rockpile Winery, "Independence Red," 2006, Rockpile, California.

Macaroon Hazelnut Ice Cream Sandwich

Macaroons are traditional French pastries that originated in Nancy, a small city in northeastern France. These petite sandwiched delights are made by placing a bit of cream or ganache between 2 very light crunchy cookies. I have altered the presentation ever so slightly to create a Frenchified version of the American ice cream sandwich.

SERVES 6

Hazelnut Ice Cream (page 309)
1¼ cups + 2 tablespoons confectioners' sugar
1 cup + 3 tablespoons almond flour
⅓ cup unsweetened cocoa powder
5 large egg whites
Pinch of cream of tartar
¾ cup granulated sugar

Prepare the ice cream ➤ Once the ice cream has been churned in the ice cream machine, spread it evenly onto a 9 × 13-inch rimmed baking sheet. It should be ½ inch thick. Freeze the ice cream until firm, at least 2 hours.

Make the macaroon batter ➤ Preheat the oven to 325°F. Mix the 1¼ cups of the confectioners' sugar with the almond flour, cocoa powder, and 2 egg whites in a small bowl to form a paste-like consistency.

Using a stand mixer fitted with the whisk attachment, whisk the remaining 3 egg whites and cream of tartar in the mixer bowl at medium speed until soft peaks begin to form. Meanwhile, place the granulated sugar and 3 tablespoons of water in a small saucepan over medium-high heat and bring to a boil for 2 minutes. With the machine running, pour the hot syrup into the egg whites. Increase the speed to high and continue to whisk until the egg whites have tripled in size and are smooth and glossy, about 4 minutes. Using a rubber spatula, fold the flour mixture into the egg whites and mix until well combined. Transfer the batter to a pastry bag.

Bake the macaroons ➤ Line 2 large baking sheets with parchment paper. Pipe the macaroon batter into twenty-four 2½-inch rounds. Let them rest until a skin begins to form over the top of the macaroon, about 10 minutes. Bake until the bottom is fully cooked but the inside remains moist, about 10 minutes. Remove from the oven and allow to cool to room temperature. Once cool, wrap the macaroons with plastic wrap and freeze until cold, about 30 minutes.

Assemble the sandwiches ➤ Remove the ice cream from the freezer. Using a 2½-inch round cookie cutter, cut the ice cream into 12 rounds. Place each ice cream round between 2 macaroons and return them to the freezer for 1 hour.

To serve ➤ Remove the macaroons from the freezer. Dust the sandwiches with the remaining 2 tablespoons of confectioners' sugar and serve immediately.

Wine suggestion ➤ Serve a Solera-style sherry from California that offers flavors of vanilla, roasted hazelnuts, and caramel, such as Galleano Winery, "Nino's Solera Sherry," NV, Cucamonga Valley, California.

Rice Pudding with Dried Plum Compote

This stovetop cooking method is much more gratifying than waiting for a three-hour proper rice pudding to come out of the oven. The result is sweet, luscious, and incredibly creamy. This recipe makes enough rice pudding to serve six with a little bit left over to enjoy the next day.

SERVES 6

Rice Pudding

1 orange
9 cups whole milk
1 pound Arborio rice, rinsed under cold water
1 cup sugar
3 cinnamon sticks
2 vanilla beans, split lengthwise and seeds scraped
2 tablespoons dark rum
1 tablespoon vanilla extract
2 cardamom pods
2 tablespoons orange blossom water

Plum Compote

10 ounces dried plums, pitted
½ cup Simple Syrup (page 314)
1½ tablespoons Grand Marnier

Make the rice pudding ➤ Using a vegetable peeler, remove the orange-colored peel from the orange then squeeze the juice from the orange. Combine the orange peel and juice, 4 cups of the milk, the rice, sugar, cinnamon sticks, vanilla beans and vanilla seeds, 1 tablespoon of the rum, the vanilla extract, and cardamom pods in a large saucepan. Cook the rice mixture over medium heat until the rice is tender, adding the remaining 5 cups of milk slowly and stirring constantly so that the rice does not stick to the bottom of the saucepan, about 40 minutes. Remove the pan from the heat, discard the vanilla bean, orange peel, cardamom pods, and cinnamon sticks and transfer the rice pudding to a large bowl. Mix in the remaining 1 tablespoon of rum and the orange blossom water. Allow the mixture to cool to room temperature. Press a sheet of plastic wrap onto the surface of the rice pudding to prevent the pudding from forming a skin. Refrigerate until ready to serve.

Make the compote ➤ Combine the dried plums, simple syrup, and 1½ cups of water in a small saucepan. Cover and simmer over low heat until the plums begin to soften and break apart, about 20 minutes. Add the Grand Marnier and cook for 5 minutes. Remove from the heat.

To serve ➤ Spoon the rice pudding into 6 bowls and top with a spoonful of the compote. Serve immediately.

Wine suggestion ➤ Serve this dish with a vin de paille (straw wine) that offers flavors of ripe apricots, spice, and maple syrup, such as Vin de Paille, "Quintessence," Tablas Creek Vineyards, 2005, Paso Robles, California.

Chocolate Feuilletine Gianduja with Coffee-Cointreau Crème Glace

New York City has an abundance of street-cart vendors selling foods ranging from classic hot dogs to halal kebabs. My favorites though are the ones selling hot fragrant candied nuts. The honey-roasted peanuts have the perfect sweet and salty crunch that I find hard to resist.

SERVES 8 TO 10

Chocolate Cake
¾ cup almond flour
½ cup + 2 tablespoons confectioners' sugar
2 large whole eggs
3 tablespoons unsweetened cocoa powder
4 teaspoons unsalted butter
2 tablespoons all-purpose flour
2 large egg whites
2 teaspoons sugar

Feuilletine
¾ cup hazelnut praline paste
2½ ounces milk chocolate (40% cocoa), chopped
1½ tablespoons unsalted butter
1½ cups feuilletine

Gianduja Mousse
2½ gelatin sheets
8 ounces gianduja chocolate (or milk chocolate)
⅓ cup sugar
4 large egg yolks
3 tablespoons heavy cream, warmed
2¾ cups cold heavy cream

3 tablespoons unsweetened cocoa powder
¼ cup honey-roasted peanuts, preferably from your local street-cart vendor
Coffee-Cointreau Crème Glace (page 308)

Make the cake ➤ Preheat the oven to 325°F. Line a 13 × 9-inch baking sheet with parchment paper. Using a stand mixer fitted with the paddle attachment, mix the almond flour, confectioners' sugar, whole eggs, and cocoa powder in the mixer bowl at medium speed for 10 minutes. While the batter is mixing, melt the butter in a small saucepan over high heat and cook, swirling the saucepan, until the butter begins to brown, about 2 minutes. Remove the brown butter from the heat.

Using a rubber spatula, transfer the batter from the mixer to a large bowl. Using the rubber spatula, carefully fold the all-purpose flour and brown butter into the batter until well combined. In a clean mixing bowl, whisk the egg whites and sugar at high speed until the mixture forms stiff peaks, about 3 minutes. Gently fold the egg whites into the batter until well combined.

Bake the cake ➤ Pour the chocolate cake batter onto the lined baking sheet and spread evenly. Bake until just set, about 10 minutes. Cool to room temperature and then refrigerate for at least 1 hour.

Invert the chocolate cake and carefully remove the parchment paper from the bottom of the cake. Replace it with a clean sheet of parchment paper (this will keep the cake from sticking when it is sliced). Place the cake back in the pan, parchment side down, and refrigerate it until you are ready to assemble.

Make the feuilletine layers ➤ Line an 18 × 13-inch rimmed baking sheet with parchment paper. Melt the hazelnut praline paste, milk chocolate, and butter in a double boiler, stirring until smooth. Fold the feuilletine into the melted chocolate mixture and stir until well combined.

Spread the mixture evenly over the parchment paper to a ⅛-inch thickness. Freeze for 20 minutes. Remove the feuilletine from the freezer and cut in half so that it is the same shape as the chocolate cake. Return to the freezer until you are ready to assemble.

Make the mousse ➤ Soak the gelatin in 2 cups of cold water to soften. Melt the chocolate in a double boiler stirring until smooth; set aside. Bring the sugar and 3 tablespoons of water to a boil in a small saucepan over medium heat and cook for 2 minutes.

continued

Using a stand mixer fitted with the whisk attachment, whisk the egg yolks in the mixer bowl until pale and fluffy, about 2 minutes. With the mixer running, pour the hot syrup over the egg yolks. Continue to whisk over high speed until the mixture has cooled.

Remove the gelatin from the water, squeeze out any excess water, and dissolve it in the warmed cream. Using a rubber spatula, fold the melted chocolate into the egg yolk mixture and then fold in the warm cream with the gelatin. Meanwhile, in a mixer fitted with the whisk attachment, whisk the cold heavy cream at high speed until it forms soft peaks, about 3 minutes. Using a rubber spatula, gently fold the whipped cream into the chocolate mixture. Refrigerate until ready to use.

Assemble the cake ➤ Remove the chocolate cake from the refrigerator. Spread a layer of mousse, about ¼ inch thick, over the cake. Freeze for 5 minutes. Remove from the freezer and place a layer of the feuilletine over the mousse. Spread another layer of the mousse, about ¼ inch thick, over the feuilletine. Return to the freezer until set, about 5 minutes. Place a second layer of feuilletine over the mousse, and then spread a final layer of mousse over the top. Freeze for a minimum of 3 hours.

Remove the cake from the freezer and, using a sharp knife, trim 1 inch from each side of the cake. Carefully remove the cake from the sheet pan and cut into 8 rectangular pieces. Refrigerate until ready to serve.

To serve ➤ Dust the cocoa powder over the top of the cake and decoratively garnish with the honey-roasted peanuts. Serve with the glace.

Wine suggestion ➤ Serve this dish with a port-inspired wine that offers flavors of raspberry jam, cherry pie, and caramel, such as Warwick Valley Winery, "Winston's Harlequin Port," NV, New York.

Duck Eggs in a Jar with Sorrel

Sorrel, a large leafy herb, resembles spinach in appearance but the flavor is sweet and almost kiwi-like. The larger leaves tend to be more acidic, so stick with smaller, sweeter leaves. You can also use tender medium-size spinach leaves in this recipe instead. I like to eat this dish with thin slices of country ham and toasted seven-grain bread.

SERVES 6

Special Equipment
Six 6-ounce lidded glass jars or ramekins

1 bunch sorrel, thick stems discarded
6 tablespoons grated Pleasant Ridge Reserve cheese (or another washed-rind, semi-aged cow's milk cheese)
6 tablespoons crème fraîche
Freshly grated nutmeg
6 farm fresh duck eggs
Sea salt and freshly ground black pepper

Preheat the oven to 375°F. Arrange six 6-ounce lidded glass jars or ramekins in a roasting pan. Divide the sorrel, then the cheese, and lastly the crème fraîche among the jars. Sprinkle a pinch of nutmeg over each. Crack a duck egg into each jar and season with salt, pepper, and another pinch of nutmeg. Close the lids of the jars or cover with heavy-duty aluminum foil.

Pour enough hot water into the roasting pan to come halfway up the sides of the jars and place the roasting pan in the oven. Bake the eggs until the whites are set but the yolks are still runny, about 12 minutes. Immediately remove the jars from the hot water and serve.

Oeuf Coque with Chive-Tarragon Mouillette

Soft-cooked eggs are a beloved French breakfast tradition. Mouillette, which translates as bread fingers, are ideal for dipping into the egg and soaking up the rich, runny yolk. If you don't have egg cups, crack the eggs open in the center and serve the eggs in their shell in small bowls.

SERVES 6

Special Equipment
Six egg cups

Tarragon-Chive Cream
¼ cup crème fraîche
¼ cup roughly chopped fresh chives
2 tablespoons chopped fresh tarragon
Sea salt and freshly ground black pepper

Mouillette
6 slices country bread

Soft-Cooked Eggs
1 tablespoon white vinegar
6 large farm fresh eggs
Pinch of freshly grated nutmeg

Make the tarragon-chive cream ➤ Combine the crème fraîche, chives, and tarragon in a small food processor fitted with a metal blade and process until green. Make sure not to overprocess or the crème fraîche will turn into butter. Season the tarragon-chive cream to taste with salt and pepper.

Make the mouillette ➤ Toast the bread and spread with the tarragon-chive cream, reserving 6 teaspoons of the cream to spoon into the eggs.

Cook the eggs ➤ Fill a medium saucepan three-fourths full with water. Add the vinegar and a pinch of salt and bring to a boil. Using a large slotted spoon, place the eggs gently into the boiling water and cook for 3 minutes. Remove the eggs from the water and place each of them in an egg cup with the oval tip facing up.

To serve ➤ Briskly tap the top of the egg with the edge of a small metal spoon until it cracks. Remove the cracked top with the spoon. Sprinkle the nutmeg over the eggs and spoon 1 teaspoon of the tarragon-chive cream over each egg. Cut the mouillette into 1-inch strips. Serve hot with an espresso spoon to scoop the egg out of the shell.

Pea, Ramp, Sausage, & Fresh Goat Cheese Frittata

A frittata is the perfect way to incorporate little bits and pieces you may have in your refrigerator; however this is not to imply that the frittata should become the dumping ground for your leftovers. I like to serve the remaining spring onion slices on the side with a handful of arugula dressed with extra virgin olive oil and lemon juice.

SERVES 6

½ cup shelled fresh English peas
6 to 8 fiddlehead ferns, trimmed and cleaned
12 large farm fresh eggs
4 ramps, leaves and bulbs thinly sliced
2 tablespoons chopped fresh chives
2 tablespoons chopped fresh tarragon
Dash of Tabasco
Dash of Worcestershire sauce
Sea salt and freshly ground black pepper
3 tablespoons extra virgin olive oil
1 pound spicy Italian sausage, casings removed
1 portobello mushroom, stem and gills removed, thinly sliced
2 green garlic cloves, finely chopped
1 medium spring onion, thinly sliced into half-moons
3 ounces crumbled Coach Farm fresh goat cheese

Preheat the oven to 375°F. Bring a small saucepan of salted water to a boil and cook the peas for 2 minutes. Drain the peas and immediately place them in a bowl of ice water. Once cool, remove the peas from the water and pat dry on a kitchen towel. Repeat this process with the fiddlehead ferns.

Vigorously whisk the eggs in a large bowl until the whites and yolks are fully combined. Stir in the peas, ramps, chives, tarragon, Tabasco, Worcestershire sauce, and salt and pepper to taste.

Heat 2 tablespoons of the olive oil in large ovenproof nonstick sauté pan over medium heat. Crumble the sausage into the pan and break up any large pieces with a wooden spoon. Sear the sausage until it's barely pink in the center, about 3 minutes. Add the fiddlehead ferns to the sausage and sauté until they are just tender, about 3 minutes. Remove the ferns from the pan and set them aside for garnish. Add the mushrooms, garlic, and half of the sliced onion to the sausage and season to taste with salt and pepper. Cook until the mushrooms have released their liquid and the onions are soft, about 5 minutes.

Pour the egg mixture over the sausage mixture and scatter the goat cheese over the top. Transfer the pan to the oven and bake the frittata until the eggs have set, about 10 minutes.

Remove the frittata from the oven. Run a silicone spatula around the edge of the frittata to loosen it from the pan. Invert the frittata onto a plate then turn it over so that the goat cheese side faces up. Drizzle with the remaining tablespoon of olive oil, garnish with the fiddlehead ferns, and serve.

Warm Vanilla Waffles

I like to enjoy these waffles several ways, depending upon what is in my refrigerator—sometimes just with butter and warm honey, or as my southern friends have taught me, with fried chicken and maple syrup. Europeans eat waffles with whipped cream, confectioners' sugar, Nutella, chocolate, jam, you name it. They consider them more of an afternoon snack than breakfast.

SERVES 6 TO 8

2¼ cups cold whole milk
1¾ tablespoons fresh yeast
3¼ cups all-purpose flour
1 tablespoon sugar
2 vanilla beans, split lengthwise and seeds scraped
Pinch of salt
2 cups warm water
5 large eggs
1¾ cups unsalted butter, melted
Nonstick cooking spray

Mix ¾ cup of the milk with the yeast in a small bowl. Whisk the flour, sugar, vanilla bean seeds, and salt in a large bowl. Whisk the 2 cups of warm water, eggs, and the remaining 1½ cups of milk in another large bowl. Add the yeast mixture and the egg mixture to the dry ingredients and whisk until well combined. Finally, stir in the melted butter until just incorporated.

Let the batter rise at room temperature until it doubles in size and begins to bubble, about 40 minutes. Using a whisk, stir the batter several times to allow some of the air to escape, and then let the batter rise 5 minutes longer. Cover with plastic wrap and refrigerate for 3 hours.

Heat a waffle iron according to the manufacturer's instructions. Spray the waffle iron with nonstick cooking spray and ladle enough batter just to cover the surface. Close and cook per the manufacturer's instructions, until golden brown, about 3 minutes. Serve immediately.

Easter Sunday Brunch Buffet

MENU

Appetizers

Seasonal Crudités with Homemade Boursin

or

Poached White Asparagus with Ramp Béarnaise

or

Mâche and Chive Blossom Salad with Deviled Quail Eggs

or

Creamy White Mushroom Scrambled Eggs

or

Duck Eggs in a Jar with Sorrel

Main Courses

Roasted Lamb Shoulder Stuffed with Merguez and Swiss Chard

or

Veal Cheeks Blanquette with Fingerling Potatoes and Black Trumpet Mushrooms

or

Halibut en Papillote with Fava Beans and Green Garlic

COCKTAIL

Jack Rabbit

DESSERTS

Gingerbread Brioche Pain Perdu

or

Mammy Louisette's Ginger-Rhubarb Tart with Vermont Double Cream Ice Cream

or

Chocolate Feuilletine Gianduja with Coffee-Cointreau Crème Glace

Mother's Day Brunch

MENU

COCKTAIL

Rhubarb Mule

Appetizers

Pea Pod and Mint Risotto with Steamed Maine Red Shrimp

or

Grilled Marinated Salmon Salad with Sugar Snap Peas,
Pea Shoots, Cucumber, Watercress, and Radishes

or

La Quercia Prosciutto and Blue Ledge Farm Crottina Salad
with Creamy Lardon Vinaigrette

Main Courses

Grilled Jamison Farm Double Lamb Chop
with Vegetable au Vert and Gorgonzola Polenta

or

Pan-Seared Arctic Char with Braised Artichokes,
Fava Beans, and Lemon-Basil Pesto

or

Breaded Maine Sea Scallops with Old Bay–Caper Butter
and Spring Onion Purée

DESSERTS

Key Lime Pavlova

or

Chocolate-Amaretto Icebox Pie with Milk Chocolate Ice Cream

or

Sour Cherry Pie with Pistachio Chantilly

Summer

In the heat of the summer, it's easy to enjoy light fare based on dazzling ingredients at their peak. I enjoy bright summer mornings by indulging in a gem-studded bowl of fresh raspberries, blackberries, and blueberries and a drizzle of locally harvested honey; or I might want something a bit more substantial like farm fresh eggs and thinly sliced country ham. Simple pastas, like a perfectly al dente bucatini or a roasted tomato soup are ideal for lunch; while warm nights make for a leisurely meal of striped bass paired with a glass of crisp North Fork Sauvignon Blanc. Basically, to me, the summer is an endless buffet of simple but elegantly prepared meals.

Summer harvests are prolific and bright colors and flavors define these market-inspired recipes. Treasures from the field—tomatoes, corn, eggplant, summer squash, shelling beans, sweet peppers—take center stage. Juicy stone fruits, berries, figs, and melon can be used in both sweet and savory dishes. Seafood, like swordfish, cod, and soft-shell crab, are in abundance during this season as well.

Summer also holds a promise of escape and adventure. I try to go on vacation at least once during the summer, even if it's just to the local beach for a long weekend. It's there that I savor exceptionally fresh fish caught only hours earlier or farm fresh produce from roadside stands that look like overgrown jewel boxes with their bright brimming wares. Other summer adventures lead me farther afield and I indulge in more exotic fare. On these journeys I always seek out local specialties and am never disappointed. Many of those trips, both near and far, have inspired several recipes in this book.

This is also the perfect time of year to let the produce do the hard work. The cooking techniques best suited to summer are easy, straightforward, and quick methods, like grilling and steaming. Cold dishes like a summer bean salad or raw tuna are a great way to celebrate the warmer months. Also, don't be afraid to experiment with new ingredients, like those curious-looking heirloom tomatoes or some deliciously briny white anchovies. Summer is a time for adventure so I like to embrace it in any, and all, forms.

July

Vegetables
Arugula
Bok Choy
Chinese Cabbage
Corn
Cucumber
Dandelion
Eggplant
Green Bean
Napa Cabbage
Red Onion
Squash Blossom
Summer Squash
Yellow Wax Bean

Herbs
Chocolate Mint
Hyssop
Lavender
Lemon Balm
Pineapple Sage
Purple Basil
Verbena

Seafood
Blue Fin Tuna
Fluke
Lobster
Mussel
Rock Shrimp
Soft-Shell Crab
Striped Bass
Swordfish

Fungi
Morel
Mousseron
Porcini
Summer Truffle

Fruit
Apricot
Huckleberry
Key Lime
Mango
Melon
Nectarine
Peach
Red and White Currant
Rhubarb
Strawberry
Sweet Cherry

August

Vegetables
Bell Pepper
Cranberry Bean
Cucumber
Dandelion
Eggplant
Green Bean
Green Garlic
Green Tomato
Heirloom Tomato
Pear Tomato
Summer Squash
Vidalia Onion
White Corn
Yellow Wax Bean

Herbs
Chocolate Mint
Dill
Hyssop
Lavender
Lemon Balm
Lemongrass
Marjoram
Pineapple Sage
Purple Basil
Sage
Savory
Thyme
Verbena

Seafood
Blue Fin Tuna
Flounder
Lobster
Mussel
Rock Shrimp
Soft-Shell Crab
Swordfish

Fungi
Chanterelle
Morel
Porcini
Summer Truffle

Fruit
Apricot
Black Mission Fig
Blackberry
Blueberry
Huckleberry
Key Lime
Melon
Peach
Plum
Raspberry
Red and White Currant
Sweet Cherry
Tristar Strawberry
Watermelon

September

Vegetables
Corn
Cranberry Bean
Cucumber
Eggplant
Green Bean
Green Garlic
Green Tomato
Heirloom Tomato
Pear Tomato
Poblano Pepper
Summer Squash
Vidalia Onion
Yellow Wax Bean
Zucchini

Herbs
Hyssop
Lavender
Opal Basil
Orange Mint
Oregano
Sage
Savory
Verbena

Seafood
Blue Fin Tuna
Chatham Cod
Mussel
Rock Shrimp
Striped Bass
Swordfish

Fungi
Chanterelle
Porcini
Summer Truffle

Fruit
Apricot
Black Mission Fig
Blackberry
Blueberry
Honey Crisp Apple
McIntosh Apple
Melon
Peach
Plum
Raspberry
Tristar Strawberry

Apricot Cosmo

Apricots in all forms take this Cosmo to another level. Try looking for small, fragrant, fresh apricots for this cocktail.

SERVES 1

1 apricot, peeled, pitted, and diced
2 ounces Absolut Citron vodka
1 ounce apricot brandy
½ ounce cranberry juice
½ ounce freshly squeezed lime juice
½ ounce Simple Syrup (page 314)
1 dried apricot slice

Muddle the diced apricot in a cocktail shaker until it reaches a pasty consistency. Add the vodka, brandy, cranberry juice, lime juice, and simple syrup and shake with ice. Strain into a martini glass. Garnish with the dried apricot slice on the rim of the glass.

White Peach Julep

The julep, a classic Southern cocktail, has become one of my favorite summer drinks. The sweetness of the white peach complements the deep caramel flavors of the bourbon.

SERVES 1

½ white peach, peeled, pitted, and diced
8 fresh mint sprigs
2½ ounces Maker's Mark bourbon
1 ounce Mathilde peach liqueur
2 dashes of Fee Brothers Peach Bitters

Muddle the peach and 7 of the mint sprigs in a cocktail shaker until fragrant. Add the bourbon, peach liqueur, and bitters. Shake and strain into a highball glass with ice and garnish with the remaining mint sprig.

Watermelon-Basil Margarita

Watermelon is the perfect fruit for a cocktail, as it adds just a hint of sweetness while the basil adds fragrance and a little bit of bite.

SERVES 1

½ cup diced peeled seedless watermelon
2 ounces Sauza Blanco tequila or other premium clear tequila
1 ounce Simple Syrup (page 314)
½ ounce freshly squeezed lime juice
2 fresh basil sprigs, torn
1 thin slice watermelon

Muddle the diced watermelon in a cocktail shaker until juicy. Add the tequila, simple syrup, lime juice, and basil sprigs and shake with ice. Strain into a cocktail glass. Garnish with the slice of watermelon on the rim of the glass.

Basil-Cucumber Mojito

Having spent quite a bit of time in Miami, the Mojito has become one of my favorite cocktails. The cucumber and basil are cooling on a hot summer day.

SERVES 1

6 cucumber slices, ¼ inch thick
2 fresh basil leaves
2 ounces Hendrick's gin or other premium gin
1 ounce freshly squeezed lime juice
1 ounce Ginger Syrup (see page 314)
Club soda

Muddle 3 slices of cucumber and the basil leaves in a cocktail shaker. Add the gin, lime juice, and syrup and shake with ice. Strain into a highball glass. Top with a splash of soda and garnish with the remaining 3 slices of cucumber floating on top.

Raspberry-Thyme Spritzer

Gin's herbaceous quality is highlighted by the addition of sweet summer thyme. The raspberries add a great tart flavor and lend their gorgeous color to the cocktail.

SERVES 1

10 fresh raspberries + 1 for garnish
1 teaspoon fresh thyme leaves
2 ounces Plymouth gin or other premium gin
1 ounce Simple Syrup (page 314)
½ ounce freshly squeezed lemon juice
Club soda
1 fresh thyme sprig

Muddle the 10 raspberries and thyme leaves in a cocktail shaker. Add the gin, simple syrup, and lemon juice, and shake with ice. Strain into a highball glass filled with ice and top with a splash of soda. Garnish with the thyme sprig and the remaining 1 raspberry.

Ginger Summer Fizz

This is hands down one of my favorite drinks. Ginger and lemongrass add so much flavor and fragrance to savory dishes, so why not try them in a cocktail? The effect is a lovely and aromatic cocktail with a bit of spice.

SERVES 1

¼ cup thinly sliced lemongrass
2 ounces Absolut Citron vodka
1 ounce Simple Syrup (page 314)
½ ounce freshly squeezed lime juice
½ ounce ginger juice (see page 96)
Club soda
1 lemongrass stalk or slice of candied ginger

Muddle the lemongrass in a cocktail shaker until fragrant. Add the vodka, simple syrup, lime juice, and ginger juice and shake with ice. Strain into a highball glass filled with ice and top with a splash of soda. Garnish with a lemongrass stalk or a slice of candied ginger.

Raspberry-Thyme Spritzer

Beefsteak Tomato, Mortadella, & Wisconsin Emmenthaler Tart

Wisconsin Emmenthaler is similar but worlds better than regular old grocery store Swiss cheese. True Emmenthaler cheese is generally richer because it is made with unpasteurized milk. It's great in this tart with its slightly piquant and somewhat sharp taste.

SERVES 6

- 1 sheet store-bought frozen puff pastry, preferably Dufour brand, thawed
- 2 tablespoons Raye's whole grain mustard
- 12 slices Wisconsin Emmenthaler cheese, ⅛ inch thick
- 6 slices mortadella, ¼ inch thick
- 3 large vine-ripened or beefsteak tomatoes, thinly sliced
- 3 thinly sliced garlic cloves
- Sea salt and freshly ground black pepper
- 4 tablespoons extra virgin olive oil

Preheat the oven to 375°F. Line a baking sheet with parchment paper. Unfold the puff pastry sheet on a cool, lightly floured surface and roll it out to a ¼-inch thickness. Trim the pastry into a 12-inch round and place it on the prepared baking sheet. Using a fork, prick the pastry in several places.

Brush the pastry with the mustard, leaving a ½-inch border. Lay 6 slices of cheese over the mustard, then top with the mortadella. Lay the remaining 6 slices of cheese over the mortadella. Arrange, the tomatoes atop the tart, slightly overlapping to form a circular pattern, then scatter the garlic over the tomatoes. Season to taste with salt and pepper and drizzle with 2 tablespoons of the olive oil.

Bake until the pastry is golden brown, the cheese is hot and bubbling, and the tomatoes are slightly caramelized, about 30 minutes.

Drizzle the tart with the remaining 2 tablespoons of olive oil and serve immediately.

Wine suggestion ➤ Serve this dish with an Alsatian white-inspired blend that offers aromas of nectarines, flowers, and spice, such as Robert Sinskey, "Abraxas," 2007, Napa Valley, California.

Bucatini with Swordfish, Eggplant Ragu, & Garlic Breadcrumbs

Bucatini pasta is a long, hollow pasta, which at first glance looks like spaghetti; but upon further inspection, you'll notice that it actually has a hole running through the middle. Its density and length make it well suited to heavier sauces like this one.

SERVES 6

Swordfish
6 tablespoons extra virgin olive oil
1½ teaspoons chili powder
1 teaspoon coriander seeds
1 teaspoon cumin seeds
1 teaspoon fennel seeds
1 teaspoon smoked paprika
½ teaspoon finely chopped garlic
½ teaspoon freshly ground black pepper
1 pound swordfish, cut into 1-inch pieces
Sea salt

Eggplant Ragu
3 tablespoons extra virgin olive oil
8 medium Japanese eggplants, cut into ½-inch cubes
2 cups chopped onions
2½ teaspoons finely chopped garlic
2 plum tomatoes, seeded and chopped
6 fresh thyme sprigs
Sea salt and freshly ground black pepper

Garlic Breadcrumbs
3 tablespoons extra virgin olive oil
½ teaspoon finely chopped garlic
6 tablespoons panko (Japanese breadcrumbs)
1 tablespoon roughly chopped fresh oregano

Pasta
12 ounces bucatini pasta
1 tablespoon finely grated lemon zest

Marinate the swordfish ➤ Stir the olive oil, chili powder, coriander, cumin, fennel, smoked paprika, garlic, and black pepper in a medium bowl until well combined. Reserve 1 tablespoon of the marinade for later use. Add the swordfish to the remaining marinade and toss to coat. Cover and refrigerate for 1 hour.

Make the ragu ➤ Heat 1 tablespoon of the olive oil in a large sauté pan over high heat until nearly smoking. Add one-third of the eggplant and sear until dark brown on all sides, about 5 minutes. Remove the eggplant from the pan and repeat the process 2 more times with the remaining eggplant and oil. Reduce the heat to medium and return all of the seared eggplant to the pan. Add the onions and garlic and sauté until the onions are soft and becoming translucent, about 5 minutes. Add the tomatoes and thyme and season to taste with salt and pepper. Sauté until the ragu begins to thicken, about 5 minutes. Add 1 cup of water. Cover and reduce the heat to medium-low, and simmer until the ragu is thick and the water has been absorbed, about 5 minutes.

Make the breadcrumbs ➤ Heat the olive oil in a small sauté pan over medium heat. Add the garlic and sauté until just lightly golden, about 1 minute. Add the panko and toss to coat. Continue to sauté until the panko is toasted, about 5 minutes. Stir in the oregano.

Cook the pasta ➤ Bring a large pot of salted water to a boil over high heat. Add the bucatini and cook until al dente, stirring often, about 10 minutes. Drain the bucatini.

Cook the swordfish ➤ While the pasta is cooking, season the swordfish with salt. Heat a large sauté pan over high heat. Add the swordfish along with its marinade and sear the fish on all sides, about 5 minutes. Gently stir the swordfish into the ragu so as not to break the fish.

To serve ➤ Divide the bucatini among 6 warm serving plates. Spoon the ragu over the pasta and drizzle with the reserved 1 tablespoon of marinade. Sprinkle with the breadcrumbs and garnish with lemon zest.

Wine suggestion ➤ Serve this dish with a full-bodied rosé that offers flavors of fresh strawberries, raspberries, and hints of summer flowers, such as Sola Rosa, 2007, Sonoma County, California.

Raw & Confit Bigeye Tuna Tonnato

Tonnato is a classic cold Italian sauce made with puréed oil-packed tuna and traditionally drizzled over veal. I know it sounds a bit strange, but the result is a thick, silken sauce, rich with flavor. It's imperative to use a good-quality oil-packed tuna to make the tonnato or it will be watery. There are a few American companies, like American Tuna in San Diego, that make terrific oil-packed tuna that can be purchased at many gourmet markets.

SERVES 6

Tonnato

1 cup mayonnaise
½ cup drained good-quality oil-packed tuna
3 anchovy fillets
2 tablespoons salt-packed capers, rinsed and drained
1 tablespoon finely chopped garlic
1 tablespoon freshly squeezed lemon juice
1 teaspoon sherry vinegar
½ teaspoon Tabasco
Sea salt and freshly ground black pepper

Confit Tuna

4 cups extra virgin olive oil
2 garlic cloves, halved
2 fresh thyme sprigs
1 fresh basil sprig
¼ teaspoon dried hot red pepper flakes
2 pieces sushi-quality bigeye tuna, 12 ounces each

Garnish

1 ripe avocado, halved, pitted, peeled, and thinly sliced
3 tablespoons pitted halved niçoise olives
2 tablespoons sliced caper berries or fried capers (see Chef's note)
1 fresh heart of palm, thinly sliced on the bias
Fresh opal basil leaves, for garnish
Extra virgin olive oil, for drizzling

Make the tonnato ➤ Purée the mayonnaise, tuna, anchovies, capers, and garlic in a blender until smooth. Add the lemon juice, vinegar, and Tabasco and continue to blend until well incorporated. Season to taste with salt and pepper and transfer to a small bowl. Cover and refrigerate for at least 2 hours.

Confit the tuna ➤ Combine the olive oil, garlic, thyme, basil, and red pepper flakes in a medium saucepan. Using a deep-fry thermometer, cook over low heat just until the temperature reaches 120°F. Place 1 piece of the tuna in the infused oil and cook for 2 minutes on each side, making sure the temperature of the oil stays at 120°F. Remove the fish from the oil and transfer to a plate. Allow the tuna to cool in the refrigerator.

To assemble and serve ➤ Using a sharp knife, slice the cooked piece of tuna into ¼-inch-thick slices. Slice the raw piece of tuna into ¼-inch-thick slices. Spoon 1 tablespoon of the tonnato sauce in the center of each of 6 chilled plates. Beginning at the top of the plate, arrange 1 slice of the cooked tuna, followed by a slice of avocado, and then a slice the raw tuna. Continue arranging the cooked tuna, avocado, and raw tuna 2 more times until a complete circle has been formed. Once all 6 plates have been assembled, garnish with the niçoise olives, caper berries, heart of palm, and basil. Season to taste with salt and pepper and drizzle with olive oil.

Chef's note ➤ To fry the capers, dust drained capers with Wondra flour and fry them in hot vegetable oil until the popping subsides. Using a slotted spoon, remove the fried capers from the oil and place them on a plate lined with paper towels to drain.

Wine suggestion ➤ Serve this dish with a crisp and fresh Pinot Grigio with flavors of Key lime, honeydew melon, and pears, such as Pinot Grigio, Palmina, 2007, Santa Barbara County, California.

TUNA have dark flesh, unlike most fish, as a result of their unique muscle tissue. The two varieties of tuna most commonly found in the marketplace are bluefin and yellowfin. Bluefin tuna can actually raise their body temperature, which allows them to live in both the colder waters off the Atlantic coast as well as the warm Pacific waters. They can grow up to 1,400 pounds and are easily the best tuna for sushi and other raw preparations. Yellowfin tuna live in primarily warm waters worldwide and are fished in the Pacific year-round and off the Atlantic coast in the warmer summer months. These fish are not nearly as large as bluefin and generally grow to 500 pounds. Yellowfin are the most commonly fished variety and if you see a sign in the market that says "tuna," it's probably yellowfin.

Summer Bean Salad with Lemon Pesto & White Anchovy Beignets

I consider white anchovies, a variety found primarily in Spain, to be the ultimate anchovy. They are lightly cured and marinated in white wine vinegar and have an incredibly subtle flavor.

SERVES 6

Beans

2 cups shelled fresh cranberry beans
½ pound yellow wax beans, cut into 2-inch pieces
½ pound haricots verts, cut into 2-inch pieces
2 cups shelled fresh fava beans

Pesto

2 cups fresh basil leaves
3 garlic cloves, roughly chopped
½ cup extra virgin olive oil
1 cup coarsely grated Sartori Stravecchio cheese (or another domestic Parmesan cheese)
2 tablespoons freshly squeezed lemon juice
Sea salt and freshly ground black pepper

Vinaigrette

12 Cerignola olives, pitted and thinly sliced
2 white anchovies, finely chopped
2 tablespoons extra virgin olive oil
1½ tablespoons freshly squeezed lemon juice
1 teaspoon chopped fresh oregano
1 teaspoon finely chopped garlic
1 teaspoon roughly chopped drained capers

Beignets

Vegetable oil for frying
¾ cup cornstarch
½ cup all-purpose flour
½ teaspoon kosher salt
½ cup chilled club soda
18 white anchovies, drained and patted dry

2 cups wild arugula

Cook the beans ➤ Place the cranberry beans in a medium saucepan and cover with 2 quarts of water. Bring to a boil, and then reduce the heat so that the water barely simmers. Cook the beans until tender, about 30 minutes. Pour the beans and their cooking liquid into a large bowl set over ice. Allow the beans to cool in the liquid. Once cool, drain the beans and place them in a large mixing bowl. Discard the liquid.

While the cranberry beans are cooling, bring a large pot of salted water to a boil. Add the wax beans and cook until tender, about 3 minutes. Using a slotted spoon, remove the beans from the saucepan and immediately place them in a bowl of ice water. Repeat this process with the haricots verts and fava beans, making sure to remove the skins from the fava beans once they have cooled in the ice water. Once all the beans have cooled, remove them from the ice water and pat dry. Place the beans in the mixing bowl with the cranberry beans.

Make the pesto ➤ Place the basil and garlic in a blender or food processor. With the machine running, add the olive oil in a thin steam to form a thick paste. Transfer to a bowl and stir in the cheese and lemon juice. Season to taste with salt and pepper. Press a sheet of plastic wrap onto the surface of the pesto to make sure the pesto doesn't brown.

Make the vinaigrette and dress the beans ➤ Whisk together the olives, anchovies, olive oil, lemon juice, oregano, garlic, and capers in a medium bowl to blend. Drizzle the vinaigrette over the beans and toss to coat. Season the bean salad to taste with salt and pepper.

Make the beignets ➤ Fill a deep heavy pot or deep fryer with 4 inches of vegetable oil. Heat the oil to 375°F or until a small drop of the batter browns quickly in the oil. Combine the cornstarch, flour, and salt in a medium bowl. Whisk in the club soda until the mixture is well combined and the consistency of heavy cream. Working in batches, dip the anchovies into the batter to coat and fry them until golden brown, about 2 minutes. Using a slotted spoon, remove the beignets from the fryer and drain them on a plate lined with paper towels.

To serve ➤ Spoon the pesto onto the center of 6 plates. Spoon the bean salad over the pesto and scatter the wild arugula over the salad. Arrange 3 of the anchovy beignets over the top of each salad and serve.

Wine suggestion ➤ Serve this dish with a crisp and summery Sauvignon Blanc that offers aromas of Meyer lemons, fresh cut grass, and white flowers, such as Sauvignon Blanc, Brander, 2007, Santa Ynez Valley, California.

Pho with Lemongrass-Ginger Pork Dumplings

I developed my love of pho during an extensive trip through Southeast Asia. It's considered the national soup of Vietnam and is typically made with beef. Traditionally, it is eaten for breakfast in Asia, but this version can be enjoyed anytime of day, all year long.

SERVES 6

Chicken Broth

3 tablespoons canola oil
3 small whole organic chickens, 3½ pounds each, quartered
1 medium onion, halved
1 piece (3 inches) peeled fresh ginger, halved lengthwise
4 garlic cloves
3 whole star anise
3 whole cloves
3 tablespoons Vietnamese fish sauce
2 tablespoons sugar
1 tablespoon whole black peppercorns
¼ teaspoon black cardamom pods
Pinch of Chinese five-spice powder
Sea salt and freshly ground black pepper

Lemongrass-Ginger Pork Dumplings

3 lemongrass stalks, tough outer leaves discarded (see page 53)
⅓ cup finely chopped peeled fresh ginger
4 garlic cloves, finely chopped
1 pound ground pork
1 shallot, diced
2 tablespoons chopped fresh cilantro
2 tablespoons chopped fresh Thai basil
2 tablespoons Vietnamese fish sauce
1 Thai chile, finely chopped
3 tablespoons canola oil

Pho

8 ounces rice vermicelli
1 cup thinly sliced snow peas
2 cups bean sprouts
½ cup thinly sliced white onion
¼ cup chopped fresh cilantro
20 fresh Thai basil leaves, roughly chopped
10 fresh mint leaves, roughly chopped
3 scallions, thinly sliced
1 Thai chile, seeded and thinly sliced
3 limes, halved

Make the broth ➤ Heat the oil in a large sauté pan over high heat. Working in batches, sear the chickens until dark brown, about 4 minutes on each side.

Heat a cast-iron pan over high heat. Add the onions and ginger, cut sides down, and cook until charred and blackened on all sides, about 3 minutes.

Fill a large stock pot with 7 quarts of cold water. Add the chickens and bring to a boil. Reduce the heat to medium and add the charred onion and ginger, garlic, star anise, cloves, 1 tablespoon of the fish sauce, the sugar, peppercorns, cardamom, five-spice powder, and a pinch of salt. Bring to a simmer, skim any foam and fat off the top, and cook for 1½ hours. Remove from the heat and cool.

Remove the chickens from the broth and reserve the meat for another use, if desired. Strain the broth into a clean large saucepan. Bring the broth to a simmer. Add the remaining 2 tablespoons of fish sauce and season to taste with salt and pepper.

Make the dumplings ➤ Combine the lemongrass, ginger, and garlic in a food processor fitted with a metal blade and process until a paste forms. Transfer the paste to a large bowl. Add the pork, shallot, cilantro, basil, fish sauce, chile, and 1 tablespoon of the canola oil and mix until well combined. Dip your hands in water and form the meat mixture into 12 patties, rewetting your hands when necessary to prevent the meat mixture from sticking to them. Heat the remaining 2 tablespoons of canola oil in a large sauté pan over medium-high heat. Sear the dumplings until browned and cooked through, about 3 minutes per side.

Assemble the pho ➤ Bring a medium saucepan of salted water to a boil. Add the rice vermicelli and cook, stirring occasionally, until tender but firm to the bite, about 2 minutes. Strain and rinse the noodles under cold water.

Bring a small pot of salted water to a boil. Add the snow peas and cook for 2 minutes. Immediately transfer the peas to a bowl of ice water. Once cool, remove the peas from the water and pat dry.

To serve ➤ Divide the vermicelli, dumplings, snow peas, bean sprouts, onion, cilantro, basil, mint, scallions, and chile among 6 large serving bowls. Ladle the hot chicken broth over the top. Serve with lime halves on the side.

Wine suggestion ➤ Serve this dish with a slightly off-dry Riesling that offers aromas of white peaches, melon, and pineapple, such as Riesling, "Off Dry," Dr. Konstantin Frank, 2007, Finger Lakes, New York.

Grilled Littleneck Clam & Bacon Pizzettas

This dough is a recipe I have been working on for years. It takes a few hours to rise so I usually make it mid-morning and by dinner time it's ready to use. I occasionally like to substitute the Fiscalini San Joaquin Gold cheese with another American cheese called Oreganzola. This creamy blue cheese should not be cooked but scattered on top of the hot pizza immediately after removing it from the grill.

MAKES 4 PIZZETTAS

Dough

1 ounce fresh yeast or 1 tablespoon dry yeast
2 tablespoons + 1 cup lukewarm water
3½ cups unbleached "oo" flour, preferably King Arthur's Italian-style "oo" flour
1 teaspoon fine sea salt

Topping

6 ounces double-smoked bacon, finely diced
4 tablespoons (about) extra virgin olive oil
4 dozen littleneck clams, shucked, roughly chopped
2 tablespoons roughly chopped fresh oregano
1 teaspoon dried oregano
½ teaspoon finely chopped garlic
½ cup grated Fiscalini San Joaquin Gold cheese (or another firm, nutty, easy-melting, aged cow's-milk cheese, similar to an aged cheddar or a young Parmesan)
Sea salt and freshly ground black pepper

Make the dough ➤ Mix the yeast, the 2 tablespoons of lukewarm water, and 2 tablespoons of the flour in a medium bowl to form a smooth paste. Cover with a dish towel and let rise for 30 minutes. Mound the remaining flour on a cool dry surface and make a well in the center. Pour the yeast mixture into the well along with the salt and the remaining 1 cup of lukewarm water.

Dip your hands in flour, mix the ingredients together, and knead the dough until it is smooth and elastic, about 10 minutes. If the dough is too sticky, work in a few more tablespoons of flour. Divide the dough into 2 equal pieces and shape each piece into a ball. Set the dough balls on the work surface, cover with the dish towel, and let rise until they have doubled in size, about 2 hours. Note: You will only need 1 ball of dough for this recipe. Cover and refrigerate the remaining ball of dough up to 2 days for another use.

Prepare the pizzettas ➤ While the dough rises, cook the bacon in a medium sauté pan over medium-low heat until the fat has rendered and the bacon is crispy, about 7 minutes. Using a slotted spoon, transfer the bacon to a plate lined with paper towels.

Once the dough has risen, knead the dough for a couple of minutes and then press and flatten the dough with the palm of your hand into a small disk. Cut the disk into 4 equal pieces. Use a rolling pin, roll out each piece of dough into a very thin 6-inch round.

Preheat a grill over medium-high heat and brush the grates with some olive oil. Brush 1 side of the pizzettas with some olive oil and place the pizzettas, oil side down, on the grill. Brush the top side of the pizzettas with more olive oil. Grill until the bottom of the dough is golden brown, about 2 minutes. Using a spatula or tongs, remove the pizettas from the grill and turn them grilled side up. Scatter the bacon, then the clams, fresh oregano, dried oregano, garlic, and lastly, the cheese over the grilled side of the pizzettas. Return the pizzettas to the grill. Close the grill cover and grill the pizzettes until the dough is cooked through and the cheese has melted, about 2 minutes.

To serve ➤ Drizzle the pizzettas with olive oil, season to taste with salt and pepper, and serve immediately.

Wine suggestion ➤ Serve this dish with a crisp white wine from the North Fork of Long Island that offers aromas of apples, melons, and a touch of sea air, such as Pinot Blanc, Palmer Vineyards, 2007, North Fork, Long Island.

Ginger-Marinated Heirloom Tomatoes with Watermelon, Burrata, & Spicy Arugula

Burrata originated in the southern region of Italy called Puglia. It's classically made with milk from water buffalos, which has more fat and protein than regular cow's milk. Burrata starts out as mozzarella curds that are warmed and stretched and then shaped into a pouch that is stuffed with mozzarella curds and heavy cream just before sealing. The result is a creamy rich outer shell of mozzarella cheese that, when cut, exudes a thick rich cream. The creaminess of the Burrata pairs perfectly with the crunchy sweetness of the watermelon and the tender heirloom tomatoes.

SERVES 6

1 piece (6 inches) fresh ginger, peeled
½ cup + 1 tablespoon extra virgin olive oil
2 tablespoons aged sherry vinegar
24 baby heirloom tomatoes or multicolored vine-ripened tomatoes, cut into 2-inch pieces
½ cup thinly sliced red onion
¼ cup roughly chopped fresh basil
Sea salt and freshly ground black pepper
2 cups 1-inch pieces red or yellow seedless watermelon
2 cups baby arugula
¼ cup cured black olives, pitted and sliced
2 pieces burrata, 8 ounces each

Grate the ginger on the large holes of a box grater. Wrap the grated ginger in a piece of cheesecloth or thin kitchen towel and squeeze over a medium bowl to extract the juice. You should have about 4 tablespoons of juice.

Whisk the ginger juice, the ½ cup of olive oil, and the sherry vinegar in a medium bowl to blend. Add the tomatoes, red onion, and half of the basil and toss until well combined. Season to taste with salt and pepper. Allow the tomatoes to marinate at room temperature for 30 minutes.

Add the watermelon to the marinated tomatoes and toss until well combined. Toss the arugula in another bowl with the remaining 1 tablespoon of olive oil and season to taste with salt and pepper.

Divide the tomato and watermelon mixture among 6 plates. Garnish with the remaining basil and the black olives. Cut each piece of burrata into 3 pieces. Spoon the burrata evenly over the tomatoes and top with the arugula. Serve immediately.

Wine suggestion ➤ Pair this dish with a spicy and aromatic Gewurztraminer that offers aromas of lychee, passion fruit, and exotic spices, such as Gewurztraminer, Navarro, 2007, Anderson Valley, California.

HEIRLOOM TOMATOES have become increasingly popular and more readily available in recent years. The definition of what constitutes an heirloom plant is highly debated. Some schools of thought say that the seeds must be at least one hundred years old, while others pick the arbitrary date of 1945 or the end of World War II. In any case, the heirloom tomato is an older, less hybridized specimen, and tastes like a real tomato and not that mealy, waxy impostor found in most grocery stores.

Heirloom tomatoes can be found in a wide variety of colors, shapes, flavors, and sizes. When choosing one, don't be put off by the apparent flaws—those misshapen and brown-flecked ones are actually what you want and signs of a great tomato; however, don't purchase bruised specimens as they will go bad quickly. Always store tomatoes at room temperature because if refrigerated they tend to become woody and loose some of their flavor.

Spicy Blue Crab Soup with Poached Eggs

This soup has several steps and one or two hard to find ingredients, but once you have tasted the spicy, fresh, and multilayered flavors you'll be hooked. The recipe was inspired by the traditional *Bun Rieu Cua*, a Vietnamese soup with tomato and tamarind-flavored broth and ground pork, crab, and shrimp meatballs.

SERVES 6

Crab Broth

10 live blue crabs, about 4 pounds total
3 large egg whites, beaten
½ cup small dried shrimp

Crab Soup

1 package (16 ounces) Vietnamese rice vermicelli
1 tablespoon rice wine vinegar
6 large eggs
3 medium tomatoes, cored and each cut into 8 wedges
1 tablespoon fine shrimp sauce (see Chef's note)
1 tablespoon sugar
5 tablespoons corn oil
5 scallions; green parts cut into thirds, white parts thinly sliced
2½ tablespoons paprika
2 tablespoons tamarind paste
2 Thai chiles, thinly sliced
1 tablespoon freshly squeezed lime juice
1 tablespoon Vietnamese fish sauce

2 cups bean sprouts
1 cup loosely packed mint leaves
1 cup loosely packed purple perilla (also called *tia to*) or fresh basil
Sriracha (Asian chile sauce), for serving

Make the crab broth ➤ Rinse the crabs thoroughly under cold running water. Bring 6 quarts of water to a boil in a 10-quart pot over high heat. Add the crabs. Cover and cook until the shells turn a vibrant reddish orange, about 8 minutes. Using tongs, transfer the crabs to a large bowl; let cool slightly. Set the pot of crab broth aside.

Working with 1 crab at a time and using a paring knife, pry off the top shell of each crab. With a small spoon, scoop out the brownish-yellow innards, also known as the mustard, and any roe that may be attached to the inside of the top shell; transfer the mustard and roe to a bowl. Place the top shells in the crab broth.

Pull off and discard the fingerlike gills attached to the bottom of the crab and rinse out any sand lodged behind the gills. Break the bottom shell in half, extract the meat with your fingers, and add the meat to the bowl of mustard and roe. Transfer the bottom shell to the crab broth.

Crack the claws. Pick the meat out of the shells and add it to the crabmeat mixture. Add the shells to the broth. After all your labor, you should have about 1 cup of the crabmeat mixture. Place the crabmeat mixture in a food processor and pulse to combine. Transfer to a bowl and stir in the egg whites.

Bring the crab broth and shells to a boil over high heat. Lower the heat to medium and simmer, without stirring, for 30 minutes. Strain the broth through a fine-mesh sieve. Transfer 15 cups of the broth to a 6-quart saucepan. Reserve any remaining broth for another use.

Combine the dried shrimp with 1½ cups of water in a heavy small saucepan and bring to a boil. Lower the heat to medium-low and simmer until the shrimp are soft, about 15 minutes. Strain the liquid into the crab broth. Purée the softened dried shrimp in a food processor to form a coarse paste then transfer it to a serving bowl to use as a condiment for the soup.

Prepare the soup ➤ While the crab broth is cooking, bring a medium pot of salted water to a boil. Add the rice vermicelli and cook, stirring occasionally, until tender but firm to the bite, about 2 minutes. Drain and rinse the vermicelli under cold water.

Heat 2 to 3 inches of water in a large wide saucepan over medium heat until just simmering. Add the vinegar. Crack the eggs into 6 small cups and slide the eggs 1 by 1 from the cup into the simmering water. Maintain the water just below a simmer, reducing the heat to low, if necessary. Cook until the whites are set and the yolks are still soft, about 2 minutes. Using a slotted spoon, remove the eggs from the water and place them in a bowl of cold water until ready to serve.

Bring the broth to a boil then reduce the heat to medium-low. Add the tomatoes, fine shrimp sauce, and sugar and simmer until the tomatoes are softened, about 20 minutes.

Heat 3 tablespoons of oil in a small saucepan over medium heat. Add the green scallion pieces and cook until wilted, about 3 minutes. Transfer the scallions to a bowl, leaving the oil in the pan. Return the pan to medium-low heat and add the remaining 2 tablespoons of oil. Add the paprika, and cook, stirring frequently, until it turns a deep, brick-red color, about 5 minutes. Set the paprika oil aside.

Finish the soup ➤ Break the reserved crab and egg white mixture into ½-inch pieces and scatter them over the soup. Simmer the soup, without stirring, until the crab mixture floats to the surface to form a somewhat puffy top layer resembling cooked egg whites, about 3 minutes. Drizzle the paprika oil over the soup. Gently stir in the tamarind, Thai chiles, lime juice, and fish sauce and sprinkle with the cooked scallions and sliced white parts of the scallions.

To serve ➤ Mix the bean sprouts, mint, and perilla in a bowl and set on the table along with the shrimp paste and Sriracha. Divide the reserved noodles among 6 serving bowls and ladle the crab soup over the noodles. Top each serving with a poached egg and garnish with a few bean sprouts and herbs. Allow each person to season their soup to taste with the shrimp paste, Sriracha, and additional herbs.

Chef's note ➤ Shrimp sauce, also called *mam tom*, is available at many Asian grocery stores.

Wine suggestion ➤ Serve this dish with a dry sparkling rosé that offers aromas of pomegranate, ginger, and figs, such as Schramsberg, "Mirabelle Rosé," NV, California.

Tuna Tartines Niçoise

Niçoise-style dishes hail from the French Provençal town of Nice and tend to include olives, tomatoes, and anchovies, all of which are featured in this tartine. I love to serve this as a main course for lunch and always with a chilled glass of rosé wine.

SERVES 6

Tartines

24 ounces high-quality oil-packed tuna, drained
6 tablespoons mayonnaise
Sea salt and freshly ground black pepper
6 slices (1 inch thick) country bread
3 tablespoons extra virgin olive oil
12 haricots verts
8 ounces bluefin tuna, sliced into eighteen ⅛-inch-thick slices
3 hard-cooked eggs (see page 306), peeled and thinly sliced
2 plum tomatoes, thinly sliced
¼ cup thinly sliced red onion
¼ cup fresh basil leaves
¼ cup niçoise olives, pitted and halved
1 tablespoon salt-packed capers, rinsed and drained

Salad

4 tablespoons extra virgin olive oil
1 tablespoon freshly squeezed lemon juice
3 cups baby arugula

Prepare the tartines ➤ Mix the oil-packed tuna and mayonnaise in a small bowl and season to taste with salt and pepper.

Heat a grill pan over high heat. Brush both sides of the bread with the olive oil. Grill until dark and crusty, about 4 minutes on each side.

Bring a small saucepan of salted water to boil. Add the haricots verts and cook for 1 minute. Remove from the hot water and immediately place them in a bowl of ice water. Once cool, drain the haricots verts and slice them in half lengthwise.

Spread the tuna mixture over 1 side of each slice of grilled bread. Season the slices of raw tuna with salt and pepper. Alternating the slices of tuna, egg, and tomato, layer each ingredient over the bread, beginning and ending with a slice of tuna. Arrange 3 pieces of haricots verts over each tartine. Scatter the red onion, basil leaves, olives, and capers over the tartines. Transfer the tartines to 6 serving plates.

To make the salad and serve ➤ Whisk 3 tablespoons of the olive oil and the lemon juice in a medium bowl. Toss the arugula in the lemon vinaigrette and season to taste with salt and pepper. Divide the salad among the plates. Drizzle the tartines with the remaining 1 tablespoon of olive oil and serve immediately.

Wine suggestion ➤ Serve this dish with a crisp and refreshing dry rosé that offers flavors of fresh-picked raspberries, strawberries, and herbs, such as Syrah Rosé, Elizabeth Spencer, 2007, Napa Valley, California.

Roasted Tomato & Fennel Soup with Sardine Crostini

In this recipe the tomatoes are roasted and the flavor is so intense and concentrated you'll be tempted to eat them all before they can be made into a soup. The sweetness from the basil cuts the intensity of the tomatoes perfectly.

SERVES 6

Soup

12 plum tomatoes, cored and quartered
3 tablespoons extra virgin olive oil
Sea salt and freshly ground black pepper
1 Spanish onion, thinly sliced
1½ cups thinly sliced fennel bulb
½ cup thinly sliced leek (white part only)
6 garlic cloves, thinly sliced
2 fresh thyme sprigs

Basil Pesto

1½ cups loosely packed fresh basil leaves
¼ cup grated Sartori Stravecchio (or another domestic Parmesan cheese)
2 garlic cloves
3 tablespoons extra virgin olive oil

Crostini

1 small baguette
6 fresh sardine fillets
1 teaspoon extra virgin olive oil

Make the soup ➤ Preheat the oven to 275°F. Toss the tomatoes with 2 tablespoons of the olive oil in a medium bowl to coat. Season to taste with salt and pepper. Arrange the tomatoes, cut side up, on a rimmed baking sheet and roast until slightly caramelized, about 45 minutes. Transfer the tomato mixture to a blender or food processor and add 1½ cups of water. Purée until smooth and pour into a medium saucepan.

Heat the remaining 1 tablespoon of olive oil in another medium saucepan over low heat. Add the onion, fennel, leek, garlic, and thyme and sauté until translucent, about 10 minutes. Remove the thyme and transfer the vegetable mixture to a blender or food processor and purée until smooth. Stir the vegetable purée into the puréed tomatoes, and season to taste with salt and pepper.

Make the pesto ➤ Place the basil, cheese, and garlic in the blender or food processor. With the machine running, add the olive oil in a thin steam until the mixture is thick and smooth. Scrape the pesto into a bowl and press a sheet of plastic wrap onto the surface of the pesto to prevent it from turning brown.

Make the crostini ➤ Preheat the broiler. Slice the bread on a bias into six ½-inch-thick slices. Arrange the slices on a baking sheet and broil until golden brown, about 2 minutes.

Heat a grill pan over high heat. Pat the sardines dry with paper towels. Brush the cut sides of the sardines with olive oil and season with salt and pepper. Grill the sardines, skin side down, for 1 minute. Turn the sardines over and grill for an additional 1 minute. Transfer the sardines to a plate. Spread 1 tablespoon of pesto over each crostini and top with 1 grilled sardine.

To serve ➤ Warm the tomato soup over medium heat. Divide the soup evenly among 6 warm bowls. Serve with the sardine crostini on the side.

Wine suggestion ➤ Serve this dish with a crisp brut-style sparkling wine that offers clean flavors of green apples, citrus, and a touch of sea air, such as Shinn Estate Vineyards, "Brut," NV, North Fork Long Island, New York.

Veal Carpaccio with Olive-Pistachio Vinaigrette & Dandelion Salad

I love to eat carpaccio on a warm summer day with a piece of grilled rustic bread. It's the perfect example of substantial ingredients used sparingly and presented in a cool and refreshing fashion. This dish is a great way to begin a summer lunch.

SERVES 6

1½ pounds veal tenderloin
18 haricots verts, thinly sliced on the bias
⅓ cup freshly squeezed lemon juice
1 teaspoon finely chopped garlic
⅔ cup extra virgin olive oil
Sea salt and freshly ground black pepper
2 hard-cooked eggs (see page 306), peeled
¾ cup toasted pistachios, finely chopped
2 tablespoons salt-packed capers, rinsed and drained
¼ cup coarsely grated Sartori Stravecchio cheese (or another domestic Parmesan cheese)
½ pound baby dandelion greens

Cut the veal crosswise into ¼-inch-thick slices. Lay 3 slices of veal flat between 2 layers of plastic wrap. Using a mallet, evenly pound the veal until it reaches a ⅛-inch thickness. Remove the top layer of the plastic wrap and invert the carpaccio onto a serving plate, leaving the other layer of plastic wrap over the veal. Refrigerate the plate of pounded veal, and repeat the process with the remaining veal.

Bring a large saucepan of salted water to a boil. Add the haricots verts and cook until just tender, about 3 minutes. Immediately transfer the haricots verts to a bowl of ice water. Once cool, place the haricots verts on a plate lined with paper towels and blot them dry.

Combine the lemon juice and garlic in a medium bowl, and slowly whisk in the olive oil. Season to taste with salt and pepper.

Separate the egg yolks from the whites and finely chop the whites and yolks separately.

Uncover the plates of carpaccio and season with salt and pepper. Spoon the lemon vinaigrette evenly over the veal. Scatter the chopped pistachios, capers, haricots verts, egg yolks, egg whites, and cheese over the veal. Scatter the dandelion greens over the carpaccio.

Wine suggestion ➤ Serve this dish with a lush Riesling that offers flavors of Asian pears, white peach, and spring flower, such as Riesling, "Kung Fu Girl," Charles Smith Wines, 2007, Columbia Valley, Washington.

Creamy Corn Risotto & Grilled Langoustine with Summer Truffles

Summer truffles are very different from their winter cousins. The taste and aroma are not nearly as strong, which make them a great addition to summer's lighter fare. Langoustines are crustaceans that look like miniature lobsters. Mostly fished in the cold waters off of Scotland, they are incredibly delicate and must be cooked within just a day or two after being caught. For this reason, they are somewhat difficult to find and always quite expensive.

SERVES 6

Corn Stock

6 ears corn, husked
1 small onion, peeled and quartered
2 celery stalks, halved lengthwise
1 leek (white and light green part only), cut into 1-inch pieces

Corn Purée and Sauté

1 tablespoon extra virgin olive oil
2 tablespoons unsalted butter
1 small onion, diced
1 teaspoon finely chopped garlic
Sea salt and freshly ground black pepper
1½ cups heavy cream
3 fresh thyme sprigs

Risotto

3 tablespoons extra virgin olive oil
1 small onion, cut into ¼-inch dice
2 cups Arborio rice
1 cup dry white wine
½ cup grated Sartori Stravecchio cheese (or another domestic Parmesan cheese)

Langoustines

12 langoustines, shell on and split in half
1 tablespoon extra virgin olive oil
1 tablespoon truffle oil
2 medium summer truffles, very thinly sliced (optional)

Make the corn stock ➤ Using a large chef's knife, cut the corn kernels off the cobs and set aside. Place the cobs in a large stockpot along with the onion, celery, and chopped leek. Add 10 cups of water and bring to a boil over high heat. Reduce the heat and simmer uncovered for 30 minutes. Strain the corn stock through a fine-mesh strainer into a bowl. Discard the solids. You should have at least 6 cups of stock.

Make the corn purée ➤ Heat the olive oil and 1 tablespoon of the butter in a medium saucepan over medium heat until the butter begins to foam. Add the onion and garlic and sauté until the onions are soft, about 5 minutes. Add 1 cup of the reserved corn kernels, season to taste with salt and pepper, and continue to cook over low heat, stirring constantly, until the kernels begin to soften, about 5 minutes. Add the cream, thyme, and 1 cup of the corn stock and continue to simmer over low heat until the mixture begins to thicken, about 10 minutes. Remove the thyme and purée the mixture in a blender until smooth.

Sauté the corn ➤ Melt the remaining 1 tablespoon of butter in a medium sauté pan over medium-high heat. Add the remaining corn kernels and sauté until the corn is tender, about 5 minutes. Season to taste with salt and pepper.

Make the risotto ➤ Heat the olive oil in a large wide saucepan over medium heat. Add the onion and sauté until the onion is translucent, about 5 minutes. Add the rice and stir to coat with the oil. Add the wine and reduce the heat to a simmer until most of the wine has evaporated. Add 1 cup of the corn stock to the pan and continue to cook, stirring constantly, until most of the stock is absorbed. Repeat the process with the remaining 4 cups of corn stock, making sure the stock has been fully incorporated after each addition before adding more. Once the rice is tender yet firm to the bite, remove the pan from the heat. Stir in the corn purée, sautéed corn, and grated cheese and season to taste with salt and pepper.

continued

Prepare the langoustines ➤ Holding the tail end of each langoustine, wrap the body around itself in the shape of a pinwheel. Secure the langoustines with a toothpick and season with salt and pepper.

While the risotto is cooking, heat the olive oil in a large sauté pan over medium-high heat. Working in batches, sear the langoustines until they are golden brown, about 2 minutes per side. Remove them from the pan and remove the toothpicks.

To serve ➤ Divide the risotto among 6 warm bowls. Arrange 2 langoustines atop each bowl of risotto. Drizzle with the truffle oil and garnish with sliced summer truffles, if desired.

Wine suggestion ➤ Serve this dish with a brut-style sparkling wine that shows flavors of ripe apples, fresh baked biscuits, and lemon zest, such as Iron Horse, "Classic Vintage Brut," 2004, Green Valley, California.

LIVE
LOBSTERS
FRESH FISH
SWEET CORN
STRAWBERRIES
BLUEBERRIES

Veal, Pork, & Ricotta Meatballs with Pea Shoot Salad

I like to eat these extraordinary meatballs alongside polenta flavored with finely chopped rosemary. They can also be served like a sandwich on a soft bun, which is what I do in some of my restaurants.

SERVES 6

Meatballs

2 tablespoons raisins, roughly chopped
2 tablespoons dry white wine
2 tablespoons extra virgin olive oil
1 cup finely chopped onion
1 tablespoon finely chopped garlic
1½ teaspoons finely chopped fresh oregano
1½ teaspoons finely chopped fresh thyme
1 head roasted garlic (see page 306)
½ pound ground beef short ribs
½ pound ground pork shoulder
½ pound ground veal short ribs
6 tablespoons fresh ricotta cheese, drained overnight
3 tablespoons grated Sartori Stravecchio cheese (or another domestic Parmesan cheese), plus more for garnish
3 tablespoons grated Meadow Creek Grayson cheese (or another washed-rind, semi-soft, pungent, cow's-milk cheese, similar to domestic Taleggio)
2 large eggs
2 tablespoons toasted pine nuts
Sea salt and freshly ground black pepper
¼ cup (about) all-purpose flour

Tomato Sauce

¼ cup + 2 tablespoons extra virgin olive oil
6 garlic cloves, peeled and thinly sliced
1 can (28 ounces) whole tomatoes
Sea salt and freshly ground black pepper
1 tablespoon (about) sugar
¼ cup chopped fresh basil leaves
1 tablespoon chopped fresh oregano

1½ cups pea shoots
Extra virgin olive oil, for drizzling

Make the meatballs ➤ Place the raisins in a small bowl and cover with the white wine. Heat the olive oil in a large sauté pan over medium heat. Add the onion and sauté until lightly browned, about 6 minutes. Add the chopped garlic, oregano, and thyme and sauté until the garlic has lightly browned, about 3 minutes. Remove the pan from the heat and allow the mixture to cool to room temperature.

Line a baking sheet with parchment paper or plastic wrap. Combine the roasted garlic, beef, pork, veal, ricotta, Sartori Stravecchio, Grayson, eggs, pine nuts, raisins, and sautéed onions and garlic in a large bowl. Season to taste with salt and pepper, and mix until well combined. Lightly flour your hands to prevent the meat mixture from sticking to them. Shape the meat mixture into 2-ounce balls. Place the meatballs on the prepared baking sheet, cover, and refrigerate overnight.

Make the tomato sauce ➤ Heat the ¼ cup of olive oil in a medium saucepan over medium-low heat. Add the garlic and cook slowly until evenly browned, about 3 minutes. Add the tomatoes and their juices and gently crush them using the back of your spoon. Season with salt, pepper, and sugar. Simmer the sauce over medium-low heat, stirring occasionally, until thickened, about 10 minutes. Stir in the basil and oregano. Season to taste, adding more salt and sugar, if necessary.

Cook the meatballs ➤ Heat the remaining 2 tablespoons of olive oil in a large sauté pan over medium heat. Sauté the meatballs until well browned on all sides, about 2 minutes. Add the meatballs to the warm tomato sauce. Cover and allow the meatballs to finish cooking, about 7 minutes.

To serve ➤ Toss the pea shoots with a drizzle of olive oil and season to taste with salt. Arrange 3 meatballs on each of 6 plates. Ladle the warm sauce over the meatballs and garnish with a drizzle of the olive oil. Garnish with Sartori Stravecchio cheese and the seasoned pea shoots.

Wine suggestion ➤ Serve this dish with a wine made from Barbera that offers aromas of fresh raspberries, strawberries, and herbs, such as Barbera "Reserve," Barboursville Vineyards, 2006, Barboursville, Virginia.

Grilled Rib-Eye Steak with Green Tomato Chimichurri & Balsamic Radicchio

Chimichurri is a marinade and sauce for grilled meat that originated in Argentina. It is typically made with parsley, cilantro, chiles, oil, and some sort of acid, like vinegar or lemon, to balance out the flavors. I was making it one night for some friends and decided to toss in some grilled green tomatoes—the smokiness and tartness were the perfect addition.

SERVES 6

Green Tomato Chimichurri

5 medium green tomatoes, sliced ½ inch thick
1 tablespoon + ½ cup extra virgin olive oil
½ cup chopped fresh cilantro
½ cup chopped fresh parsley
2 tablespoons finely chopped red onion
2 tablespoons white wine vinegar
1 teaspoon dried hot red pepper flakes
1 teaspoon finely chopped garlic
1 teaspoon kosher salt
½ teaspoon freshly ground black pepper

Balsamic Radicchio

1 cup extra virgin olive oil
½ cup balsamic vinegar
⅓ cup freshly squeezed lemon juice
2 tablespoons honey
2 teaspoons kosher salt
1 teaspoon freshly ground black pepper
½ teaspoon dried hot red pepper flakes
2 medium heads of radicchio, cut into 4 wedges, core intact

Rib-Eye Steaks

4 tablespoons unsalted butter, softened
3 rib-eye steaks, preferably dry-aged, 30 to 40 ounces each, 2 inches thick
2 tablespoons fine sea salt
2 tablespoons freshly ground black pepper

Make the chimichurri ➤ Preheat the grill to medium-high heat. Brush the tomato slices with the 1 tablespoon of olive oil and grill until well charred on each side, about 2 minutes per side. Once the tomatoes are cool enough to handle, roughly chop them and place them in a medium bowl. Stir in the remaining ½ cup of olive oil, the cilantro, parsley, onion, vinegar, pepper flakes, garlic, salt, and pepper.

Grill the balsamic radicchio ➤ Combine the olive oil, vinegar, lemon juice, honey, salt, black pepper, and red pepper flakes in a medium bowl. Place the radicchio in a shallow baking dish and pour the marinade over. Allow the radicchio to marinate for 15 minutes.

Remove the radicchio from the marinade, reserving the marinade, and grill the radicchio until crispy, about 1 minute on each side. Remove from the heat and arrange on a serving platter. Drizzle with some of the reserved marinade.

Grill the steaks ➤ Brush the butter on both sides of the steaks and season with salt and pepper. Cook the steaks to medium-rare doneness, about 7 minutes on each side. To check for doneness, insert an instant-read thermometer in the thickest part of the meat. The temperature reading should be 130° to 135°F for medium-rare doneness.

Place the steaks on a cutting board, cover loosely with foil, and let rest 10 to 12 minutes.

To serve ➤ Cut the steaks into 1-inch-thick slices. Serve with the chimichurri and grilled radicchio on the side.

Wine suggestion ➤ Serve this dish with a juicy, spicy Malbec that shows flavors of boysenberry, figs, and black licorice, such as Bodegas Catena Zapata Alta, 2005, Mendoza, Argentina.

Fried Soft-Shell Crabs with Szechuan Peppercorns & Tangy Barbecue Sauce

Until a few years ago, it was actually illegal to purchase Szechuan peppercorns in the United States. However, they are now widely available and unlike the pungent spicy flavors of white or black peppercorns, Szechuan peppercorns add a more floral and lemony essence.

SERVES 6

Soft-Shell Crabs

12 soft-shell crabs, cleaned (see page 27)
4 cups (about) buttermilk
Vegetable oil for frying
2 cups Japanese rice flour
1 tablespoon + 1½ teaspoons ground Szechuan peppercorns
1 tablespoon garlic powder
1 tablespoon kosher salt
1 teaspoon Hungarian paprika
½ teaspoon cayenne pepper
½ teaspoon chili powder

Citrus Barbecue Sauce

1½ teaspoons coriander seeds
1½ teaspoons cumin seeds
1½ teaspoons whole allspice
1 tablespoon extra virgin olive oil
1 large sweet onion, grated
2 garlic cloves, crushed
½ teaspoon cayenne pepper
2 tablespoons light brown sugar
1 tablespoon cider vinegar
⅓ cup ketchup
1 tablespoon Dijon mustard
1 tablespoon Worcestershire sauce
3 tablespoons freshly squeezed orange juice
1 tablespoon freshly squeezed lemon juice
1 tablespoon orange zest
2 teaspoons lemon zest
Sea salt and freshly ground black pepper

Soak the crabs ➤ Place the crabs in a large plastic resealable bag. Pour in enough buttermilk to completely cover the crabs and refrigerate for 1 hour.

Make the sauce ➤ Toast the coriander, cumin, and allspice in a small sauté pan over high heat until fragrant, about 2 minutes. Once cool, crush the spices using a mortar and pestle until coarsely ground.

Heat the olive oil in a medium saucepan over medium heat. Add the onion, garlic, toasted spices, and cayenne and cook until the onion is soft, stirring often to make sure none of the spices burn, about 5 minutes. Add the brown sugar and vinegar and stir until well combined. Stir in the ketchup, mustard, Worcestershire sauce, and 1 cup of water. Simmer uncovered until thickened, about 15 minutes. Remove from the heat and cool slightly.

Stir in the orange juice, lemon juice, and citrus zests. Transfer the sauce to a blender and purée until smooth. Pass the sauce through a fine-mesh strainer set over a clean saucepan. Season to taste with salt and pepper.

Fry the crabs ➤ Fill a deep heavy pot or a deep fryer with 4 inches of vegetable oil. Heat the oil to 375°F or until a small drop of the flour mixture browns quickly in the oil.

While the oil is heating, combine the rice flour, the 1 tablespoon of ground Szechuan peppercorns, the garlic powder, salt, paprika, cayenne pepper, and chili powder in a large shallow bowl. Using a slotted spoon or tongs, remove the crabs, a few at a time, from the buttermilk and toss in the flour mixture to coat.

Gently lower the crabs, 1 at a time, into the hot oil. Fry the crabs until crispy and cooked through, about 4 minutes. Using a slotted spoon, remove the crabs from the oil and drain on paper towels. Season to taste with salt and the remaining 1½ teaspoons of ground Szechuan peppercorns.

To serve ➤ Arrange the soft-shell crabs on individual plates or on a large platter with the warm barbecue sauce on the side.

Wine suggestion ➤ Serve the dish with a dry, refreshing rosé made from Grenache that offers aromas of framboise, fresh raspberries, and a touch of rose petals, such as Grenache Rosé, "Purisima Mountain," Beckmen Vineyards, 2007, Santa Barbara County, California.

SOFT-SHELL CRABS are blue crabs caught just after shedding their tough outer shells. This results in a completely edible crab, shells and all. Soft shells are primarily fished in the warm waters of the Chesapeake Bay and the Gulf of Mexico. They are a real delicacy and are available from May to September. Make sure the crabs you buy are still alive to ensure freshness, and ask your fishmonger to clean the crabs before you purchase them.

Chatham Cod with Curried Eggplant & Kaffir Lime Leaves

Kaffir lime leaves add so much flavor and fragrance. They are worth seeking out at your local Asian market. The leaves will keep for several weeks in the freezer, so buy some when you run across them in the market. The eggplant curry is so good on its own that you can serve it along with the rice for a lighter and simpler meal.

SERVES 6

Curry

6 medium Japanese eggplants, cut crosswise into 1-inch-thick slices
Sea salt and freshly ground black pepper
5 tablespoons grapeseed oil
1 medium onion, chopped
10 kaffir lime leaves
1 tablespoon finely chopped peeled fresh ginger
1 tablespoon Thai red curry paste, preferably Mae Ploy brand
1 can (13.5 ounces) unsweetened coconut milk
1 cup Chicken Stock (page 303)
2 tablespoons Vietnamese fish sauce

Cod

4 tablespoons extra virgin olive oil
6 skinless Chatham cod fillets, 1½ inches thick, 7 ounces each

Fleur de sel
1 lime, cut into 6 wedges
Lemongrass Sticky Rice (page 256)

Make the curry ➤ Toss the eggplant in a medium bowl and season with salt and pepper, ensuring that all the pieces are seasoned.

Heat 2 tablespoons of the grapeseed oil in a large sauté pan over high heat. Add half of the eggplant and sear until dark brown, about 3 minutes on each side. Remove the eggplant from the pan and transfer to a plate. Repeat the process with the remaining eggplant and 2 tablespoons of the remaining grapeseed oil.

Wipe out the pan, reduce the heat to medium, and add the remaining 1 tablespoon of grapeseed oil. Add the onion, kaffir lime leaves, ginger, and curry paste and sauté until the onions are translucent, about 5 minutes. Deglaze with the coconut milk, chicken stock, and fish sauce. Bring to a boil. Add the seared eggplant back to the pan and cook until heated through, making sure the eggplant does not break apart, about 2 minutes.

Cook the fish ➤ Heat 2 tablespoons of the olive oil in a large sauté pan over medium-high heat. Season the cod with sea salt and pepper on both sides. Sear 3 of the cod fillets until golden brown, about 3 minutes on each side. To check for doneness, insert an instant-read thermometer in the thickest part of the cod fillet. The temperature reading should be 165° to 175°F. Remove the fillets from the pan and repeat the process for the remaining 3 fillets.

To serve ➤ Spoon the eggplant curry into 6 warm shallow bowls. Arrange the fish on top of the eggplant, sprinkle lightly with fleur de sel, and garnish with the kaffir lime leaves from the sauce and a wedge of lime. Serve the rice on the side.

Wine suggestion ➤ Serve this dish with an exotically fruity Viognier that offers aromas of ripe mangoes, peaches, and honeysuckle, such as Viognier, K Vintners, 2007, Columbia Valley, Washington.

Grilled Striped Bass with Smoky Tomato Butter

Smoked cherry tomatoes and the caramelized roasted shallots complement the fine taste and texture of the striped bass. Striped bass will become tough if overcooked, so make sure to grill the fish until just barely cooked through.

SERVES 6

Smoked Cherry Tomatoes

1 cup cherry tomatoes, halved
½ cup fresh baby basil
¼ cup extra virgin olive oil
1 teaspoon freshly squeezed lemon juice
Sea salt and freshly ground black pepper

Smoky Tomato Butter

1 cup hickory wood chips, soaked in water
2 plum tomatoes, peeled, quartered, and seeded
2 sticks (8 ounces) unsalted butter, softened
¼ cup finely chopped shallots
1 tablespoon finely chopped chives
1 tablespoon freshly squeezed lemon juice

Roasted Shallots

3 shallots, peeled and halved lengthwise
¼ cup extra virgin olive oil

Striped Bass

3 whole striped bass, cleaned, about 2 pounds each
Extra virgin olive oil for brushing
Sea salt and freshly ground black pepper

Prepare the smoked cherry tomatoes ➤ Preheat the oven to 150°F. Place the tomatoes, cut side down, on a rack set over a rimmed baking pan. Bake until the tomatoes are dried, about 1 hour. Remove from the oven.

Make the smoked tomato butter ➤ Drain the hickory wood chips. Line the bottom of a pot and a steamer insert with aluminum foil. Place the chips in the bottom of the pot and heat the chips over a burner until they are smoking. Place the plum tomatoes in the steamer insert and set the steamer insert over the smoking wood chips in the pot. Cover tightly with the lid and smoke the tomatoes over medium heat for about 5 minutes. Remove the tomatoes from the smoker and cool. Reserve the smoker for later use. Once the tomatoes have cooled, roughly chop them.

Mix the chopped smoked tomatoes, butter, shallots, chives, and lemon juice in a medium bowl. Season to taste with salt and pepper. Transfer the butter onto a sheet of plastic wrap and roll it up into a log shape and seal tightly. Store the butter in the refrigerator for up to 3 days.

Smoke the dried cherry tomatoes ➤ Heat the prepared smoker over high heat. Place the oven-dried cherry tomatoes in the steamer insert in the smoker, cover tightly, and smoke the tomatoes over medium heat for 5 minutes. Remove the tomatoes from the smoker.

Roast the shallots ➤ Preheat the oven to 350°F. Place the shallots on a sheet of foil. Season the shallots to taste with salt and pepper and drizzle with the olive oil. Wrap the foil around the shallots to seal tightly. Place the foil packet on a baking sheet and roast the shallots for 30 minutes.

Cook the striped bass ➤ Preheat an outdoor grill or a grill pan over high heat. Brush the bass with olive oil and season with salt and pepper. Grill until the flesh is opaque and cooked through, about 6 minutes on each side.

To serve ➤ Place the bass on a large platter. Cut the tomato butter into ½-inch-thick slices and place 3 slices of butter over each fish. Arrange 2 shallot halves between the butter slices. Toss the smoked cherry tomatoes with the basil, olive oil, and lemon juice in a small bowl. Season the cherry tomato mixture to taste with salt and pepper and scatter it evenly over the fish.

Wine suggestion ➤ Serve this dish with a crisp Sauvignon Blanc that offers mouthwatering flavors of grapefruit, white peaches, and minerals, such as Sauvignon Blanc, Saracina, 2007, Mendocino County, California.

Spiced Grilled Long Island Duck with Plum Mostarda & Hudson Valley Foie Gras

I love to make this dish for parties because so much of it can be made in advance, and all I have to do is grill the duck just before eating. It's a festive and rich meal that actually takes little time. You can also make the mostarda with any stone fruits, like peaches, nectarines, or fresh plums, you happen to find at the market.

SERVES 6

Duck

6 whole star anise
3 tablespoons loose Earl Grey tea
4 teaspoons whole cloves
2 teaspoons Szechuan peppercorns
1 teaspoon ground cinnamon
½ teaspoon green cardamom pods
½ teaspoon whole black peppercorns
6 Long Island duck breasts, 10 ounces each
Sea salt

Plum Mostarda

½ cup dry white wine
2 tablespoons red wine vinegar
1 tablespoon dried cherries
1 tablespoon golden raisins
1 tablespoon sugar
1 tablespoon yellow mustard seeds
Zest of 1 lemon
½ Granny Smith apple, peeled, cored, and diced
4 plums, pitted and diced
2 tablespoons plum jam
1 cup Sauternes
4 fresh basil leaves, thinly sliced

3 slices foie gras terrine, ¼ inch thick
3 slices toasted brioche, ½ inch thick

Season the duck ➤ Blend the star anise, tea, cloves, Szechuan peppercorns, cinnamon, cardamom pods, and black peppercorns in a coffee grinder until a fine powder forms.

Using a sharp knife, trim the fat from the duck breasts then score the fat on top of the duck breast in a diagonal pattern, making sure not to cut into the flesh. Season the duck breasts with salt and evenly coat both sides with the spice mixture. Cover and refrigerate overnight.

Make the mostarda ➤ Combine the wine, vinegar, dried cherries, raisins, sugar, mustard seeds, and lemon zest in a small saucepan over medium heat and bring to a boil. Boil until the raisins and cherries are plump and rehydrated, about 3 minutes. Add the apple, reduce the heat, and simmer for 1 minute. Add the plums and cook until tender, about 3 minutes. Stir in the plum jam. Bring the Sauternes to a boil in another medium saucepan. Pour the hot Sauternes over the mostarda and stir to combine. Strain the mostarda through a fine-mesh strainer set over a clean bowl. Stir the basil into the liquid. Reserve both the liquid and the solids separately.

Grill the duck ➤ Preheat the grill to high heat. Once the grill is very hot, grill the duck breasts, skin side down, until the skin is crispy, about 3 minutes. Turn the duck breasts over and cook for 2 minutes more. Remove the duck breasts from the heat and let rest, loosely tented with aluminum foil, for 5 minutes.

To serve ➤ Place the foie gras slices on top of the toasted brioche, trimming the crusts of the brioche to fit the size of the foie gras. Cut each slice of brioche in half. Arrange the brioche toasts on 6 warm plates. Spoon the mostarda solids evenly over the foie gras. Cut the duck breast into ¼-inch-thick slices and fan them over the mostarda. Drizzle with the warm liquid from the mostarda and serve immediately.

Wine suggestion ➤ Serve this dish with a big and succulent Pinot Noir that offers enticing flavors of crème de framboise, juicy plums, and a touch of toasty vanilla, such as Pinot Noir, "Steven," Dierberg, 2005, Santa Maria Valley, California.

D'ARTAGNAN purveys some of the most incredible duck and foie gras. They sell several breeds of ducks including Long Island or Pekin, Moulard, and Muscovy, and seasonally, Mallard duck. All of their products are antibiotic and hormone free, and raised on small farms with careful attention to humane care. The Long Island or Pekin duck has smaller breasts and is quite lean. I tend to cook with this breed the most. Moulard, a hybrid of a Pekin and Muscovy, is the duck that provides foie gras. This "cross" results in a very large duck with a uniquely flavored meat. Muscovy duck has a thinner skin than the others, and is lower in fat. The meat is lean, tender, and full flavored.

Poached Halibut in Heirloom Tomato & Lemon Balm Water

Lemon balm, a member of the mint family, has a gentle lemon scent with mild mint undertones. The delicate fragrance and flavor makes lemon balm a perfect match for halibut, which is so mild and moist. Poaching the halibut in the tomato and lemon balm water allows the flavors to permeate the fish.

SERVES 6

Tomato and Lemon Balm Water

4 pounds heirloom tomatoes, cored and quartered
2 garlic cloves, smashed
10 fresh basil sprigs, leaves only, stems reserved
10 fresh lemon balm sprigs, leaves only, stems reserved

Halibut

6 skinless East Coast halibut fillets, 7 ounces each
Sea salt and freshly ground black pepper
6 tablespoons extra virgin olive oil

2½ pounds heirloom tomatoes, peeled and cut into 2-inch pieces
Fleur de sel

Make the tomato and lemon balm water ➤ Combine the tomatoes, garlic, basil leaves, and lemon balm leaves in the food processor fitted with a metal blade and blend until smooth. Secure a large colander over a mixing bowl and line the colander with piece of cheesecloth. Pour the puréed tomatoes into the colander. Place the colander and bowl in the refrigerator and allow the liquid to strain into the bowl overnight.

Transfer the tomato liquid to a medium saucepan; discard the mixture in the cheesecloth. Boil the tomato liquid until reduced by half, about 10 minutes. While the liquid is reducing, use a ladle to remove any foam from the surface. Remove from the heat and strain the liquid through a coffee filter and into a clean small saucepan. You may have to pass the liquid through a coffee filter twice until it is completely clear. Set the saucepan over very low heat.

Cook the halibut ➤ Preheat the oven to 300°F. Scatter the reserved stems of the basil and lemon balm in a roasting pan. Season the halibut with salt and pepper. Arrange the halibut over the stems and pour the warm tomato water around the halibut. Drizzle with 3 tablespoons of the olive oil and cover tightly with foil. Steam the fish in the oven until the flesh is opaque and cooked through, about 8 minutes.

To serve ➤ Season the heirloom tomatoes to taste with salt and pepper. Arrange the tomatoes on 6 warm serving plates. Drizzle the tomatoes with the warm poaching liquid. Arrange the halibut in the center of the plate. Sprinkle with fleur de sel and drizzle with the remaining 3 tablespoons of olive oil.

Wine suggestion ➤ Serve this dish with an elegant Chardonnay that offers flavors of crisp apples, lemon zest, and vibrant minerality, such as Chardonnay, "Tinaquaic Vineyard," 2007, Foxen Winery, Santa Maria Valley, California.

Oven-Roasted Chicken with Vegetables Provençal

A good friend of mine from the Pays Niçois region used to make this dish when I visited. The roasted vegetable medley is a classic ratatouille with the addition of chickpeas. I like to make this dish a day ahead if possible so the flavors of the chicken and the herbes de Provence will permeate the vegetables and vice versa.

SERVES 6

1 cup dried chickpeas, soaked for 12 hours in cold water
3 medium beefsteak tomatoes, cut into 1-inch pieces
2 yellow summer squash, cut into 1-inch pieces
2 zucchini, cut into 1-inch pieces
1 medium eggplant, cut into ½-inch pieces
1 green bell pepper, seeded and cut into 1-inch pieces
1 red bell pepper, seeded and cut into 1-inch pieces
½ Spanish onion, cut into 1-inch pieces
5 garlic cloves, cut in half
2 bay leaves
¼ cup extra virgin olive oil + 1 tablespoon for brushing the chicken
Sea salt and freshly ground black pepper
1 whole organic chicken, 4½ to 5 pounds
3 tablespoons herbes de Provence

Drain the chickpeas and transfer them to a large saucepan. Cover the chickpeas with cold salted water and simmer until tender, about 2 hours. Drain the peas and allow them to cool.

Preheat the oven to 375°F. Scatter the tomatoes, squash, zucchini, eggplant, bell peppers, onion, garlic, and bay leaves in a large roasting pan. Drizzle the ¼ cup of olive oil over the vegetables, season with salt and pepper, and toss to coat.

Brush the chicken with the remaining 1 tablespoon of olive oil and season with salt and pepper and the herbes de Provence. Arrange the chicken on top of the vegetables.

Roast the chicken and vegetables until the skin of the chicken is golden brown and crisp and the juices run clear when the chicken is pierced with a knife at the joint of the leg, about 50 minutes. To check for doneness, insert an instant-read thermometer in the thickest part of the thigh, making sure not to touch the bone. The temperature reading should be 165° to 175°F.

Carefully transfer the chicken to a cutting board. Turn the oven temperature down to 325°F. Return the roasting pan with vegetables to the oven and cook until soft but still holding their shape, about 1 hour. Skim the excess fat off the top of the vegetables, add the chickpeas to the vegetables, and roast until the chickpeas are heated through and the flavors have combined, about 20 minutes.

Cut the chicken into 8 pieces by gently pulling the legs away from the body and cutting the legs and the thigh off in 1 piece. Cut the legs and the thighs apart at the joints. Cut the breasts away from the main breast bone, scraping the breast meat away from the bone with the knife, and cut each breast in half. Place the chicken, skin side up, on top of the vegetables and rewarm in the oven.

Serve the chicken and the ratatouille on a large serving platter.

Wine suggestion ➤ Serve this dish with a lush Chardonnay that offers flavors of red delicious apples, crème brûlée, and a touch of pineapple, such as Chardonnay, Ramey Wine Cellars, 2006, Sonoma Coast, California.

Marsala-Braised Osso Buco with Grapes

This dish is perfect enjoyed in the late summer weeks when grapes are just beginning to appear at the farmers' market. I like to serve this dish with a simple starch, like pasta with parsley and butter or couscous, and a side of grilled summer vegetables. I recommend you make this dish in the morning and allow it to rest all day. By the time you reheat it, the flavors have fully developed and the meat is meltingly tender.

SERVES 6

1 cup dry sweet Marsala
¼ cup sultana raisins
6 crosscut veal shanks (osso buco), 10 ounces each
Sea salt and freshly ground black pepper
¼ cup extra virgin olive oil
2 medium shallots, diced
3 garlic cloves, peeled and cut in half
1 fresh thyme sprig
1 bay leaf
2 tablespoons Armagnac or cognac
1½ cups green seedless grapes
¾ cup Chicken Stock (page 303)
½ cup Veal Stock (page 304)
2 tablespoons chopped fresh parsley

Pour 3 tablespoons of the Marsala over the raisins in a small bowl and allow them to soak until the raisins soften and plump, about 30 minutes.

Preheat the oven to 350°F. Season the shanks with salt and pepper. Heat an ovenproof sauté pan large enough to hold the shanks in 1 layer over high heat. Add the olive oil and heat until nearly smoking. Sear the shanks on all sides until browned, about 5 minutes per side. Remove the shanks from the pan and reduce the heat to medium. Pour off all but 2 tablespoons of the fat from the pan and add the shallots, garlic, thyme, and bay leaf to the pan. Sauté until slightly softened, about 3 minutes. Add the Armagnac and the remaining Marsala and simmer until reduced by half, about 3 minutes. Add the raisins and their soaking liquid. Using a wooden spoon, scrape up any browned bits from the bottom of the pan and stir them into the sauce. Add the grapes, chicken stock, and veal stock. Return the osso buco to the pan and bring the liquid to a simmer.

Once the liquid has come to a simmer, cover the pan tightly with aluminum foil. Place the pan in the oven and cook until the meat is very tender and starting to fall off the bone, about 1½ hours. Transfer the shanks to a serving platter.

Simmer the braising liquid over high heat until reduced to a thick sauce that will coat the back of a spoon. Stir in half of the chopped parsley.

Spoon the sauce over the shanks and garnish with the remaining parsley.

Wine suggestion ➤ Serve this dish with a jammy Zinfandel that offers flavors of ripe blackberries, brandied cherries, and allspice, such as Zinfandel, "Rancho Bello Vineyard," Ottimino, Russian River Valley, California.

Grilled Montauk Tuna Stuffed with Herbs & Tapenade

Montauk, located at the very end of Long Island, is blessed with terrific seafood, ranging from striped bass, to bluefish, fluke, and, of course, amazing bluefin tuna. The farms around this area also supply a bounty of produce, like terrific white and yellow corn. I like to marry the two by serving grilled tuna with steamed or grilled corn on the cob.

SERVES 6

1 cup fresh basil leaves, roughly chopped
¼ cup store-bought black olive tapenade
2 tablespoons salt-packed capers, rinsed and roughly chopped
1 anchovy, rinsed and chopped
1 finely chopped Thai chile
3 bluefin tuna steaks, 14 ounces each
⅓ cup + 2 tablespoons extra virgin olive oil
4 tablespoons freshly squeezed lemon juice
2 tablespoons chopped fresh oregano
1½ tablespoons chopped fresh rosemary
1 tablespoon cracked black peppercorns
1 tablespoon finely chopped garlic
3 baby artichokes
Sea salt and freshly ground black pepper
1 tablespoon balsamic vinegar
2 ounces Sartori Stravecchio (or another domestic Parmesan cheese), shaved
2 tablespoons fresh parsley leaves
1 lemon, cut into 6 wedges
Cerignola olives, cut in half (optional)

Prepare the tuna ➤ Mix the basil, tapenade, capers, anchovy, and chile in a small bowl. Using a sharp paring knife, make an incision along 1 side of each tuna steak. Move the knife back and forth to make a pocket. Divide the stuffing into 3 equal parts and stuff the tuna steaks. Place the steaks in a shallow nonreactive baking dish.

Mix the ⅓ cup of olive oil with 3 tablespoons of the lemon juice, oregano, rosemary, peppercorns, and garlic in a small bowl. Pour the marinade over the fish and marinate in the refrigerator for 4 hours.

Prepare the artichokes ➤ Using a paring knife, trim an artichoke of all external green leaves as well as the green exterior of the stem. Once the artichoke has been trimmed down to the tender, yellow-hued leaves, cut it in half. Using a mandoline or a very sharp knife, very thinly slice the artichoke. Transfer the slices to a bowl of cold water with the remaining 1 tablespoon of lemon juice. Repeat this process quickly with the remaining artichokes, making sure they do not turn brown.

Grill the tuna ➤ Preheat a grill or grill pan to medium-high heat. Remove the fish from the marinade and season with sea salt and pepper. Grill until the tuna is well seared but still medium-rare, about 3 minutes per side. Remove the tuna from the grill and cut it into 1-inch-thick slices.

To serve ➤ Transfer the tuna to a platter, drizzle with the remaining 2 tablespoon of olive oil and the balsamic vinegar. Garnish with the shaved cheese, parsley leaves, artichoke slices, lemon wedges, and halved olives, if desired.

Wine suggestion ➤ Serve this dish with a mouthwatering Pinot Blanc that offers flavors of nectarine, pear, and crisp acidity, such as Pinot Blanc, "Reserve," Lieb Cellars, 2007, North Fork Long Island, New York.

Steamed Lobster in Gingered Lime–Scallion Broth with Baby Bok Choy

The combination of ginger and lime results in a truly enchanting flavor, which is well suited for both savory and sweet dishes alike. This very light broth pairs quite well with other shellfish, such as shrimp and mussels, or firmer white fish.

SERVES 6

6 live lobsters, 2 pounds each
½ cup Chablis or another dry white wine
3 cups Vegetable Stock (page 304)
6 shiitake mushrooms, stemmed and thinly sliced
2 tablespoons matchstick-size strips peeled fresh ginger
1½ tablespoons ginger juice (see page 96)
6 baby bok choy
4 tablespoons cold unsalted butter, diced
4 scallions, thinly sliced on the bias
2 tablespoons chopped fresh cilantro
2 tablespoons freshly squeezed lime juice
Zest of 2 limes
Pinch of cayenne pepper

Prepare the broth ➤ Holding the lobster body in 1 hand and the tail in the other hand, twist the lobster until the body and tail separate. Repeat with the remaining 5 lobsters. Using the back of a chef's knife, crack the claws off the lobster bodies just below the knuckles. Reserve the bodies for making lobster stock or freeze them for another use.

Bring a large saucepan of water to a boil over high heat. Add the lobster claws and cook until the shells become bright red and the claw meat is just barely cooked through, about 8 minutes. Transfer the claws to a bowl of ice water. Once cool, remove the claw meat from the shells.

Using a chef's knife, cut the lobster tails in half lengthwise and discard any intestines that may be clinging to the tail. Leave the meat in the shells. Bring the Chablis to boil in a large saucepan. Add the lobster tails, flesh side down, and the vegetable stock. Cover and cook until the lobster meat is just barely cooked through, about 3 minutes. Remove the tails from the broth.

Using a fine-mesh strainer, strain the broth into a clean medium saucepan over medium heat. Add the shitake mushrooms, ginger, and ginger juice to the broth and simmer until the ginger is soft, about 3 minutes. Strain the broth again through a fine-mesh strainer and into a large saucepan, reserving the mushrooms and ginger.

Finish the broth ➤ Bring a medium pot of salted water to a boil over high heat. Add the bok choy and cook until crisp-tender, about 3 minutes. Immediately transfer the bok choy to a bowl of ice water and allow to cool.

Using an immersion blender, blend the cold butter into the strained broth until emulsified. Return the reserved mushrooms and ginger, lobster claw meat, and blanched bok choy to the broth along with the scallions, cilantro, lime juice, lime zest, and cayenne and continue to cook over low heat for 2 minutes.

To serve ➤ Divide the lobster tails among 6 large shallow bowls. Arrange the claw meat and 1 bok choy over each lobster tail. Spoon the sauce and vegetables over the lobster tails and claws and serve.

Wine suggestion ➤ Serve this dish with an exotic white Rhone blend that offers rich flavors of guava, minerals, and Asian spices, such as Tensley, "Blanc," 2007, Santa Barbara County, California.

Sablé of Marinated Tristar Strawberries, Cream Chiboust, & Lemon Verbena Sorbet

A pastry chef by the name of Chiboust developed this lightened pastry cream in France in the mid 19th century. It's a great filling for any tart because it has the lightness of whipped cream and the silken texture of pastry cream. Lemon verbena is a perennial shrub native to South America. It has a clean sharp lemon scent and is used to make tea and add flavor to everything from jams to poultry to sorbet.

SERVES 6

Sablé

¾ cup all-purpose flour
½ cup almond flour
¼ cup + 1 teaspoon confectioners' sugar
4 tablespoons unsalted butter, softened + 2 tablespoons unsalted butter, cold

Cream Chiboust

2½ gelatin sheets
4 large eggs, separated
1 tablespoon + 1 teaspoon + ⅓ cup sugar
1 tablespoon all-purpose flour
⅓ cup + 1 tablespoon freshly squeezed lemon juice
¼ cup + 1 teaspoon heavy cream
1 tablespoon light corn syrup

Strawberries

½ cup sugar
½ cup roughly chopped Tristar strawberries
2 pints Tristar strawberries, trimmed and cut in half

Lemon Verbena Sorbet (page 313)
12 small fresh mint leaves

Make the sablé ➤ Preheat the oven to 325°F. Line a baking sheet with parchment paper. Combine the all-purpose flour, almond flour, and confectioners' sugar in a large bowl. Add the softened butter and mix with a fork or your fingertips until the mixture resembles course crumbs.

Press the dough onto the prepared baking sheet and bake until golden brown, about 10 minutes. Let the biscuit cool completely.

Once cool, transfer the biscuit to a food processor and pulse until the biscuit resembles a fine powder. Transfer the powder to the bowl of a stand mixer fitted with the paddle attachment. Mix in the cold butter at medium speed until just combined. The dough should now resemble graham cracker crumbs. Divide the crumb mixture evenly among six 6-ounce glass or ceramic ramekins, pressing the mixture evenly onto the bottom.

Make the chiboust ➤ Soak the gelatin sheets in a bowl with 2 cups of cold water until softened, about 5 minutes. Whisk together the egg yolks, the 1 tablespoon plus 1 teaspoon of sugar, and the flour in a large bowl until pale and frothy, about 3 minutes.

Combine the lemon juice and heavy cream in a small saucepan over medium heat. Once the lemon juice and cream begin to boil, slowly pour the cream over the egg mixture, whisking constantly so that the eggs do not cook. Let cool. Pass the custard through a fine-mesh strainer and into a clean saucepan. Bring to a boil over medium heat, whisking constantly, until the mixture thickens, about 3 minutes. Transfer to a clean mixing bowl. Remove the softened gelatin sheets from the water, squeeze out any excess water, and whisk them into the pastry cream until well dissolved. Press a sheet of plastic wrap onto the surface of the pastry cream to prevent a skin from forming and refrigerate until ready to use. Whisk the pastry cream to loosen it before folding in the meringue.

Combine the remaining ⅓ cup of sugar with the corn syrup and 2 tablespoons of water in small saucepan and bring to a boil. Using a stand mixer fitted with a whisk attachment, whisk the egg whites in the mixer bowl until soft peaks form. With the mixer running, slowly pour the hot syrup into the egg whites and whisk on high speed until the mixture has completely cooled and forms stiff, glossy peaks. Using a rubber spatula, fold the egg whites into the pastry cream until fully incorporated.

Transfer the mixture to a pastry bag and pipe into the ramekins. Cover and refrigerate at least for 4 hours before serving.

continued

Prepare the strawberries ➤ Bring the sugar and ½ cup of water to a boil in a small saucepan over medium heat. Remove from the heat and cool. Once cool, add the chopped strawberries to the syrup. Using a handheld immersion blender, blend the strawberries until smooth. Pass through a strainer set over a medium bowl, discarding any solids and seeds. The consistency will resemble a thick juice. Add the 2 pints of halved strawberries and marinate for 30 minutes.

To serve ➤ Using a slotted spoon, lift the strawberries from the syrup and spoon them over the top of the chiboust. Spoon some of the syrup over the strawberries and place a scoop of the sorbet on top of each serving. Garnish with mint sprigs and serve.

Wine suggestion ➤ Serve this dish with a late harvest Riesling that offers flavors of lemon, white spices, and honey, such as White Riesling, "Ethos–Late Harvest," Château St. Michelle, 2006, Columbia Valley, Washington.

TRISTAR STRAWBERRIES are an heirloom variety of strawberries. I love working with them because they have such a wonderful, rich berry flavor. The berries are small to medium in size and are a darker red than most other varieties. The local farms start harvesting these berries at their peak during mid to late summer. They are surprisingly hearty given their small size, and the plants will produce berries well into the fall if they are continuously harvested.

Roasted Peach Melba with Vermont Double Cream Ice Cream & Crystallized Lavender

The peach Melba was created by a famous French chef, Auguste Escoffier, in honor of famed Australian soprano Nellie Melba. Peaches were supposedly her favorite fruit and the chef, so taken by her performance, was inspired to invent this dessert. The peaches are the star of the show, but this dessert is not complete without ice cream. If I am short on time, I serve the peaches with Ronnybrook Farm Dairy vanilla ice cream.

SERVES 6

Poached Peaches

3 ripe peaches
2 vanilla beans, split lengthwise and seeds scraped, scraped beans cut into 3 equal pieces, for garnish
3 tablespoons honey
2 tablespoons Kirsch
1 tablespoon grenadine
2 teaspoons unsalted butter
1 teaspoon almond extract

Crystallized Lavender

1 large egg white
1 teaspoon dried lavender flowers
¾ teaspoon sugar

Vermont Double Cream Ice Cream (page 311)
6 teaspoons red currant jelly
Caramelized almonds (see page 132)

Poach the peaches ➤ Bring a medium saucepan of water to a boil. Using a paring knife, make a shallow "X" on the bottom of the peaches. Immerse the peaches in the boiling water for 30 seconds, and then immediately transfer them to a bowl of ice water. Once cool, the peach peel should slide off the peaches with little effort. Once peeled, cut the peaches in half and discard the pits.

Combine the vanilla beans and seeds, honey, Kirsch, grenadine, butter, almond extract, and ½ cup of water in a large saucepan over medium-low heat. Add the peaches, cover, and simmer until the peaches are tender, stirring occasionally so that the peaches cook evenly, about 15 minutes. Allow the peaches to cool in the liquid. The peaches should be cooled to room temperature before serving.

Crystallize the lavender ➤ Line a baking sheet with parchment paper. Brush the parchment paper with the egg white. Evenly scatter the lavender over the baking sheet, and using your fingers, lightly press the lavender into the egg white to ensure it is coated. Sprinkle the sugar over the lavender. Allow the lavender to dry out for at least 2 hours.

To serve ➤ Scoop the ice cream into 6 ice cream coupe glasses or other shallow bowls. Arrange a peach half, cut side down, on top of the ice cream in each bowl, and drizzle each peach with 1 tablespoon of the cooking liquid. Spoon 1 teaspoon of the red current jelly over each peach. Garnish with the caramelized almonds, crystallized lavender, and the sliced vanilla bean from the cooking liquid.

Wine suggestion ➤ Serve this dish with a sweet wine made from a blend of Sauvignon Blanc and Semillon that offer flavors of roasted peaches, honey, and jasmine, such as Beringer Private Reserve, "Nightingale," 2004, Napa Valley, California.

Plum Tarte Tatin with Huckleberry & Frozen Almond Milk

Huckleberries resemble blueberries in appearance and taste. The sweetness of the huckleberries makes them an ideal match with the more tart red plums.

SERVES 6

Special Equipment
Six 3½-inch Flexipan molds

Puff Pastry and Almond Cream
1 sheet store-bought frozen puff pastry, preferably Dufour brand, thawed
¾ cup almond flour
¾ cup confectioners' sugar
6 tablespoons unsalted butter, softened
1 large egg

Caramelized Almonds
3 tablespoons Simple Syrup (page 314)
2 teaspoons orange blossom water
⅓ cup sliced almonds
2 teaspoons sugar

Caramel
1 cup sugar
3 tablespoons light corn syrup
3 tablespoons unsalted butter

Huckleberry Compote
⅓ cup sugar
¾ cup huckleberries

6 ripe red plums
Almond Milk Sorbet (page 311)

Prepare the puff pastry ➤ Line 2 baking sheets with parchment paper. Unfold the puff pastry on a lightly floured cool surface. Using a lightly floured rolling pin, roll out the pastry to a ⅛-inch thickness. Using a 3½-inch cookie cutter, cut 6 disks from the puff pastry and transfer them to 1 of the prepared baking sheets. Freeze for a minimum of 1 hour.

Using a stand mixer fitted with the paddle attachment, mix the flour, sugar, butter, and egg in the mixer bowl at medium speed until well combined and fluffy, about 2 minutes. Remove the puff pastry from the freezer and spread 2 tablespoons of the almond cream evenly over each of the 6 disks. Return to the freezer and freeze for at least 1 hour.

Caramelize the almonds ➤ Preheat the oven to 325°F. Combine the simple syrup and orange blossom water in small bowl. Add the almonds and mix until the almonds are well coated. Spread the almonds evenly over the second prepared baking sheet and sprinkle the sugar over the almonds. Bake until light golden brown, about 10 minutes.

Make the caramel ➤ Cook the sugar, corn syrup, and 3 tablespoons of water in a small saucepan over medium-high heat, swirling the pan every so often, until the mixture is deep amber in color, about 4 minutes. Remove from the heat and add the butter, whisking until well incorporated. Immediately divide the hot caramel evenly into six 3½-inch Flexipan molds. Allow to cool to room temperature.

Make the huckleberry compote ➤ Bring the sugar and 2 tablespoons of water to a boil in a heavy small saucepan over medium-low heat. Add the huckleberries and cook until the huckleberries just begin to release their juices, about 2 minutes. Transfer to a small bowl and refrigerate until cold.

Assemble the tarts ➤ Preheat the oven to 375°F. Cut the plums in half and remove the pits. Cut each plum half into 4 slices and arrange about 8 slices evenly over the caramel in each mold. Place 1 puff pastry round, almond cream side down, atop the plum in each mold. Transfer the molds to a baking sheet. Bake until the puff pastry is cooked through and golden brown, about 20 minutes. The puff pastry will have puffed up significantly from the moisture in the plums.

To serve ➤ While still warm, invert each mold and serve the tarts plum side up. Scatter the almonds over each tart. Serve each tart with a scoop of the sorbet topped with a spoonful of huckleberry compote.

Wine suggestion ➤ Serve this dish with a late harvest Chardonnay that offers flavors of baked apples, puff pastry, and almond candy, such as Chardonnay Late Harvest, "Eloquence," Raymond, 2005, Napa Valley, California.

New York Ricotta Cheesecake with Hibiscus Poached Cherries

Being a New Yorker, I owe my allegiance to New York–style cheesecake, which incorporates both cream cheese and heavy cream. The result is incredibly creamy and tangy. The addition of ricotta here adds a hint of texture. The sweetness of the cheesecake is perfectly offset by the slightly acidic and very floral hibiscus tea. The tea is actually dried leaves of the tropical hibiscus flower.

SERVES 6

Special Equipment
Six 2¾-inch ring molds (1¾ inches high); kitchen torch

Hibiscus Poached Cherries
- ½ cup dried hibiscus flowers
- 3 tablespoons sugar
- 1½ cups halved pitted cherries

Orange Sablé Crust
- 3 tablespoons + 1 teaspoon unsalted butter
- 3 tablespoons + 1 teaspoon sugar
- 1 large egg yolk
- 2 teaspoons orange zest
- ½ cup + 2 tablespoons all-purpose flour
- 1 teaspoon baking powder
- Pinch of salt

Cheesecake
- 1⅔ cups cream cheese, softened
- ¾ cup ricotta cheese
- ¼ cup + 8 tablespoons sugar
- ¾ teaspoon vanilla extract
- 1 large egg
- 2 large egg whites
- ¾ cup heavy cream
- 1 tablespoon unsalted butter, melted

Fresh mint for garnish

Poach the cherries ➤ Bring 2 cups of water to a boil and add the dried hibiscus. Remove from the heat. Cover and let infuse for at least 8 hours. Strain the hibiscus flowers from the liquid and discard.

Combine the sugar and the hibiscus tea in a small saucepan over medium heat. Simmer for 10 minutes. Remove from the heat and stir in the cherries. Let cool to room temperature, then transfer to a small bowl. Cover and refrigerate for at least 4 hours.

Make the orange sablé crust ➤ Preheat the oven to 325°F. Prepare six 2¾-inch ring molds (1¾ inches high) by wrapping aluminum foil around the bottom and sides of each mold. Using a stand mixer fitted with the paddle attachment, beat the butter in the mixer bowl until light and fluffy.

Using the stand mixer fitted with the whisk attachment, beat the sugar, egg yolk, and orange zest in another mixer bowl at high speed until the mixture doubles in volume, about 3 minutes. Change the attachment on the stand mixer back to the paddle. Add the creamed butter to the yolk mixture and mix until just combined. Sift together the flour, baking powder, and salt into a medium bowl. Using a rubber spatula, slowly fold the flour mixture into the butter mixture until just combined. Divide the dough evenly among the molds and, using your fingers, press firmly until uniform. Place the molds on a baking sheet and bake until golden brown, about 10 minutes. The cooked dough should resemble a cookie.

Make the cheesecake ➤ Preheat the oven to 300°F. Using a stand mixer fitted with the paddle attachment, beat the cream cheese, ricotta, ¼ cup plus 2 tablespoons of the sugar, and vanilla in a clean mixer bowl at medium speed until smooth, about 4 minutes. Mix in the egg and egg whites. Add the heavy cream and mix for 1 minute.

Brush the inside of the ring molds containing the orange sablé with the melted butter. Pour the cheesecake batter into the prepared ring molds, filling them three-fourths of the way to the top. Place the ring molds in a roasting pan and pour enough hot water into the roasting pan to come halfway up the sides of the molds. Bake until the cheesecakes have set in the center, about 30 minutes. Remove the cheesecakes from the water and cool for 15 minutes. Refrigerate the cheesecakes for at least 3 hours or until they have cooled thoroughly. Dip a paring knife in warm water and run it around the sides of the cheesecakes. Carefully unmold the cheesecakes.

To serve ➤ Place the cheesecakes in the center of 6 serving plates and sprinkle 1 tablespoon of the remaining sugar evenly over the top of each cheesecake. Using a kitchen torch, caramelize the sugar, making sure not to burn it. Arrange the poached cherries around the cheesecakes and drizzle them with some of the liquid. Top each cheesecake with 2 cherry halves and garnish with mint.

Wine suggestion ➤ Serve this dish with a frizzante, sweet wine made from Muscat that offers flavors of lychee, orange blossoms, and a touch of jasmine, such as Muscat Frizzante, "Semi-Sparkling," Tualatin Estate, 2006, Willamette Valley, Oregon.

Mum's Warm Apricot Tarte Fine with Chamomile Sorbet

When I visit my parents in the south of France each summer my mother makes this spectacular dessert. It's quite possibly one of my favorite summer desserts. The name *Tarte Fine* literally means a tart with a very fine or thin flaky crust. If you are unable to find ripe apricots, you can easily substitute peaches in this recipe. For an additional twist, whisk a few tablespoons of pistachio paste into the almond cream and scatter toasted pistachio halves over the top of the tart when it is removed from the oven.

SERVES 6

Almond Cream

½ cup almond flour
½ cup confectioners' sugar
½ stick (2 ounces) unsalted butter, softened
1 large egg

Dough

2¾ cups all-purpose flour
4 teaspoons sugar
½ teaspoon salt
1 stick (4 ounces) cold unsalted butter, cut into ½-inch pieces
7 tablespoons vegetable shortening
¾ teaspoon white vinegar

Apricot Sauce and Topping

4 apricots, pitted and chopped
3 tablespoons Simple Syrup (page 314)
1 teaspoon freshly squeezed lemon juice
15 apricots, pitted and cut into thin slices
6 tablespoons sugar

Chamomile Sorbet (page 312)

Make the almond cream ➤ Combine the flour, sugar, butter, and egg in the bowl of a stand mixer fitted with the paddle attachment and mix at medium speed until well combined and fluffy, about 2 minutes.

Make the dough ➤ Using a stand mixer fitted with the paddle attachment, mix the flour, sugar, and salt in the mixer bowl until well combined. Add the butter and vegetable shortening and continue to mix until crumbly, about 1 minute. Add 3 tablespoons of cold water and the vinegar and mix until completely absorbed. Wrap the dough in plastic wrap and refrigerate for 1 hour.

Using a lightly floured rolling pin, roll out the dough on a cool, lightly floured surface to a ⅛-thick thickness. Press the dough into a 9 × 9-inch baking pan and trim off any excess dough hanging over the edge. Freeze for 1 hour.

Make the apricot sauce ➤ Blend the chopped apricots, simple syrup, and lemon juice in a blender until smooth. Strain the sauce through a fine-mesh strainer set over a small bowl and discard the solids. Cover and refrigerate.

Assemble the tart ➤ Preheat the oven to 350°F. Remove the tart shell from the freezer. Spread the almond cream evenly over the bottom of the tart shell. Arrange the apricot slices over the almond cream. Sprinkle the top with sugar and bake until the crust is cooked through and golden brown, and the apricots are tender, rotating the pan halfway through, about 45 minutes. Let the tart cool for 10 minutes.

To serve ➤ Cut the tart into squares and spoon the apricot sauce on the side of each piece. Serve with a scoop of the sorbet atop the apricot sauce.

Wine suggestion ➤ Serve this dish with a sweet wine made from Muscat with aromas of apricots, orange blossoms, and dried fruits, such as Muscat "Vin de Glaciere," Pacific Rim, 2006, Washington.

Honey Roasted Black Mission Figs & Amaretti Whipped Cream

The best time of year to make this dessert is late summer and early fall when figs are at their peak sweetness. Black Mission figs are my favorite but Brown Turkey figs and bright green Kadota figs can be used as well. The almond cookie whipped cream is great with just about any fruit. Try this recipe with summer fruits like peaches, plums, cherries, or nectarines.

SERVES 6

6 tablespoons honey
¼ cup ruby port
12 fresh black Mission figs, halved
1 cup heavy cream
1½ tablespoons confectioners' sugar
2 tablespoons amaretto or other almond liqueur
¾ cup roughly chopped amaretti cookies

Heat the honey and port in a medium sauté pan over low heat and simmer for 1 minute. Add the figs and continue to cook, stirring gently, until the figs are tender, about 2 minutes. Make sure not to overcook the figs as they may fall apart. Remove the pan from the heat and allow to cool.

Using a stand mixer fitted with the whisk attachment, whisk the heavy cream and sugar in the mixer bowl at medium speed until soft peaks form, about 3 minutes. Using a rubber spatula, gently fold in the liqueur and cookies until well combined. Cover and refrigerate until ready to serve. Do not make the whipped cream more than 2 hours in advance or the cookies will become soggy.

Arrange the figs on a large serving platter and serve with the amaretti whipped cream on the side.

Wine suggestion ➤ Serve this dish with a sweet cream sherry that offers flavors of dried figs, almonds, and raisins, such as Cream Sherry, Stone Hill Winery, NV, Missouri.

Blackberry Clafoutis with Lime–Cottage Cheese Ice Cream

Clafoutis, a French dessert, is a layer of fresh fruit topped with a pancake-like batter and baked in the oven. Baked, the clafoutis tastes like a cooked custard, bursting with ripe fruit. You can make this dessert with all types of berries.

SERVES 6

Special Equipment
Six 3½-inch ring molds (¾ inch high)

Tart Crust
2 sticks (8 ounces) cold unsalted butter, cut into ½-inch pieces
¾ cup confectioners' sugar
½ teaspoon vanilla extract
2 cups all-purpose flour

Clafoutis Batter
2 cups fresh blackberries
1¼ cups sugar
⅓ cup all-purpose flour
2 large eggs
Pinch of salt
½ cup + 3 tablespoons whole milk

Lime–Cottage Cheese Ice Cream (page 309)

Make the crust ➤ Using a stand mixer fitted with the paddle attachment, mix the butter and sugar in the mixer bowl at medium speed until just incorporated, about 1 minute. Add the vanilla, then the flour, and mix until the dough reaches a crumbly consistency. Wrap the dough with plastic wrap and refrigerate for 1 hour.

Line a rimmed baking sheet with parchment paper. Using a floured rolling pin, roll out the dough on a lightly floured surface to a ⅛-inch thickness. Cut the dough into six 5-inch disks and fit each dough disk into a 3½-inch ring mold (¾ inch high), trimming off any excess dough that hangs over the sides. Place the prepared ring molds on the prepared baking sheet and freeze for 1 hour.

Preheat the oven to 325°F. Bake the tarts until golden brown, about 20 minutes. Cool for at least 20 minutes. Maintain the oven temperature.

Make the clafoutis batter ➤ Combine the blackberries and ¾ cup of the sugar in a large bowl and toss until well combined.

Whisk the flour, eggs, salt, and the remaining ½ cup of sugar in another large bowl to blend. Add the milk and continue to whisk until the mixture forms a paste-like consistency.

Assemble the tarts ➤ Place just enough blackberries in the tart shells to cover the bottom (about 8 blackberries per tart). Fill the remainder of the tart shells with the clafoutis batter. Bake the tarts until the center of the filling is completely set, about 15 minutes. Cool on a wire rack.

To serve ➤ Once the tarts have cooled to room temperature, carefully remove the ring molds. Transfer the tarts to plates and serve at room temperature with a scoop of ice cream.

Wine suggestion ➤ Serve this dish with a sweet late harvest Viognier offering flavors of honeyed peaches, vanilla, and candied citrus, such as Viognier, "Late Harvest," 2005, Barboursville, Virginia.

Caramelized Mascarpone Cheese Tarts with Grilled Nectarines

What could be easier than throwing a couple of peaches or nectarines on the hot grill when you are finished cooking your steaks? Grilled fruit is truly a summer luxury and should be enjoyed as much as possible. I have paired the grilled nectarines with a sweet, creamy cheese tart; however, you can also serve grilled fruit with honey and ricotta or whipped mascarpone.

SERVES 6

Special Equipment
Six 3½-inch ring molds (¾ inch high); pie weights or dried beans; kitchen torch

Tart Dough
9 tablespoons cold unsalted butter
2 tablespoons sugar
2 cups all-purpose flour
2 large egg yolks
Pinch of salt
¼ cup heavy cream

Mascarpone Filling
1¼ cups mascarpone
½ cup sour cream
¼ cup + 2 tablespoons sugar
½ vanilla bean, split lengthwise and seeds scraped
Pinch of salt
5 large egg yolks
1 tablespoon heavy cream

6 nectarines
½ cup turbinado sugar

Make the dough ➤ Using a stand mixer fitted with the paddle attachment, mix the butter and sugar in the mixer bowl at medium speed until light and fluffy, about 2 minutes. Add the flour, egg yolks, and salt and continue to mix at medium speed until just incorporated. With the mixer running, slowly add the heavy cream and mix until it is completely absorbed and the dough is uniform, about 1 minute. Wrap the dough in plastic wrap and refrigerate for at least 1 hour.

Bake the tarts ➤ Preheat the oven to 325°F. Line a baking sheet with parchment paper. Using another sheet of parchment paper, cut out 6 paper rounds to fit six 3½-inch ring molds (¾ inch high). Using a lightly floured rolling pin, roll out the dough on a lightly floured surface to a ⅛-inch thickness. Cut the dough into six 5-inch disks. Fit the dough disks into the 6 ring molds. Transfer the ring molds to the baking sheet. Line the dough with the paper rounds and fill with pie weights or dried beans. Bake the tarts until the dough is golden brown and cooked through, about 20 minutes. Allow the tarts to cool, then gently remove the beans and parchment paper.

Make the filling ➤ Reduce the oven temperature to 300°F. Using a stand mixer fitted with the paddle attachment, mix the mascarpone, sour cream, sugar, scraped vanilla bean seeds, and salt in the mixer bowl at low speed until just incorporated. Add the egg yolks and heavy cream and continue to mix on low speed until well combined. Pour the filling into the prebaked tart shells, and then bake until the filling has just set, about 15 minutes. Place the tarts on a wire rack to cool to room temperature. Refrigerate the tarts for at least 4 hours or until thoroughly chilled.

Grill the nectarines ➤ Preheat an outdoor grill or grill pan over medium-low heat. Cut each nectarine in half and remove the pits. Grill the nectarine halves until grill marks are apparent and the nectarines have softened, about 3 minutes on each side.

To serve ➤ Remove the tarts from the refrigerator and sprinkle with the turbinado sugar. Using a kitchen torch, caramelize the sugar on each tart. Serve the tarts with two grilled nectarines halves on the side.

Wine suggestion ➤ Serve this dish with an Ice Wine made from Semillon that offers flavors of ripe pineapples, dried apricots, and fresh acidity, such as Semillon Ice Wine, Covey Run, 2005, Yakima Valley, Washington State.

Warm Olive Oil Biscuit with Raspberry Jubilee

This cake, or biscuit, is often referred to as a *pompe*, or a pump, in the south of France. It is a leavened pastry made with olive oil and orange blossom water and generally served during the winter holidays with sugared almonds.

SERVES 6

Special Equipment

Six 2¾-inch ring molds (1¾ inches high)

Biscuits

¾ teaspoon dry yeast
Pinch of sugar + 4 tablespoons
1 cup all-purpose flour
½ teaspoon salt
Zest of 1 orange
1 large egg
2 teaspoons extra virgin olive oil
4 tablespoons cold unsalted butter, diced
2 teaspoons unsalted butter, at room temperature
2 cups Simple Syrup (page 314)
¼ cup orange blossom water
Confectioners' sugar, for garnish

Raspberry Jubilee

½ cup + 2 tablespoons light brown sugar
3 tablespoons unsalted butter
¼ cup Kirsch
2 tablespoons Grand Marnier
½ cup freshly squeezed orange juice
Zest of 2 oranges
Zest of 1 lemon
2 teaspoons vanilla extract
2 cups fresh raspberries

Make the biscuits ➤ Mix the yeast, the pinch of sugar, and 2 tablespoons of warm water in a small bowl and let sit for 5 minutes. Using a stand mixer fitted with the paddle attachment, beat the flour, salt, and orange zest in the mixer bowl at low speed. Add the yeast mixture and continue mixing until incorporated. Add the egg and olive oil and mix at medium speed until just combined. Replace the paddle attachment with the hook attachment. Slowly add the cold butter and continue to mix at medium speed until the mixture forms a ball, about 15 minutes.

Line a baking sheet with parchment paper. Place six 2¾-inch ring molds (1¾ inches high) on the baking sheet. Divide the dough into 6 pieces. Using your hands, roll the dough into small balls and place each ball inside the ring mold. Allow the dough to rise, uncovered, in a warm place until it doubles in size, about 45 minutes. Some oil may seep from the bottom of the dough, but this is normal.

Preheat the oven to 350°F. Spread a generous ¼ teaspoon of room temperature butter over the top of each biscuit and sprinkle the remaining 4 tablespoons of sugar over the butter. Bake until a knife inserted into a biscuit comes out clean, about 12 minutes. Cool for 30 minutes.

Make the raspberry jubilee ➤ Using a wooden spoon, stir the brown sugar and butter in a medium sauté pan over medium-low heat until the brown sugar dissolves, about 2 minutes. Reduce the heat and add the Kirsch and Grand Marnier and simmer until the alcohol has cooked off, about 2 minutes. Add the orange juice, orange zest, lemon zest, and vanilla and continue to simmer until the mixture begins to thicken, about 4 minutes. Remove the pan from the heat and very gently fold in the raspberries, making sure they do not break.

To serve ➤ Carefully remove the biscuits from the ring molds. Combine the simple syrup and orange blossom water in a large shallow dish. Quickly dip the biscuits into the syrup just to moisten them ever so slightly. Arrange a biscuit in the center of each plate and dust with confectioners' sugar. Spoon the raspberry jubilee on the side of the biscuits and drizzle any remaining syrup over the top of the biscuits. Serve immediately.

Chef's note ➤ The raspberry jubilee must be prepared and served the same day or else the raspberries will begin to brown.

Wine suggestion ➤ Serve this dish with a vin glace–style sweet wine that offers aromas of dried tropical fruits, peach, and candied orange peel, such as Signature Vin Glace, King Estate, 2006, Willamette Valley, Oregon.

Tomato and Chorizo Eggs Cocotte

To simplify this dish, you can make the tomato-chorizo mixture the day before. On the morning you are serving the eggs, bring the tomato-chorizo mixture to room temperature and assemble the ramekins. Also, if you prefer something a bit spicier, use dried hot red pepper flakes instead of the much milder Espelette pepper.

SERVES 6

2 tablespoons extra virgin olive oil
¼ pound Spanish chorizo, casing removed, thinly sliced
2 garlic cloves, sliced
1 small onion, finely diced
½ fresh poblano chile, seeded and thinly sliced
4 medium vine-ripened tomatoes, seeded and diced
Pinch of Espelette pepper
Pinch of sugar
Sea salt and freshly ground black pepper
¾ cup grated Monterey Jack cheese
6 large farm fresh eggs

Heat the olive oil in a medium sauté pan over high heat. Add the chorizo and sauté until lightly browned, about 2 minutes. Transfer the chorizo to a small bowl and leave the oil in the pan. Reduce the heat to medium, add the garlic, and sauté until golden brown, about 1 minute. Add the onion and poblano chile and cook until the onion is soft, about 4 minutes. Add the tomatoes, Espelette pepper, and sugar and cook over low heat until very thick and the consistency of jam, about 15 minutes. Season to taste with salt and pepper. Stir in the sautéed chorizo.

Preheat the oven to 375°F. Divide the tomato mixture equally among the six 8-ounce ramekins and top with the cheese. Break an egg into each of the ramekins.

Place the ramekins in a large roasting pan and fill the pan with enough hot water to come halfway up the sides of the ramekins. Bake until the egg whites are just set and the yolks are runny, about 12 minutes. Serve warm.

Blue Crab & Corn Omelet

This blue crab mixture is amazing in an omelet and maybe even better as a sandwich. I have yet to decide. If you have crab mixture left over, mix it with a little mayonnaise and a spicy Asian chile sauce, like Sriracha, and make a sandwich on grilled bread with watercress.

SERVES 6

2 ears corn
12 large farm fresh eggs
Sea salt and freshly ground black pepper
1 small heirloom tomato, finely chopped
½ small onion, finely chopped
½ small red bell pepper, finely chopped
1 jalapeño chile, seeded and diced
3 tablespoons chopped fresh cilantro
¼ teaspoon Old Bay seasoning + pinch for garnish
¼ teaspoon Tabasco
¾ pound jumbo lump blue crabmeat
1 tablespoon extra virgin olive oil
5 ounces grated sharp cheddar cheese

Bring a small saucepan of salted water to a boil and cook the corn for 8 minutes. Remove the corn and place it under cold running water. Once cool enough to handle, cut the corn kernels off the cob.

Whisk the eggs in a large bowl until blended, then stir in the corn kernels. Season with salt and pepper.

Combine the tomato, onion, bell pepper, and jalapeño in a medium bowl. Stir in the cilantro, the ¼ teaspoon of Old bay seasoning, and the Tabasco, and then gently fold in the crabmeat. Season to taste with salt and pepper.

Heat the oil in a large skillet over medium-low heat. Pour the egg mixture into the skillet. As the eggs set, lift the edges of the omelet and tilt the pan slightly to allow the uncooked egg to reach the pan's hot surface. When the eggs are nearly completely set, cover the pan and cook until the surface looks dry, about 1 minute longer. Scatter the cheese and the crab mixture over half of the omelet. Fold the uncovered portion of the omelet over the filling and sprinkle the top with the remaining pinch of Old Bay seasoning.

Transfer the omelet to a large serving platter and serve immediately.

BLT, Fried Egg, & Cheese Sandwich

When I think of the quintessential American breakfast sandwich it consists of bacon, eggs, and cheese. This version is slightly more involved than the one you get at your neighborhood diner or deli and it can be served to even the most discerning company. I like to enjoy the sandwich dipped in Heinz ketchup.

SERVES 6

12 slices country bread, about 1 inch thick
6 tablespoons extra virgin olive oil
12 slices double-smoked bacon
2 large vine-ripened tomatoes, each cut into 3 slices
Sea salt and freshly ground black pepper
6 slices Pleasant Ridge Reserve cheese (or another washed-rind, semi-aged cow's-milk cheese)
6 large eggs
6 tablespoons mayonnaise
1 bunch arugula, large stems removed
Tabasco

Preheat an outdoor grill or grill pan to medium heat. Brush both sides of the bread with some of the olive oil. Grill the bread until browned and crisp on both sides, about 2 minutes per side. Grill the bacon until the fat has mostly rendered and the bacon is crisp, about 2 minutes per side. Drain the bacon on a plate lined with paper towels. Brush the tomatoes with some of the olive oil and season them with salt and pepper. Grill the tomatoes on both sides until just barely charred, about 2 minutes.

Place a slice of cheese on 6 slices of the grilled bread and transfer to the hot grill. Close the cover of the grill until the cheese has just melted.

Heat 2 tablespoons of the olive oil in a nonstick pan over medium-high heat. Crack 3 eggs into the pan, making sure to keep the yolks intact. Season the eggs with salt and pepper. Once the egg white is set, gently flip the eggs over and cook 20 seconds longer. Remove the eggs from the pan. Fry the remaining eggs.

Spread the mayonnaise over 1 side of the remaining 6 slices of grilled bread and top with several leaves of arugula. Top each sandwich with an egg, a dash of Tabasco, a slice of grilled tomato, and 2 slices of grilled bacon. Place the 6 grilled bread slices, melted cheese side down, on the sandwiches and serve warm.

Memorial Day Barbecue

MENU

COCKTAIL
Basil-Cucumber Mojito

Appetizers
Summer Bean Salad with Lemon Pesto
and White Anchovy Beignets
or
Grilled Littleneck Clam and Bacon Pizzettas

Main Courses
Grilled Rib-Eye Steak with
Green Tomato Chimichurri and Balsamic Radicchio
or
Grilled Montauk Tuna Stuffed with Herbs and Tapenade

Smoked Fingerling Potato Salad

DESSERTS
Roasted Peach Melba with Vermont Double Cream Ice Cream and Crystallized Lavender
or
Mum's Warm Apricot Tarte Fine with Chamomile Sorbet

Fourth of July Picnic

MENU

COCKTAIL

White Peach Julep

Appetizers

Beefsteak Tomato, Mortadella, and Wisconsin Emmenthaler Tart

or

Ginger-Marinated Heirloom Tomatoes with Watermelon, Burrata, and Spicy Arugula

Main Courses

Oven-Roasted Chicken with Vegetables Provençal

or

Bucatini with Swordfish, Eggplant Ragu, and Garlic Breadcrumbs

DESSERTS

New York Ricotta Cheesecake with Hibiscus Poached Cherries

or

Sablé of Marinated Tristar Strawberries, Cream Chiboust, and Lemon Verbena Sorbet

Fall

The fall has always meant gradual but great change for me. Growing up, the endless summer days spent roaming the neighborhood with fellow mischief-makers were replaced by the seemingly eternal drudgery in the schoolroom. Vivid green leaves morphed into brilliant yellow, orange, and red hues. And, as the summer heat gave way to shorter days and brisker temperatures, the fall harvest provided a bounty of new ingredients and my appetite for heartier fare returned. I began to long for crisp, juicy apples and pears, earthy mushrooms and nuts, and all varieties of cabbages and potatoes.

The farmer's almanac may insist that fall officially begins on September 21, but my fall menus tend to reflect the lingering warmth of summer and the gentle crossover to earthier flavors. More substantial appetizers like creamy risottos, velvety soups, and foie gras offer a rich beginning to a meal. However, if an Indian summer lingers, lighter options, like chilled raw fish or crispy octopus with a bright citrus vinaigrette, are the answer. Longer cooking techniques, like slow roasting and braising for meat and poultry, become a focus, but don't put the grill away just yet.

The cooler temperatures also bring grapes to their peak ripeness. The fall grape harvest at vineyards across America is one of the busiest and most festive times of year. Depending upon the type of grapes grown, as well as acreage, the wine harvest at various vineyards can last for a few days or several weeks. During the harvest, the grapes are picked, processed, and fermented, and many vineyards host dinners to celebrate the occasion.

I love to participate in the harvest as I did throughout my early years in France. Harvest dinners are joyous events, and undoubtedly a convivial affair is born amongst people with shared passions for wine and food. The wine harvest menu pulls from some of my favorite dinners in the past.

Thanksgiving is perhaps my favorite holiday. It becomes an all-day affair where everyone can pitch in, but I insist on roasting the turkey myself. The aroma of the roasting turkey permeates the whole house and provides inspiration for friends and family who are busy setting the table, replete with seasonal gourds, dried sheaves of wheat, and, of course, many different wine glasses for the pairings.

October

Vegetables
Acorn Squash
Artichoke
Butternut Squash
Chinese Cabbage
Fingerling Potato
Fresh Shelling Bean
Leek
Napa Cabbage
Pumpkin
Red Cabbage
Salsify
Savoy Cabbage
Spaghetti Squash
Sunchoke
Swiss Chard

Fungi
Black Trumpet
Hedgehog
Matsutake
Porcini
White Truffle

Seafood
Black Bass
Black Cod
Flounder
Rock Shrimp
Salmon

Poultry & Game
Partridge
Pheasant
Venison
Wild Boar

Fruit
Blueberry
Bosc Pear
Concord Grape
Honey Crisp Apple
McIntosh Apple

Nuts
Chestnut
Hazelnut
Walnut

November

Vegetables
Artichoke
Butternut Squash
Cauliflower
Chinese Cabbage
Fingerling Potato
Napa Cabbage
Pumpkin
Red Cabbage
Rutabaga
Salsify
Savoy Cabbage
Spaghetti Squash
Sunchoke
Swiss Chard

Fungi
Black Truffle
Black Trumpet
Hedgehog
Matsutake
Porcini
White Truffle

Seafood
Black Bass
Black Cod
Lobster
Nantucket Bay Scallop
Rock Shrimp
Wild Salmon

Poultry & Game
Partridge
Pheasant
Venison
Wild Boar

Fruit
Bosc Pear
Concord Grape
Cranberry
Honey Crisp Apple
McIntosh Apple
Meyer Lemon
Pomegranate

Nuts
Chestnut
Hazelnut
Walnut

December

Vegetables
Brussels Sprout
Butternut Squash
Cabbage
Endive
Fennel
Fingerling Potato
Kale
Parsnip
Rutabaga
Salsify
Sunchoke
Turnip

Fungi
Black Truffle
Black Trumpet
Porcini
White Truffle

Seafood
Black Cod
Nantucket Bay Scallop
Skate
Stone Crab

Poultry & Game
Partridge
Pheasant
Venison
Wild Boar

Fruit
Blood Orange
Bosc Pear
Cranberry
Date
Honey Crisp Apple
Kumquat
Mandarin
McIntosh Apple
Meyer Lemon
Persimmon
Pomegranate
Quince

Nuts
Chestnut
Walnut

Red Apple & Bourbon Fizz

Red Apple & Bourbon Fizz

The deep caramelized flavor of Maker's Mark bourbon combined with the crispy sweetness of a red apple turns this cocktail into a grown-up version of a caramel apple.

SERVES 1

2 ounces Maker's Mark bourbon
1 ounce apple juice
1 ounce apple syrup, preferably Monin brand
¾ ounce freshly squeezed lemon juice
Splash of ginger ale
2 thin red apple slices

Combine the bourbon, apple juice, apple syrup, and lemon juice in a cocktail shaker. Shake with ice and strain over fresh ice in a highball glass. Top with a splash of ginger ale and garnish with the apple slices.

Pumpkin Patch

This sweet, creamy cocktail has all the aroma and flavor of fall. It's richly flavored and best served at the end of the night.

SERVES 1

2 ounces Coole Swan Irish cream liqueur or other Irish cream liqueur
1½ ounces Stoli Vanil vodka
1 ounce pumpkin syrup, preferably Monin brand
Freshly grated nutmeg

Combine the Irish cream liqueur, vodka, and pumpkin syrup in a cocktail shaker. Shake with ice and strain into a martini glass. Garnish with grated nutmeg.

Concord Spritzer

Grape-distilled vodka has a subtle grape flavor and aroma. This method for making vodka has become rather popular, and several makers in the United States specialize in this process.

SERVES 1

2 ounces Cîroc vodka
  or other grape-distilled vodka
2 ounces fresh Concord grape juice
1 ounce Simple Syrup (page 314)
½ ounce freshly squeezed lemon juice
Club soda
Small grape cluster

Combine the vodka, grape juice, simple syrup, and lemon juice in a cocktail shaker. Shake with ice and pour into a highball glass. Top with a splash of club soda and garnish with the grape cluster on the rim of the glass.

Cranberry-Mint Martini

I like to make this drink for any and all my holiday celebrations. It's easy to mix a larger quantity and serve at holiday gatherings.

SERVES 1

2 ounces cranberry juice
2 ounces Finlandia cranberry vodka
½ ounce grenadine
½ ounce Simple Syrup (page 314)
8 fresh mint leaves, 7 torn,
  1 whole leaf for garnish

Combine the cranberry juice, vodka, grenadine, simple syrup, and 7 torn mint leaves in a cocktail shaker. Shake with ice and strain into a martini glass. Smack the whole mint leaf in the palm of your hand to release the oils and drop it into the drink.

59-02

Pigs in a Blanket "Ritz Carlton"

This is my French twist on one of the most delicious American treats I have ever had. I find it absolutely impossible to eat just one. Make sure to use a very high-quality puff pastry or try to purchase some from your local baker, as it will make all the difference.

SERVES 6

2 sheets store-bought frozen puff pastry, preferably Dufour brand, thawed
¼ cup all-purpose flour
2 large eggs
2 tablespoons whole milk
6 Schaller and Weber wieners (beef and pork)
2 cups grated Roth Käse Grand Cru Gruyère cheese
½ cup sauerkraut, drained
¼ cup Raye's yellow mustard

Unfold the puff pastry on a lightly floured, cool surface. Using a lightly floured rolling pin, roll out the pastry to a ¼-inch thickness and cut it into 6 rectangles that are about 7 × 3 inches.

Preheat the oven to 375°F. Line a baking sheet with parchment paper. Place the flour in a shallow bowl and whisk together the eggs and milk in another shallow bowl. Roll 1 wiener in the flour and then dip it into the egg mixture and place it on a piece of puff pastry. Repeat with the remaining wieners. Top each wiener with ¼ cup of the cheese and then wrap the puff pastry tightly around the wiener, pinching the ends to seal completely.

Place the pigs in blankets, seam side down, on the prepared baking sheet; brush them with the remaining egg mixture and evenly scatter the remaining ½ cup of cheese on top, pressing to adhere. Bake until the pastry is golden brown and completely cooked through, about 25 minutes.

Slice each pig in a blanket into 6 pieces and serve with the sauerkraut and a dollop of mustard on top.

Wine suggestion ➤ What's better with this American classic than a cold, frothy beer? I recommend serving a Belgian-inspired witte (wheat) beer with these addictive treats, such as Ommegang "Witte," Cooperstown, New York.

Hamachi & Hearts of Palm Salad with Raye's Whole Grain Mustard Dressing

Slender, ivory-colored hearts of palm are the inner core of the trunk of certain varieties of palm trees. Fresh hearts of palm are a bit more subtle than the canned type and have a much crispier texture and nutty flavor. You can order them online or they may be at your farmers' market depending upon how tropical your climate is. However, if you are unable to find fresh hearts of palm, you can use a high-quality canned or jarred variety. This recipe also calls for yuzu juice, a highly acidic and very fragrant Japanese citrus. Bottled yuzu juice can be found at many Asian markets.

SERVES 6

¼ cup sugar
⅓ cup white wine vinegar
6 tablespoons yuzu juice
4 tablespoons extra virgin olive oil
1 tablespoon Raye's whole grain mustard
3 teaspoons mustard oil
Sea salt and freshly ground black pepper
2 ripe avocados, peeled, pitted, and sliced into 30 pieces
12 ounces sushi-quality hamachi, sliced into 30 pieces
2 teaspoons freshly squeezed lemon juice
1 celery stalk, peeled and thinly sliced
2 ounces fresh hearts of palm, thinly sliced
¼ cup celery leaves

Combine the sugar with 2 tablespoons of water in a small saucepan and simmer over high heat until syrupy. Add the vinegar and continue to simmer until reduced to ⅓ cup. Pour the syrup into a medium nonreactive bowl and cool. Whisk in the yuzu juice, 2 tablespoons of the olive oil, mustard, 1 teaspoon of the mustard oil, and 6 tablespoons of water. Season the sauce to taste with salt and pepper.

Place 5 avocado slices in the center of each of 6 plates. Place 1 hamachi slice over each avocado slice and season the fish with the remaining 2 tablespoons of olive oil, the lemon juice, and salt and pepper. Scatter the celery, hearts of palm, and celery leaves evenly over the fish and spoon the sauce around the plate and on top of the fish. Drizzle with the remaining 2 teaspoons of mustard oil and serve immediately.

Wine suggestion ➤ Pair this dish with a crisp, dry Riesling from New York's Finger Lake Region with aromas of citrus, peach, and minerals, such as Dry Riesling, "HJW Vineyard," Hermann J. Wiemer, 2007, Finger Lakes, New York.

Crispy Octopus & Cranberry Bean Salad with Blood Orange Vinaigrette

There are several steps in this dish—blanching, grilling, braising, and then frying—but it's worth all the effort. The result is an octopus that is incredibly tender but crisp at the same time.

SERVES 6

Octopus

3½ to 4 pounds baby octopus
1 cup kosher salt
2 tablespoons extra virgin olive oil
1 onion, cut into 1-inch pieces
2 celery stalks, cut into 1-inch pieces
1 medium carrot, cut into 1-inch pieces
½ fennel bulb, cut into large dice
1 bottle (750 ml) dry red wine
3 cups Chicken Stock (page 303) or Vegetable Stock (page 304)
3 fresh thyme sprigs
1 bay leaf
1 teaspoon whole black peppercorns
2 quarts vegetable oil for frying
2 tablespoons Wondra flour

Cranberry Bean Salad

1 pound fresh cranberry beans, rinsed
Sea salt and freshly ground black pepper
1 red bell pepper
1 yellow bell pepper
1 tablespoon finely chopped fresh oregano
1 tablespoon finely chopped rinsed preserved lemon rind

Blood Orange Vinaigrette

1 cup freshly squeezed blood orange juice (about 4 oranges)
¼ cup extra virgin olive oil
1 tablespoon freshly squeezed Meyer lemon juice

2 cups arugula

Prepare the octopus ➤ Preheat the oven to 300°F. Place the octopus in an 8-quart saucepan, add the kosher salt, and fill with enough cold water to cover the octopus by 2 inches. Bring to a rapid boil over high heat, and then immediately transfer the octopus to a colander in the sink. Discard the salted cooking water. Once cool, cut around the base of the octopus head to separate the head from the rest of the body. Discard the head and cut the tentacles apart and blot the tentacles dry.

Heat a large grill pan over high heat. Brush the tentacles with 1 tablespoon of olive oil and grill the tentacles for 2 to 3 minutes on each side, being sure to get even color on all sides.

While the octopus is grilling, heat the remaining 1 tablespoon of olive oil in a large Dutch oven over medium-high heat. Add the onion, celery, carrot, and fennel and sauté until soft and caramelized, about 10 minutes. Add the wine, stock, thyme, bay leaf, and peppercorns and bring to a boil. Transfer the grilled octopus to the wine mixture. Cover with a lid or foil and place in the oven. Cook until the octopus is very tender, about 1½ hours. Cooking times for octopus vary widely, so test the octopus with a paring knife after 1 hour. The octopus should cut easily and be quite tender when done.

Transfer the octopus to a medium bowl with 3 cups of the braising liquid and cool. Discard the remaining braising liquid and vegetables.

Cook the cranberry beans ➤ Place the beans and 5 cups of water in a medium saucepan. Bring to a boil over high heat, then lower the heat and simmer, partially covered, until the beans are just tender, about 45 minutes. Season to taste with salt and pepper. Set the beans aside to cool completely in the liquid. Drain the liquid from the cooled beans and discard the liquid.

Make the vinaigrette ➤ Bring the blood orange juice to a simmer in a small saucepan. Cook over medium heat until the juice is reduced by half then pour the reduced juice into a medium nonreactive bowl. Whisk the reduced juice with the olive oil and Meyer lemon juice. Season to taste with salt and pepper.

Make the cranberry bean salad ➤ On a grill pan or under a broiler, char the red and yellow peppers until blackened on all sides. Place the peppers in a bowl and cover with plastic wrap. Set aside until cool. Peel the peppers and remove the seeds. Slice the peppers into thin strips and toss them in a large bowl with the cooked cranberry beans, the oregano, preserved lemon rind, and 2 tablespoons of the vinaigrette.

Fry the octopus ➤ Fill a deep heavy pot with 4 inches of the vegetable oil and heat the oil to 375°F. Remove the octopus from the braising liquid and pat dry. Working in batches, sprinkle the octopus tentacles evenly with the flour and carefully lower the tentacles into the hot oil. Do not crowd the pot. Fry the tentacles until golden brown and crispy, about 2 minutes. With a slotted spoon, transfer the octopus to a plate lined with paper towels, season lightly with salt, and allow the excess oil to drain.

To assemble and serve ➤ Toss the arugula with 1 tablespoon of the vinaigrette and season to taste with salt and pepper.

Spoon the cranberry bean salad onto 6 serving plates. Arrange the fried octopus and arugula over the bean salad and drizzle with the remaining vinaigrette.

Wine suggestion ➤ Pair this dish with a crisp Tocai Friulano from the Hudson River Valley with notes of citrus, kiwi, and herbs, such as Tocai Friulano, Millbrook, 2006, Hudson River Valley, New York.

Homemade Gnocchi, Lamb Sausage, & Swiss Chard with Fennel Beurre Blanc

The potatoes for the delicious gnocchi are baked on a mound of salt to draw the moisture out of the potato, so the gnocchi dough will not be gluey.

SERVES 6

Gnocchi

2 cups kosher salt
2¼ pounds russet potatoes, scrubbed
½ cup + 3 tablespoons all-purpose flour
1 large egg
2 tablespoons extra virgin olive oil
¼ teaspoon freshly grated nutmeg
Sea salt and freshly ground black pepper

Sausage and Chard

1 pound lamb sausage (not Merguez)
1 bunch Swiss chard, leaves only

Fennel Beurre Blanc

1 tablespoon extra virgin olive oil
1 cup diced fennel bulb
¾ cup finely chopped shallots
5 fresh thyme sprigs
10 whole black peppercorns
1 teaspoon fennel seeds
1 cup dry white wine
½ cup white wine vinegar
½ cup heavy cream
2 sticks (8 ounces) cold unsalted butter, cut into 1-inch pieces

½ cup grated Dancing Ewe Farm's Caciotta cheese (a cow's-milk cheese with a firm exterior and rich creamy interior, and a buttery and slightly nutty flavor)

Make the gnocchi ➤ Preheat the oven to 375°F. Mound the salt in the center of a baking sheet. Nestle the potatoes into the salt and bake until a knife easily pierces the center of the potato, about 1 hour. Remove the potatoes from the oven and let cool. When cool enough to handle, peel the potatoes and pass them through a ricer or food mill and into a large bowl, or mash them thoroughly with a potato masher.

Mix the mashed potatoes with the ½ cup of flour, the egg, oil, nutmeg, and salt and pepper to taste. If the dough is too sticky, add a little more flour. Divide the dough into 6 pieces. On a lightly floured surface, roll each piece into a ¾-inch-thick rope. Cut each rope into 1-inch pieces.

Oil a large rimmed baking sheet. Bring a large saucepan of salted water to a boil. Add one third of the gnocchi to the boiling salted water and cook until they float to the surface, about 2 minutes. Using a slotted spoon, remove the gnocchi, draining them well, and set them on the prepared baking sheet to cool. Cook the remaining gnocchi in the same way. At this point, the gnocchi can be made up to 24 hours in advance. Cover them with plastic wrap and refrigerate until ready to use.

Cook the sausage and chard ➤ Preheat an outdoor grill or grill pan over high heat and grill the sausages until cooked through, about 10 minutes. Let the sausages rest for 5 minutes and then cut them on the bias into ¼-inch-thick slices.

Bring a large pot of salted water to a boil and cook the chard for 2 minutes. Using a slotted spoon, remove the chard from the boiling water and immediately transfer it to a bowl of ice water. Once cool, remove the chard from the water, squeeze out any excess water, and then roughly chop it.

Make the beurre blanc ➤ Heat the olive oil over medium-low heat in a medium sauté pan. Add the fennel, shallots, thyme, peppercorns, and fennel seeds. Sauté until the vegetables are tender, about 10 minutes. Increase the heat to medium. Add the wine and vinegar and simmer until reduced by half, about 4 minutes. Add the heavy cream and continue to simmer until the cream has reduced by half, about 3 minutes. Remove from the heat and strain the sauce into a medium saucepan over low heat. Whisk the pieces of cold butter, 1 at a time, into the sauce, making sure each piece has melted before adding another. Season the beurre blanc to taste with salt.

To assemble and serve ➤ Bring the beurre blanc to a simmer and add the gnocchi, sausage, and Swiss chard. Simmer until heated through. Immediately divide the mixture among 6 warm shallow serving bowls, scatter the cheese over, and serve.

Wine suggestion ➤ Serve this with a zesty and rich Chardonnay that offers notes of tropical fruit, orange rind, and hazelnuts, such as Chardonnay, "Rosemary's Vineyard," Talley, 2006, Arroyo Grande Valley, California.

Duck Confit & Parsnip Risotto with Sage-Garlic Brown Butter

This risotto is particularly indulgent due to the richness of the duck confit and creamy parsnip purée that are added at the end. The finished dish is much looser than a classic risotto because of the purée. The risotto and a light salad are a wonderful combination for a brisk fall evening.

SERVES 6

Duck Confit
4 Hudson Valley Farm confit duck legs
1 tablespoon unsalted butter

Parsnip Purée and Sauté
3 medium parsnips, peeled; 2 sliced into ½-inch-thick rounds, 1 sliced into ¼-inch-thick rounds
1 cup heavy cream
6 tablespoons unsalted butter
Sea salt and freshly ground black pepper

Risotto
4 cups Chicken Stock (page 303)
3 tablespoons extra virgin olive oil
½ cup diced onion
1 tablespoon finely chopped garlic
1 teaspoon thyme leaves
2 cups Arborio rice
1⅓ cups dry white wine
1 cup grated Sartori Stravecchio cheese (or another domestic Parmesan cheese)

Sage-Garlic Brown Butter
3 tablespoons unsalted butter
1 tablespoon finely chopped garlic
6 thinly sliced fresh sage leaves

Sauté the duck ➤ Pick the meat from the legs of the duck, and discard the skin and bones; you should have about 10 ounces of meat. Melt the butter in a large sauté pan over medium heat. Once the butter begins to foam, add the duck meat and sauté until warm.

Cook the parsnips ➤ Combine the 2 sliced parsnips, cream, and 5 tablespoons of the butter in a medium saucepan. Cook over medium heat until the parsnips are tender, about 20 minutes. Transfer to a blender and purée until smooth. Season to taste with salt and pepper.

Melt the remaining 1 tablespoon of butter in a medium sauté pan over medium heat. Once the butter is foaming, add the remaining sliced parsnip and sauté until golden brown on both sides, about 2 minutes.

Make the risotto ➤ Heat the chicken stock in a small saucepan until warm. Heat the olive oil in large heavy saucepan over medium heat. Add the onion, garlic, and thyme and sauté until the onion is translucent, about 5 minutes. Add the rice and stir to coat with the oil. Increase the heat to medium-high and add the wine. Simmer until most of the wine has evaporated. Reduce the heat to medium-low and ladle 1 cup of the warm broth into the rice. Cook, stirring constantly, until most of the broth has been absorbed. Add the remaining broth in 3 more additions, stirring constantly and making sure the broth is absorbed before adding more. Season to taste with salt and pepper.

When the risotto is tender, yet still firm in the center, stir in the parsnip purée, duck confit, and cheese.

Make the sage-garlic brown butter ➤ Melt the butter in a small sauté pan over medium heat. Add the garlic and cook until the garlic is golden brown and the butter is beginning to brown, about 3 minutes. Stir in the sage.

To serve ➤ Spoon the risotto into 6 warm shallow bowls, top with the sautéed parsnips and drizzle with the brown butter. Serve immediately.

Wine suggestion ➤ Pair this dish with a full-bodied, juicy, spicy Pinot Noir with notes of black cherries, roasted herbs, and fresh acidity, such as Pinot Noir, Dumol, 2006, Russian River Valley.

Langoustine with Marinated Matsutake Mushrooms & Sunchokes

Langoustines are wonderfully sweet and sometimes very hard to find. If you can't find fresh ones, use fresh jumbo prawns or small spiny lobster tails. Matsutake mushrooms are very prized in both Japanese and Korean cuisine. The mushrooms have rich, smoky, earthy flavors and have become increasingly popular in the United States. They are grown abundantly throughout Asia and in the Pacific Northwest.

SERVES 6

Sunchokes

1 pound sunchokes, peeled and cut into ½-inch dice
2 cups whole milk
2 tablespoons extra virgin olive oil
1 tablespoon freshly squeezed lemon juice
½ teaspoon finely chopped garlic
Sea salt and freshly ground black pepper

Dressing

½ cup + 2 tablespoons grated Pleasant Ridge Reserve cheese (or another washed-rind, semi-aged cow's-milk cheese)
¼ cup extra virgin olive oil
2 tablespoons freshly squeezed lemon juice
Pinch of dried hot red pepper flakes

Mushrooms and Greens

2 tablespoons extra virgin olive oil
1 tablespoon freshly squeezed lemon juice
½ teaspoon finely chopped garlic
3 matsutake mushrooms, thinly sliced
2 cups baby mustard greens

Langoustines

18 langoustines, shelled
1 tablespoon extra virgin olive oil

Cook the sunchokes ➤ Place the sunchokes and milk in a medium saucepan. Bring to a simmer over medium heat and cook, partially covered, until the sunchokes are tender and can be easily pierced with a knife, about 35 minutes. Drain in a colander and rinse under cold water. Place the sunchokes in a medium bowl along with the olive oil, lemon juice, and garlic. Mix together with a fork until the sunchokes are slightly crushed. Season to taste with salt and pepper.

Make the dressing ➤ Mix the cheese, olive oil, lemon juice, and red pepper flakes in a small bowl.

Prepare the mushrooms ➤ Preheat the broiler. Combine the olive oil, lemon juice, and garlic in a small bowl. Set the lemon vinaigrette aside.

Place the mushrooms on a rimmed baking sheet and season to taste with salt and pepper. Drizzle half of the lemon vinaigrette over the mushrooms. Broil the mushrooms until they are just slightly brown on the edges, about 5 minutes.

Sear the langoustines ➤ Holding the tail end of each langoustine, wrap the body around itself in the shape of a pinwheel. Secure the langoustine with a toothpick and season with salt and pepper. Heat the olive oil in a large sauté pan over medium-high heat. Working in batches, sear the langoustines until they are golden brown, about 2 minutes per side. Remove the langoustines from the pan and remove the toothpicks.

To assemble and serve ➤ Place the baby mustard greens in a medium bowl, season to taste with salt and pepper, and drizzle with the remaining lemon vinaigrette.

Place a spoonful of the sunchokes in the center of 6 plates. Top the sunchokes with a spoonful of the dressing. Place 3 seared langoustines around the sunchokes, and top with the mushrooms and dressed baby mustard greens.

Wine suggestion ➤ Pair this dish with a full-bodied Sauvignon Blanc that has a touch of oak aging with notes of figs, honeydew melon, and hints of fresh-cut grass, such as Sauvignon Blanc, Rudd, 2007, Napa Valley, California.

Nantucket Bay Scallops with Smoked Fingerling Potato Salad, Endive, & McIntosh Apple

McIntosh apples grow abundantly in New England, making them one of my local favorites. The red and green skin conceals a tender-crisp, pale flesh that is not overly sweet and adds the perfect crunch to this salad.

SERVES 6

Potato Salad

2 slices thick-cut bacon
¾ pound fingerling potatoes
Kosher salt
1 cup hickory wood chips, soaked in water
½ cup mayonnaise
2 tablespoons store-bought barbecue sauce
1 tablespoon mustard oil
1 tablespoon sherry vinegar
2 tablespoons chopped fresh parsley
1 tablespoon finely diced celery
1 tablespoon finely diced red onion
1 teaspoon chopped fresh tarragon
Sea salt and freshly ground black pepper

Scallops

1 tablespoon canola oil
1½ pounds Nantucket Bay scallops

Salad

3 tablespoons extra virgin olive oil
1 tablespoon freshly squeezed lemon juice
½ teaspoon finely chopped garlic
1 head endive, sliced on the bias into ½-inch strips
1 small McIntosh apple, peeled and cut into matchstick-size strips
1 bunch watercress, large stems removed

Make the potato salad ➤ Cook the bacon in a small sauté pan over medium heat until crispy, about 5 minutes. Drain on a plate lined with paper towels. Once cool, roughly chop the bacon.

Place the potatoes in a large pot and cover them with cold water. Bring the water to a boil over high heat and salt liberally with kosher salt. Reduce the heat to a simmer and cook until the potatoes are tender, about 18 minutes. Drain the potatoes. When they are cool enough to handle, peel off the skins.

Line the bottom of a pot with heavy-duty aluminum foil. Drain the hickory wood chips and place them in the pot. Heat the wood chips over a burner until they are smoking. Place the potatoes in a steamer insert and set the insert in the pot. Cover tightly with a lid, allowing no smoke to escape from the pot. Smoke the potatoes over medium heat for about 5 minutes.

Whisk the mayonnaise, barbecue sauce, mustard oil, and sherry vinegar in a large bowl to blend. Add the warm potatoes to the dressing and, using a fork, crush the potatoes into the vinaigrette. Fold in the chopped bacon, parsley, celery, onion, and tarragon and season to taste with sea salt and pepper. Let the salad stand for 20 minutes to allow all the flavors to incorporate, stirring occasionally.

Prepare the scallops ➤ Heat the canola oil in a large sauté pan over medium-high heat. Season the scallops with salt and pepper. When the pan is smoking hot, add the scallops. Sear the scallops on 1 side until caramelized, about 2 minutes. Once the scallops have caramelized, swirl the pan several times and continue to cook for 2 more minutes. Transfer the scallops to a plate lined with paper towels to absorb any excess moisture.

Assemble the salad ➤ Whisk the olive oil, lemon juice, and garlic in a medium bowl to blend. Season to taste with salt and pepper. Toss the endive, apple, and watercress in the vinaigrette to coat.

To serve ➤ Spoon the potato salad in the center of 6 plates. Place the scallops over the potato salad and then top with the watercress salad. Serve immediately.

Wine suggestion ➤ This dish is perfect with an un-oaked Chardonnay that offers notes of green apple, lemon zest, and tangerines, such as Chardonnay, "Clone 76 Inox," Melville, 2006, Sta. Rita Hills, California.

NANTUCKET BAY SCALLOPS have a rather short season and are typically available only November through April. These thimble-shaped mollusks are actually a tad bit larger, but also sweeter, than Taylor Bay scallops. They live in protected bays, harbors, and salt ponds from North Carolina to Canada. The best species come from Nantucket and Cape Cod.

Wild Mushroom Manicotti Gratinée with Fines Herbes

The traditional Neapolitan manicotti uses freshly made crêpes while other Italian versions call for fresh or dried pasta. I prefer the traditional method using crêpes.

SERVES 6

Manicotti Filling

4 tablespoons extra virgin olive oil
2 pounds mixed wild mushrooms
2 tablespoons chopped shallots
2 teaspoons finely chopped garlic
Sea salt and freshly ground black pepper
2 tablespoons chopped fresh chives
8 ounces herbed Boursin cheese
½ cup grated Vermont Shepherd Farm's cheese (or another raw sheep's-milk cheese)
1 large egg
1 large egg yolk
1 tablespoon chopped fresh parsley

Crêpes

1 cup all-purpose flour
3 large eggs
1 tablespoon finely grated Vermont Shepherd Farm's cheese (or another raw sheep's-milk cheese)
1 tablespoon kosher salt
1 teaspoon chopped fresh chives
1 teaspoon chopped fresh parsley
1 teaspoon sugar
2 tablespoons (about) extra virgin olive oil

Mushroom Sauce

2 tablespoons extra virgin olive oil
½ pound white mushrooms, sliced
2 tablespoons diced shallots
1 teaspoon finely chopped garlic
½ cup vermouth
1 cup Chicken Stock (page 303)
½ cup heavy cream

½ cup grated Vermont Shepherd Farm's cheese (or another raw sheep's-milk cheese)
Sage-Garlic Brown Butter (page 166)

Make the filling ➤ Heat the olive oil in a large sauté pan over medium heat. Add the mushrooms and sauté until lightly brown, about 8 minutes. Add the shallots and garlic and continue to cook until the shallots have softened, about 2 minutes. Season with salt and pepper. Place half of the mushrooms in a bowl and stir in 1 tablespoon of the chopped chives. Set these sautéed mushrooms aside until you are ready to assemble the dish.

Transfer the other half of the mushrooms to a food processor fitted with a metal blade. Process until finely chopped. Place the chopped mushrooms in a large bowl and fold in the remaining 1 tablespoon of chives, the cheeses, egg, egg yolk, and parsley. Season the mushroom filling to taste with salt and pepper.

Make the crêpes ➤ Whisk 1½ cups of water with the flour, eggs, cheese, salt, chives, parsley, and sugar in a large bowl to blend.

Heat a 6-inch crêpe pan over medium-high heat. Brush the pan with some of the olive oil to coat. Pour 2 tablespoons of batter into the center of the pan and swirl to spread evenly. Cook the crêpe for 30 seconds, turn it over, and cook the crêpe for an additional 10 seconds. Repeat the process with the remaining batter, adding more oil as needed, and making about 20 crêpes total.

Make the sauce ➤ Heat the olive oil in a large sauté pan over medium-high heat. Add the mushrooms and sauté until lightly brown, about 5 minutes. Add the shallots and garlic and continue until the shallots have softened, about 2 minutes. Deglaze the mushrooms with the vermouth and simmer until the vermouth has reduced by half, about 3 minutes. Add the chicken stock and heavy cream and simmer until the cream has begun to thicken, about 3 minutes. Transfer to a blender or food processor and blend until smooth. Season to taste with salt and pepper.

Bake the manicotti ➤ Preheat the oven to 350°F and preheat the broiler. Divide the mushroom filling evenly among the crêpes, about 2 tablespoons per crêpe. Roll up the crêpes and place them in a shallow baking dish. Bake until the filling is hot, about 10 minutes. Remove the manicotti from oven. Scatter the ½ cup of Vermont Shepherd Farm's cheese over the manicotti. Broil until the cheese is melted and golden brown, about 2 minutes.

To serve ➤ Rewarm the mushroom sauce and sautéed mushrooms and spoon them over the manicotti. Drizzle with the brown butter and serve immediately.

Wine suggestion ➤ Serve this dish with a crisp and complex Pinot Gris from the Willamette Valley of Oregon with notes of tropical fruits, peach, and stony minerality, such as Pinot Gris, Lange, 2007, Willamette Valley, Oregon.

Butternut Squash Soup with Foie Gras & Wild Mushroom Crostini

This is not your average butternut squash soup. The spices add fragrance and heat while the mushrooms and foie gras add a depth and richness, making this a new classic.

SERVES 6

Soup

2 tablespoons extra virgin olive oil
1 cup diced shallots
1 fresh thyme sprig
2 medium butternut squash (about 2 pounds each), peeled and cut into 1-inch pieces
6 cups Chicken Stock (page 303)
1½ cups heavy cream
½ teaspoon ground cinnamon
½ teaspoon ground nutmeg
¼ teaspoon cayenne pepper
Sea salt and freshly ground black pepper

Crostini

1 small baguette, sliced into six ½-inch-thick slices
3 tablespoons extra virgin olive oil
1 small white onion, finely chopped
3 small porcini mushrooms, trimmed and finely chopped
6 ounces black trumpet mushrooms, trimmed and finely chopped
1 teaspoon finely chopped garlic
1 teaspoon chopped fresh sage
2 tablespoons heavy cream
8 ounces foie gras, cut into medium dice

3 tablespoons Vermont Butter and Cheese Company crème fraîche, for garnish

Make the soup ➤ Heat the olive oil in a large heavy saucepan over medium heat. Add the shallots and thyme and cook until tender, about 4 minutes. Add the squash and cook until it just begins to soften, 10 minutes. Add the chicken stock and bring to a simmer. Lower the heat and continue cooking, covered, until the squash is very tender and can be cut with a spoon, about 20 minutes. Remove the thyme. Add the cream, cinnamon, nutmeg, and cayenne and season to taste with salt and black pepper.

Purée the soup in a blender in 2 batches, then pass the soup through a fine-mesh strainer into a clean medium saucepan.

Make the crostini ➤ Preheat the broiler. Arrange the baguette slices in a single layer on a baking sheet. Drizzle the crostini with 1 tablespoon of the olive oil and broil until golden brown, about 1 minute.

Heat the remaining 2 tablespoons of olive oil in a medium sauté pan over medium heat. Add the onion and sauté until soft and lightly brown, about 5 minutes. Add the porcini and black trumpet mushrooms and garlic and sauté until the mushrooms are golden brown and softened, about 8 minutes. Add the sage and season to taste with salt and pepper. Stir in the cream.

Season the foie gras with salt and pepper. Heat a medium pan over high heat. Once the pan is very hot, sear the foie gras on all sides, about 45 seconds on each side. Drain the seared foie gras on a plate lined with paper towels, and then fold it into to the mushroom mixture.

To serve ➤ Top each crostini with 2 tablespoons of the mushroom mixture. Rewarm the soup and divide it among 6 soup bowls. Garnish the soup with a generous spoonful of crème fraîche. Serve immediately with the crostini on the side.

Wine suggestion ➤ Pair this dish with a rosé sparkling wine from California with notes of fresh berries, red flowers, and a touch of fresh baked biscuits, such as Brut Rosé, Roederer Estate, NV, Anderson Valley, California.

Roasted Root Vegetable Salad with Marcona Almonds

The first time I had this salad was at The Wolseley, a famous restaurant and café in London. The Wolseley is a grand place with a menu devoted to brasserie-style dining. The Marcona almonds in this salad hail from Spain and are shorter, rounder, sweeter, and more delicate than regular almonds.

SERVES 6

- 1 small butternut squash, peeled, seeded, and cut into 6 wedges
- 1 small acorn squash, peeled, seeded, and cut into 6 wedges
- 1 small celery root, peeled and cut into 6 wedges
- 1 small yam, peeled and cut into 6 wedges
- 1 large golden beet (leaves reserved for garnish), peeled and cut into 6 wedges
- 1 turnip, peeled and cut into 6 wedges
- 1 medium parsnip, peeled and cut into 6 wedges
- 2 medium shallots, peeled and cut into 3 pieces each
- ¼ cup extra virgin olive oil
- Sea salt and freshly ground black pepper
- ¼ cup Marcona almonds
- 1½ tablespoons sherry vinegar
- Sage-Garlic Brown Butter (page 166), warm
- Zest from ½ lemon

Preheat the oven to 375°F. Toss the vegetables with the olive oil in a large bowl and season to taste with salt and pepper. Arrange the vegetables in a roasting pan or on a large rimmed baking sheet, making sure the beets and the turnips stay together since they will roast longer. Roast the vegetables until the squash and parsnips are tender, about 30 minutes. Remove all the vegetables except the beets and the turnips from the roasting pan, transfer them to a platter, and cover with foil. Return the beets and turnips to the oven and roast for 20 minutes more.

Place the almonds on a baking sheet and toast until they turn golden brown, about 5 minutes. Once they are cool enough to handle, roughly chop the almonds. Stir the almonds and sherry vinegar into the warm brown butter.

Once the turnips and beets are completely roasted, add them to the platter of vegetables. Drizzle the vegetables with the brown butter and chopped nuts. Garnish with the reserved beet leaves and lemon zest.

Wine suggestion ➤ Serve this dish with a nutty Chardonnay that offers flavors of ripe apples, mango, and smoky oak, such as Chardonnay, "Connor Lee Vineyard," Buty Winery, 2006, Columbia Valley, Washington.

Partridge Barbajuans

Barbajuans are a specialty from the French Riviera, specifically Monaco. These fried dumplings are typically filled with Swiss chard or other greens and cheese.

SERVES 6

Special Equipment
Meat grinder

Dough
1 cup all-purpose flour
Pinch of sea salt
1 tablespoon extra virgin olive oil

Filling
1 tablespoon canola oil
2 partridges, 8 to 10 ounces each
Sea salt and freshly ground black pepper
2 ounces bacon, cut into ¼-inch-thick pieces
4 cipolline onions, peeled and quartered
2 cups dry red wine
1 cup Chicken Stock (page 303)
1 bouquet garni (1 dark green leek leaf, 3 fresh thyme sprigs, 1 bay leaf, 10 whole black peppercorns; see page 305)
6 Swiss chard leaves, ribs removed
4 ounces foie gras terrine, cut into ¼-inch pieces

1 large egg, beaten to blend
½ cup all-purpose flour, for dusting
Vegetable oil for deep frying

Make the dough ➤ Using a stand mixer fitted with the hook attachment, beat the flour and pinch of salt in the mixer bowl at low speed and gradually add ⅓ cup of water and the olive oil. Mix until the dough is smooth, about 3 minutes. Wrap the dough in plastic wrap and refrigerate for at least 1 hour.

Prepare the filling ➤ Preheat the oven to 350°F. Heat the oil in a large ovenproof saucepan over medium-high heat. Season the partridges with salt and pepper. When the oil is nearly smoking, sear the partridges on all sides. Add the bacon and cipolline onions and cook until the onions are tender, about 5 minutes. Add the wine and bring to a boil. Add the chicken stock and bouquet garni. Cover and transfer the saucepan to the oven. Braise until the partridges are tender and the thigh meat shreds easily with a fork, about 1 hour. Remove the pan from the oven, uncover, and allow the partridges to cool in the braising liquid.

Strain the braising liquid, reserving the partridge and the solids, into a clean saucepan. Discard the bouquet garni. Simmer the braising liquid over medium-high heat until the liquid is thick enough to coat the back of a spoon, about 15 minutes. Remove from the heat and cool.

Finely chop the bacon and onions and place them in a large bowl. Using your hands, pick the meat from the partridge, discarding the bones and the skin. Transfer the meat to the bowl with the bacon and onions and set aside.

Meanwhile, bring a large pot of salted water to a boil. Add the chard and cook until tender, about 4 minutes. Drain the chard and immediately transfer it to a bowl of ice water. Once cool, drain the chard, squeeze out any excess water, and roughly chop it. Place the chard in the bowl with the partridge mixture.

Grind the partridge-chard mixture through a meat grinder fitted with a large die. Return the ground mixture to the bowl and stir in the cooled reduced braising liquid. Gently stir in the foie gras until fully incorporated. Season to taste with salt and pepper.

Assemble the barbajuans ➤ Divide the dough in half. Using a lightly floured rolling pin, roll out each piece of dough on a lightly floured surface into a sheet 2 feet long and 5 inches wide. Using 1 tablespoonful of filling for each mound, mound the filling in 2 rows of 18 on 1 strip of dough, spacing them 1 inch apart. Brush the second sheet of dough lightly with the beaten egg and lay it, egg side down, over the filling. Press lightly around the filling, making sure the dough has sealed properly and air bubbles are removed. Cut into thirty-six 1½-inch squares; dust with flour.

Fry and serve the barbajuans ➤ Heat the vegetable oil in a large heavy pot to 375°F. Working in batches, fry the barbajuans until golden brown, about 3 minutes. Using a slotted spoon, transfer the barbajuans to a plate lined with paper towels to absorb the excess oil. Season to taste with salt and serve immediately.

Wine suggestion ➤ Serve this dish with a dark and earthy Pinot Noir that offers flavors of blackberries, cigar tobacco, and tea leaves, such as Pinot Noir, Hanzell, 2005, Sonoma County, California.

Venison Bolognese Pappardelle with Kale & Vermont Shepherd Cheese

When possible, I like to use fresh pasta, which cooks very quickly and is less dense than dried pasta. Fresh pasta is available in most local markets. If you aren't able to find fresh pappardelle, use Pasta Setaro, a very high-quality dried pasta.

SERVES 6

Sage Oil
1 cup vegetable oil
½ cup fresh sage leaves

Bolognese
2 cans (28 ounces each) whole tomatoes
5 tablespoons extra virgin olive oil
1 pound venison stew meat, coarsely ground
Sea salt and freshly ground black pepper
2 cups finely diced onion
1 small carrot, finely chopped
1 celery stalk, finely chopped
½ teaspoon finely chopped garlic
¼ cup tomato paste
1½ cups dry white wine
1 tablespoon sugar
1 bouquet garni (1 dark green leek leaf, 2 fresh rosemary sprigs, 2 fresh thyme sprigs, 4 fresh sage leaves, 1 bay leaf; see page 305)
1 cup heavy cream

Kale
½ bunch kale, leaves sliced into ½-inch strips (about 8 cups)
2 tablespoons unsalted butter
¼ cup finely diced shallots
½ teaspoon finely chopped garlic

Pasta
1 pound fresh spinach and egg pappardelle
¾ cup grated Vermont Shepherd Farm's cheese (or another raw sheep's-milk cheese)

Make the sage oil ➤ Purée the oil and sage leaves in a blender until smooth. Set a fine-mesh strainer over a bowl. Line the strainer with a double layer of cheesecloth. Scrape the sage purée into the strainer and let stand until all of the oil has drained into the bowl, about 1 hour. Discard the solids from the strainer.

Make the Bolognese ➤ Drain both cans of tomatoes into a strainer set over a large bowl; reserve the juice. Cut the tomatoes into quarters and place them in the bowl with the juice.

Heat the olive oil in a large heavy saucepan over medium-high heat until nearly smoking. Add the venison and sear until brown, about 10 minutes. Season to taste with salt and pepper. Add the onion, carrot, celery, and garlic. Cook until the vegetables are tender, about 8 minutes. Add the tomato paste, stir to coat the vegetables, and cook for 3 minutes. Deglaze with the wine and continue to cook over medium-high heat until the wine has reduced by half, about 4 minutes. Add the tomatoes and their juices, the sugar, and bouquet garni. Gently simmer uncovered over low heat until the tomatoes have broken down and the sauce has thickened, about 45 minutes. Season the sauce to taste with salt and pepper and remove the bouquet garni.

Prepare the kale ➤ Bring a large pot of salted water to a boil. Add the kale and cook until tender, about 5 minutes. Using a slotted spoon, immediately transfer the kale to a bowl of ice water. Once cool, remove the kale from the water and squeeze out any excess water.

Melt the butter in a medium sauté pan over medium heat. Once the butter begins to foam, add the shallots and garlic and sauté until tender, about 3 minutes. Add the kale and sauté until all the water has cooked out and the kale is tender, about 8 minutes. Season to taste with salt and pepper and add the kale to the Bolognese sauce.

Cook the pasta ➤ Bring a large pot of salted water to boil. Add the pappardelle and cook, stirring frequently, until the pappardelle is al dente. Drain the pasta.

To serve ➤ Divide the pasta among 6 warm bowls. Stir the cream into the Bolognese sauce and spoon the sauce over the pasta. Drizzle with the sage oil and top with the grated cheese.

Wine suggestion ➤ Pair this dish with a Cabernet Franc from North Fork of Long Island that offers aromas of black cherries, earth, and a touch of gaminess, such as Cabernet Franc, Pellegrini Vineyards, 2004, North Fork of Long Island, New York.

FARM STORE
CHERRY GROVE
FARM
FRESH HEIRLOOM
EGGS + PORK
CHEESE
MON-FRI 11-6
SAT 10-5

Farm Store

Pan-Seared East Coast Halibut with Caramelized Cauliflower & Hazelnuts

East coast halibut is one of the most versatile fish, and for this reason it's considered a chef's favorite. Halibut can actually reach upwards of seven hundred pounds, which is surprising given their delicate flavor and texture.

SERVES 6

Hazelnut Cream
1 tablespoon unsalted butter
½ cup hazelnuts, skins removed and roughly chopped
¾ cup fish stock
¾ cup heavy cream

Caramelized Cauliflower Cream
2 tablespoons unsalted butter
½ pound cauliflower, sliced ½-inch thick
¾ cup heavy cream
Sea salt and freshly ground black pepper

Brussels Sprouts
¾ pound medium Brussels sprouts, trimmed and halved
3 tablespoons unsalted butter
¼ cup hazelnuts, roughly chopped
½ teaspoon finely chopped garlic
4 fresh sage leaves, thinly sliced

Halibut
6 skinless halibut fillets, 6 ounces each
4 tablespoons extra virgin olive oil

Make the hazelnut cream ➤ Melt the butter in a small saucepan over low heat. Add the hazelnuts and toast them until golden brown, stirring occasionally to keep them from burning, about 3 minutes. Add the fish stock and heavy cream and simmer for 5 minutes. Transfer to a blender or a food processor fitted with a metal blade and purée until smooth.

Make the cauliflower cream ➤ Melt the butter in a large sauté pan over medium-high heat. Add the sliced cauliflower and cook until the slices are golden brown, about 2 minutes per side. Add the heavy cream and simmer until the cream has been reduced by half, about 2 minutes. Purée the cauliflower mixture in a blender until smooth. Season to taste with salt and pepper.

Cook the Brussels sprouts ➤ Bring a large pot of salted water to a boil. Add the Brussels sprouts and cook until tender when pierced with a knife, about 5 minutes. Immediately transfer the sprouts to a bowl of ice water. Once cool, drain the sprouts.

Melt the butter in a large sauté pan over medium-high heat until foamy. Add the hazelnuts and sauté until they just begin to color, about 2 minutes. Add the Brussels sprouts and continue cooking until the sprouts and hazelnuts are browned, about 5 minutes. Add the garlic and sage and cook until the garlic and sage soften, about 1 minute. Season to taste with salt and pepper.

Sauté the halibut ➤ Season the halibut with salt and pepper. Heat 2 tablespoons of the olive oil in a large sauté pan over medium-high heat. Place 3 halibut fillets in the pan and cook until the fish begins to turn opaque, about 3 minutes. Turn the fish over and cook until the flesh is opaque and begins to flake, about another 3 minutes. The thickness of the fish will determine the cooking time. Remove the fish from the pan and cover it with foil to keep warm. Repeat with the remaining 2 tablespoons of olive oil and 3 halibut fillets.

To serve ➤ Place a spoonful of cauliflower cream in the center of 6 plates. Top the cauliflower cream with the halibut, spoon the hazelnut cream on top of the fish, and scatter the Brussels sprouts around the fish. Serve immediately.

Wine suggestion ➤ Serve this dish with a white wine made from Roussanne that offers aromas of roasted almonds, honey, and lime zest, such as Roussanne, Doyenne, 2007, Yakima Valley, Washington.

Sautéed Black Cod with Bacon, Artichokes, & Sherry Vinaigrette

Many assume that artichokes are in season just in the spring, but the fall harvest produces particularly sweet and tender artichokes. The best way to pick out a prized artichoke is by color and sound. The artichoke should have an even green color, no dark or black spots, and make a squeaking sound when squeezed.

SERVES 6

Artichokes

4 large globe artichokes
2 tablespoons freshly squeezed lemon juice
3 tablespoons extra virgin olive oil
¾ pound sunchokes, peeled and thinly sliced
1 tablespoon fresh thyme leaves
Sea salt and freshly ground black pepper
½ cup dry white wine
2 cups heavy cream
6 ounces double-smoked bacon, diced

Vinaigrette

½ cup extra virgin olive oil
2 tablespoons sherry vinegar
½ cup chopped fresh parsley
1 tablespoon diced shallots
1 teaspoon finely chopped garlic

Cod

4 tablespoons extra virgin olive oil
6 skinless black cod fillets, 6 ounces each

Trim the artichokes ➤ Trim 1½ inches to 2 inches off the top of the artichokes, making sure that you have cut enough off the top so that the pale green inner leaves are visible. Using a very sharp paring knife, trim off the outer dark green leaves of the artichoke, leaving only the very tender pale green leaves. Using a peeler or sharp paring knife, peel the tough outer green layer off the stem. Cut the artichokes in half and scoop out the purple leaves and hairs that cover the artichoke heart. Soak the artichokes in a bowl of cold water mixed with 1 tablespoon of the lemon juice until ready to use.

Make the purée ➤ Cut the artichokes lengthwise into thin slices. Heat 2 tablespoons of the olive oil in a large heavy pan. Sauté half of the artichoke slices over low heat until tender and lightly browned, about 4 minutes. Add the sunchokes and thyme and season to taste with salt and pepper. Cook, stirring occasionally, until the sunchokes begin to soften, about 10 minutes. Add the wine and simmer until the wine is reduced by half, about 5 minutes. Add the heavy cream. Cover and simmer, stirring occasionally, until the artichokes and sunchokes are very tender, about 20 minutes. Remove from the heat and cool slightly. Transfer the mixture to a blender or a food processor fitted with a metal blade and purée until smooth. Season to taste with salt and pepper.

Sauté the artichokes ➤ Heat the remaining 1 tablespoon of olive oil in large sauté pan. Add the bacon and cook over medium-low heat until the bacon is crisp. Using a slotted spoon, remove the bacon from the pan. Add the remaining artichoke slices to the pan with the bacon fat. Sauté the artichokes until they are golden brown, about 5 minutes. Stir in the remaining 1 tablespoon of lemon juice. Return the bacon to the pan and season to taste with salt and pepper.

Make the vinaigrette ➤ Whisk the oil and vinegar in a small bowl to blend. Stir in the parsley, shallots, and garlic and season to taste with salt and pepper.

Sauté the cod ➤ Heat 2 tablespoons of the olive oil in a large sauté pan over medium-high heat. Season the cod with salt and pepper. Place 3 pieces of cod in the pan and cook until lightly browned, about 3 minutes per side. Repeat the process with the remaining 2 tablespoons of olive oil and 3 pieces of cod.

To serve ➤ Place a generous spoonful of the artichoke purée in the center of each of 6 warm plates. Spoon the sautéed artichokes and bacon on top of the purée. Place the fish over the artichokes and finish with a spoonful of the sherry vinaigrette.

Wine suggestion ➤ Serve this dish with a white "Bordeaux Blend" From Washington State with aromas of melons, honeysuckle, and fresh herbs, such as DeLille Cellars, "Chaleur Estate Blanc," 2007, Columbia Valley, Washington.

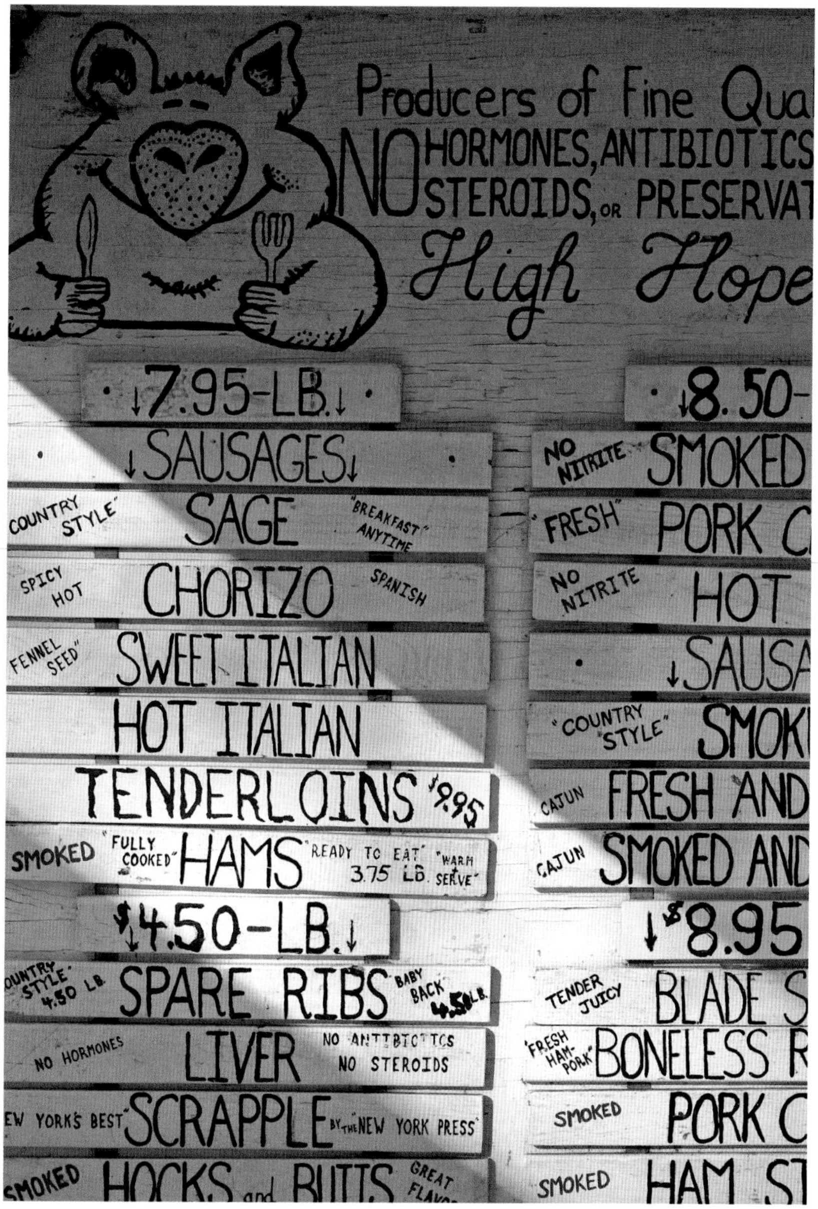

Herb-Crusted Black Bass with Hen of the Woods Bouillon

Black bass is a saltwater fish caught in the Atlantic from the coast of Maine all the way down to the warm waters of Florida. They generally prefer warmer waters and the peak of their season runs late summer through early fall.

SERVES 6

Broth and Mushrooms
2 fresh thyme sprigs
1 bay leaf
Sea salt and freshly ground black pepper
1 pound hen of the woods mushrooms, cut into 1-inch pieces
2 tablespoons extra virgin olive oil

Black Bass
1 cup fresh breadcrumbs
½ cup grated Sartori Stravecchio cheese (or another domestic Parmesan cheese)
2 tablespoons finely chopped fresh parsley
1 tablespoon finely chopped garlic
1 large egg
6 black bass fillets, 8 ounces each

Sauce
1 tablespoon cold unsalted butter
2 tablespoons chopped fresh chives
1 tablespoon truffle oil + more for garnish

Make the broth ➤ Combine 3 cups of water with the thyme, bay leaf, and a pinch of salt in a medium saucepan fitted with a steamer insert. Place the mushrooms in the steamer insert and bring the water to a boil. Cover and steam the mushrooms for 10 minutes. Remove the mushrooms from the saucepan. Using a fine-mesh strainer, strain the steaming liquid into a clean saucepan and simmer over medium-high heat to reduce the liquid by half. This will yield about 1½ cups of mushroom broth.

Roast the mushrooms ➤ Preheat the oven to 375°F. Place the steamed mushrooms on a baking sheet, drizzle with olive oil, and season to taste with salt and pepper. Roast the mushrooms in the oven until they begin to brown, about 12 minutes. Maintain the oven temperature to bake the fish.

Prepare the black bass ➤ Combine the breadcrumbs, cheese, parsley, and garlic in a medium bowl. Whisk the egg in another bowl until the white and yolk are fully combined. Place the fish on an oiled baking sheet and season with salt. Brush the top side of each fillet with the beaten egg. Gently press the breadcrumb mixture onto the egg coating over the fish, making sure to cover the top of the fish entirely. Bake the fish until the breadcrumbs are golden brown and the fish has cooked through, about 6 minutes.

Make the sauce ➤ Bring the mushroom broth to a simmer over medium-high heat. Whisk in the cold butter, then the chives, the 1 tablespoon of truffle oil, and the roasted mushrooms. Season to taste with salt and pepper.

To serve ➤ Divide the sauce and mushrooms among 6 warm bowls. Place the fish in the sauce and drizzle with a bit more truffle oil.

Wine suggestion ➤ Serve this dish with a Pinot Gris that offers flavors of citrus, pears, and fine herbs, such as Pinot Gris, Adelsheim, 2006, Willamette Valley, Oregon.

Stuffed Amish Chicken Bourgeoise

The stuffing in this recipe has amazing flavor and texture. It can be used to stuff different kinds of poultry like turkey and pheasant. The name "bourgeoise" is due to the expensive and rich ingredients like butter, wild mushrooms, foie gras, and chestnuts, which usually only the bourgeoise, or upper class, could afford.

SERVES 6

- 3 ounces foie gras
- 4½ sticks (1 pound + 2 ounces) unsalted butter, softened
- 1 ounce fresh chanterelle mushrooms, chopped
- 1 ounce fresh porcini mushrooms, chopped
- Sea salt and freshly ground black pepper
- ½ cup finely chopped shallots
- 2 teaspoons finely chopped garlic
- ½ cup brandy
- 2 cups panko (Japanese breadcrumbs)
- 1 cup cooked chestnuts, chopped
- 2 tablespoons chopped fresh chives
- 2 tablespoons chopped fresh parsley
- 2 large Amish chickens, 3 to 4 pounds each

Prepare the stuffing ➤ Preheat the oven to 375°F. Heat a small nonstick pan over high heat. Sear the foie gras until caramelized, about 45 seconds on each side. Quickly transfer the foie gras to a cold plate. Refrigerate the foie gras until firm. Once the foie gras is cool and firm, cut it into small dice.

Melt 2 tablespoons of the butter in a medium sauté pan over medium heat until foaming. Add the chanterelle and porcini mushrooms and sauté until tender, about 4 minutes. Season the mushrooms to taste with salt and pepper. Transfer the mushrooms to a large bowl and wipe the pan clean.

Melt another 2 tablespoons of butter in the pan over medium heat until foaming. Add the shallots and garlic and sauté until tender, about 5 minutes. Add the brandy and simmer until it is reduced and nearly dry. Add the shallots and garlic to the mushrooms. Fold the diced foie gras, the remaining 4 sticks of butter, the panko, chestnuts, chives, and parsley into the mushrooms and mix until well combined. Season to taste with salt and pepper.

Stuff the chickens ➤ With a chef's knife or cleaver, cut off the chicken wings at the joint closest to the breast. Gently work your fingers between the skin and flesh of the chickens to loosen the skin. Spread the prepared mushroom stuffing under the skin of the breasts and thighs, distributing it evenly to cover the flesh. Season the chickens liberally with salt and pepper and tie the legs together with kitchen string.

Roast the chickens ➤ Place the chickens, breast side up, in a large roasting pan or on a rimmed baking sheet. Roast the chicken, basting them with pan drippings every 10 to 15 minutes, until the skin is golden brown and crisp and the juices run clear when the chicken is pierced with a knife at the joint of the leg, about 1 hour. To check for doneness, insert an instant-read thermometer in the thickest part of the thigh, making sure not to touch the bone. The temperature reading should be 165° to 175°F. Once fully cooked, transfer the chickens to a cutting board.

To serve ➤ Cut the chickens into 4 pieces by gently pulling the legs away from the body and cutting the leg and the thigh off in 1 piece. Cut the breasts away from the main breast bone, scraping the breast meat away from the bone with the knife. Arrange the chicken pieces on a large platter allowing diners to choose their favorite light and dark meat pieces.

Wine suggestion ➤ Serve this with a French-inspired red Rhône blend that is dark and delicious with aromas of black fruits, forest floor, and baking spices, such as Tablas Creek, "Esprit de Beaucastel," 2006, Paso Robles, California.

AMISH CHICKENS are heritage breeds, meaning they are not crossbred and typically have more developed flavor due to being raised cage free. The ample space to roam around and a certified organic diet produces superior, not to mention healthier, poultry. Amish chickens are given this designation because they are raised on small Amish or Mennonite family farms.

Roasted Veal Chop with Artichokes & Black Trumpet Ragout

Black trumpet mushrooms are also referred to as Horns of Plenty because of their trumpet or horn-shaped appearance. These mushrooms are particularly delicious and have a buttery flavor and chewy, almost meaty texture. I love to eat them simply sautéed with butter and garlic or, as here, paired with artichokes and cream.

SERVES 6

Black Trumpet Ragout

4 tablespoons unsalted butter
1 large onion, cut into medium dice
8 ounces black trumpet mushrooms, trimmed and cleaned
1 tablespoon finely chopped garlic
1 cup dry white wine
2 cups heavy cream
1 tablespoon chopped fresh parsley
Sea salt and freshly ground black pepper

Veal Chops

6 bone-in veal chops, frenched and cleaned, 14 ounces each

Artichokes

Vegetable oil for frying
3 small globe artichokes, trimmed (see page 182) and cut into 6 wedges each

Make the ragout ➤ Melt 2 tablespoons of the butter in a medium sauté pan over medium-low heat. Once the butter begins to foam, add the onion and sauté until well caramelized, about 10 minutes.

While the onions are caramelizing, heat a large sauté pan over medium heat. Add the remaining 2 tablespoons of butter and sauté the mushrooms until tender and golden brown, about 5 minutes. Add the garlic and cook for 2 minutes. Add the caramelized onion and deglaze with the wine. Continue cooking until the wine has reduced to just a tablespoon of liquid, about 5 minutes. Add the cream and bring to a boil. Reduce the heat to low and simmer until the cream is very thick, about 8 minutes. Add the parsley and season to taste with salt and pepper.

Cook the chops ➤ While the ragout is simmering, place the broiler rack about 4 inches away from the heat source and preheat the broiler. Season the veal chops with salt and pepper. Broil the chops until they are pink when cut in the center, about 7 minutes per side for medium-rare doneness. To check for doneness, make a small cut near the bone or insert an instant-read thermometer in the thickest part of the meat. The temperature should be 140°F to 150°F. Remove from the heat, tent with aluminum foil and let rest.

Blanch the artichokes ➤ Fill a deep heavy saucepan or deep fryer with 3 inches of vegetable oil. Heat the oil to 300°F. Blanch the artichokes in the oil until the leaves are golden brown and the artichokes are tender when pierced with a knife, about 5 minutes. Drain on a plate lined with paper towels. Season to taste with salt and pepper.

To serve ➤ Arrange the veal chops on 6 serving plates. Spoon the ragout evenly over the veal chops and top each with 3 pieces of artichoke. Serve immediately.

Wine suggestion ➤ Serve this dish with a classic American Chardonnay that is full and crisp with notes of baked apples, stony minerals, and fresh acidity, such as Chardonnay, Hanzell, 2005, Sonoma County, California.

A Real Steak au Poivre with Green Oak & Homemade Boursin

You can use whatever mix of peppercorns you prefer. I like to make variations on the recipe using other peppercorns such pink, white, green, Szechuan, or even Jamaican, commonly referred to as allspice. This recipe is great with dry-aged New York strip or rib-eye steak, or even duck breast, which my father makes at home. You can also simplify the meal by purchasing Boursin from your local cheese shop.

SERVES 6

- 6 tablespoons whole black peppercorns
- 6 Black Angus beef tenderloin fillets, 10 to 12 ounces each
- Kosher salt
- 3 tablespoons unsalted butter
- 2 tablespoons canola oil
- ¼ cup finely diced shallots
- ¼ cup cognac or Armagnac
- ½ cup Veal Stock (page 303)
- ½ cup heavy cream
- Sea salt and freshly ground black pepper
- Homemade Boursin (page 30)
- 3 heads baby green oak lettuce, cut in half lengthwise

Prepare the fillets ➤ Using the bottom of a heavy skillet, roughly crush the peppercorns. Generously salt both sides of the fillets with kosher salt and then press each side of the fillets into the cracked peppercorns, encrusting the steaks as lightly or heavily as you desire.

Melt the butter with the oil in a large heavy sauté pan over medium heat. Once the foam of the butter begins to subside, the pan is hot enough. It is important that the pan not be too hot and smoking or the pepper will burn. Sear each side of the fillets until well browned and the pepper begins to form a crust, about 5 minutes. To check for doneness, insert an instant-read thermometer into the thickest part of the meat. The temperature should read 130° to 135°F for medium-rare doneness. Transfer the fillets to a warm platter, tent with aluminum foil, and let rest while making the sauce.

Make the sauce ➤ Pour out all but 2 tablespoons of the fat in the pan. Place the pan over medium heat and add the shallots. Sauté until the shallots are just tender, stirring with a wooden spoon to scrape up any browned bits from the bottom of the pan, about 1 minute.

Lean away from the stove (averting your face) and pour the cognac into the pan; tilt the edge of the pan slightly over the burner flame to ignite the alcohol. The cognac will flame for a few seconds as the alcohol burns off. Add the stock and bring to a boil. Simmer for 1 minute to thicken the sauce. Add the cream and simmer until thickened to sauce-like consistency, stirring occasionally, about 2 minutes. Season the sauce to taste with sea salt and ground black pepper.

To serve ➤ Spread 2 tablespoons of the Boursin over the cut side of each halved head of lettuce. Place 1 fillet on each of 6 warm plates and spoon the sauce over the fillets. Set the lettuce alongside the fillets and serve.

Wine suggestion ➤ Serve a spicy, juicy Syrah with aromas of black cherries, black peppercorns, and baking spices, such as Syrah, "Colson Canyon," Tensley, 2006, Santa Barbara County, California.

Jamison Farm Rack of Lamb with Salsify & Walnuts & Jurançon-Chanterelle Jus

I have a love-hate relationship with lamb because sometimes it can be very fatty and have an incredibly overt gaminess. But with the right lamb a dish can be exquisite. Over the past few years, I have been able to find grass-fed lamb, which lends a cleaner and fresher flavor to meat as opposed to the overly gamey taste of grain-fed lamb.

SERVES 6

Jurançon-Chanterelle Jus

3 tablespoons unsalted butter
¼ cup chopped shallots
1 teaspoon finely chopped garlic
1 pound baby chanterelles, trimmed and washed
1 tablespoon fresh thyme leaves
1 cup Jurançon wine
¾ cup Veal Stock (page 303)
Sea salt and freshly ground black pepper

Lamb

3 Jamison Farm racks of lamb, 12 to 14 ounces each
2 tablespoons extra virgin olive oil

Salsify and Walnuts

¾ pound salsify, peeled, cut into ¼-inch-thin rounds and stored in water until ready to cook
2 tablespoons unsalted butter
½ cup walnuts, coarsely chopped
1 teaspoon finely chopped garlic
1 tablespoon chopped fresh parsley

Make the jus ➤ Melt the butter in large sauté pan over medium heat. Add the shallots and garlic and sauté until soft, about 1 minute. Add the chanterelles and thyme and sauté until the chanterelles release their juices, about 3 minutes. Continue to cook until the chanterelles are nicely browned, about 8 minutes. Deglaze with the wine, bring the mixture to a boil, and simmer to reduce the liquid by half, about 4 minutes. Add the veal stock and simmer about 5 minutes. Season to taste with salt and pepper

Cook the lamb ➤ Preheat the oven to 450°F. Season the lamb generously with salt and pepper. Heat the olive oil in a large sauté pan over medium-high heat until nearly smoking. Place the lamb racks, fat side down, in the pan and sear until browned, about 5 minutes. Turn the racks over so they are fat side up. Transfer the skillet to the oven and roast for 7 minutes. Turn the racks fat side down again, and roast in the oven about 10 minutes for medium-rare doneness. To check for doneness, make a small cut near the bone and insert an instant-read thermometer in the thickest part of the meat. The temperature should read 140° to 150°F for medium-rare doneness. Remove the lamb from the oven, tent with aluminum foil, and let rest.

Cook the salsify and walnuts ➤ While the lamb is cooking, bring a medium saucepan of salted water to a boil. Drain the salsify and place it in the boiling water. Cook the salsify until tender when pierced with a knife, about 8 minutes. Drain the salsify and pat dry with a paper towel.

Melt the butter in a medium sauté pan over medium-high heat. Sauté the salsify until lightly brown, about 3 minutes. Reduce the heat to medium, add the walnuts and garlic, and sauté until the garlic is fragrant and the walnuts are lightly toasted, about 2 minutes. Add the parsley and season to taste with salt and pepper.

To serve ➤ Cut each rack of lamb into 4 double chops. Place the lamb chops on a large platter. Spoon the jus over the lamb chops and garnish with sautéed salsify and walnuts.

Wine suggestion ➤ Serve this dish with a "Right Bank" red Bordeaux-inspired blend from the North Fork of Long Island that offers aromas of cassis, tobacco, and toasty oak notes, such as Raphael, "La Fontana," 2005, North Fork of Long Island, New York.

JAMISON FARM is located in the rolling foothills of Appalachia. The founders, John and Sukey Jamison, have been raising lambs for over thirty years in a natural and humane environment, long before it was considered chic. During the warmer months, the lambs graze on hillside grasses and clover and are hand-fed hay and corn during the winter. The lambs' 100% natural diet and lifestyle yield meat that is lean, firm, tender, delicate, pink, and free of hormones, antibiotics, herbicides, and insecticides.

Roasted Turkey with Chestnut-Sausage Stuffing, Cranberry-Grenadine Relish, & Rosemary Gravy

Thanksgiving is my favorite American holiday because it's all about the bird. You don't have to wait until Thanksgiving to enjoy this meal though. It's perfect for a Sunday night dinner and then you can enjoy leftover turkey all week.

SERVES 6 TO 8

Cranberry-Grenadine Relish

1 cup dried cherries
1 cup freshly squeezed orange juice
1 cup grenadine
½ cup water
2 cinnamon sticks
1 bay leaf
1 tablespoon finely chopped peeled fresh ginger
3 cups fresh cranberries (or thawed frozen)

Turkey

2 sticks (8 ounces) unsalted butter, softened
2 tablespoons chopped fresh rosemary
Sea salt and freshly ground black pepper
1 turkey, 10 to 12 pounds
2 medium onions, sliced ½ inch thick
4 celery stalks
1 carrot, halved lengthwise

Chestnut-Sausage Stuffing

1 tablespoon extra virgin olive oil
1 pound pork sausage, casings removed
1 stick (4 ounces) unsalted butter
1 large onion, cut into ½-inch dice
2 celery stalks, cut into ½-inch dice
4½ cups cubes (¾-inch) crustless country-style bread
9 ounces roasted chestnuts, peeled and sliced
2 large eggs, beaten to blend
2 tablespoons roughly chopped fresh marjoram leaves
2 tablespoons roughly chopped fresh sage leaves
2 tablespoons roughly chopped fresh thyme leaves

continued

Make the relish ➤ Combine the cherries, orange juice, grenadine, water, cinnamon sticks, bay leaf, and ginger in a medium saucepan over low heat. Bring to a simmer and cook until the cherries are tender, about 10 minutes. Add the cranberries and cook until the cranberries are soft but still intact, about 15 minutes. Allow to cool for 10 to 15 minutes.

Discard the cinnamon sticks and bay leaf. Purée half of the mixture in a blender or food processor until smooth, and then stir it back into the remaining half of the relish.

Roast the turkey ➤ Preheat the oven to 350°F. Combine the butter with the rosemary in a small bowl and season with salt and pepper. Gently work your fingers between the skin and flesh of the turkey. Stuff the rosemary butter under the skin, distributing it evenly over the breasts and the legs to cover the flesh. Truss the turkey and season with salt and pepper.

Place the onions, celery, and carrot in the center of a large roasting pan. Place the turkey directly on top of the vegetables. Pour 2 quarts of cold water into the roasting pan. Roast the turkey uncovered for 1 hour. Rotate the pan and place a foil tent over the turkey, then roast until the juices run clear when the turkey is pierced with a knife at the joint of the leg, about 1½ hours. To check for doneness, insert an instant-read thermometer into the leg of the turkey. The temperature should register 165° to 175°F. Remove the turkey from the oven, cover it loosely with foil, and let it rest for 1 hour. The turkey will continue to cook as it rests. Reserve the roasting pan with all the pan drippings to make the gravy.

Make the stuffing ➤ While the turkey is roasting, heat the oil in a large sauté pan over medium heat. Add the sausage and sauté, breaking it up with a fork, until it is cooked through, about 8 minutes.

Melt the butter in a large skillet over medium heat until it foams. Add the onion and celery. Cover and cook until soft, but not browned, about 12 minutes.

Mix the cooked onion and celery, bread cubes, chestnuts, eggs, marjoram, sage, thyme, and rosemary in a large bowl. Warm the chicken stock and pour it into the stuffing. With a slotted spoon, transfer the sausage to the bowl with the stuffing and mix well. Season to taste with salt and pepper.

Butter an 11 × 8-inch baking dish. Transfer the stuffing to the baking dish. Cover with foil and bake for 30 minutes. Remove the foil. Turn on the broiler and broil the stuffing until the top is browned, about 1 minute.

1 tablespoon roughly chopped fresh rosemary leaves
½ cup Chicken Stock (page 303)

Rosemary Gravy
2 fresh rosemary sprigs
¼ cup heavy cream
2 tablespoons unsalted butter
¼ cup Wondra flour

Make the gravy ➤ Pour all of the juices from the reserved roasting pan into a medium saucepan and skim off the excess fat. Place the saucepan over medium-high heat. Add the rosemary and simmer until the juices are reduced to 3 cups, about 20 minutes. Whisk in the cream. Melt the butter in a medium saucepan over medium heat. When the butter begins to foam, stir in the flour. Cook the flour for 1 minute, stirring constantly so it does not burn. Slowly whisk in the reduced turkey pan juices and continue to cook, whisking occasionally, until the gravy has reached desired consistency, about 5 minutes.

To serve ➤ Carve the turkey, making sure each portion includes some of the skin. Serve with the relish, stuffing, and gravy on the side.

Wine suggestion ➤ Serve this holiday classic dish with a Pinot Noir from Oregon's Willamette Valley that offers flavors of dried cherries, violets and earth, such as Pinot Noir "Thea's Selection," Lemelson Vineyards, 2006, Willamette Valley, Oregon.

Roasted Pheasant with Braised Cabbage & Chestnuts

Pheasant, like most wild game, tends to be a bit drier than farm-raised animals. I like to braise it on top of cabbage, because it keeps the pheasant moist and the cabbage absorbs a lot of flavor from the bird.

SERVES 6

Braised Cabbage

1 cup peeled cooked chestnuts
¼ pound thick-cut bacon (at least ½ inch thick)
1 teaspoon canola oil
10 cipolline onions, peeled and thinly sliced
1 teaspoon finely chopped garlic
½ cup Armagnac
1 head Napa cabbage, sliced into ½-inch-thick strips
2 cups vin de paille or another off-dry, straw-colored wine
Sea salt and freshly ground black pepper

Pheasant

12 thin bacon slices
2 pheasants, 2½ pounds each
1 teaspoon canola oil
10 to 12 fresh sage leaves

Braise the cabbage ➤ Preheat the oven to 350°F. Spread the chestnuts on a rimmed baking sheet and toast them in the oven until golden brown and fragrant, about 10 minutes. When cool enough to handle, cut them in half. Maintain the oven temperature to braise the cabbage.

Cut the bacon into strips 1 inch long and ½ inch wide, making sure that each lardon contains both meat and fat.

Heat the oil in a large sauté pan over medium heat. Add the bacon lardons and cook until they are brown and crispy and the fat has been rendered, about 10 minutes. Add the cipolline onions and reduce the heat to low. Cook the onions, stirring every so often, until they caramelize, about 5 minutes. Add the garlic and cook until softened, about 2 minutes. Deglaze with the Armagnac and increase the heat to medium. Simmer until the liquid is fully evaporated. Add the cabbage and vin de paille and simmer to reduce the liquid by half, about 10 minutes. Add the chestnuts and season to taste with salt and pepper. Arrange the cabbage mixture in a 13 × 9-inch baking dish and braise in the oven for 20 minutes.

Roast the pheasants ➤ While the cabbage is braising, layer 6 slices of bacon over the breast of each pheasant. Tuck the ends of the bacon between the legs and the breasts and truss the pheasants. Season to taste with salt and pepper.

Heat the oil in a large sauté pan over medium heat. Place the pheasants, bacon side down, in the pan and sear until the bacon begins to crisp, about 5 minutes.

Remove the pheasant from the sauté pan and place them on top of the cabbage, bacon side up. Scatter sage leaves around the pheasant. Roast until the juices run clear when a pheasant thigh is pierced with a knife, about 45 minutes.

To serve ➤ Carve the pheasants, making sure each portion includes some of the bacon. Serve with the cabbage and chestnuts.

Wine suggestion ➤ Serve this dish with a jammy red wine made from Grenache that offers notes of plums, dried flowers, and spices, such as Grenache, Jaffurs, 2006, Santa Barbara County, California.

Aromatic Stuffed Suckling Pig

There is nothing more festive than a suckling pig. In Russia they serve it as part of the traditional Christmas feast. In fact, the first time I made a suckling pig was when I was living in Russia and celebrating a grand occasion with many friends. This recipe is stuffed with incredibly luxurious and flavorful ingredients like foie gras, nuts, and cheese, making it well-suited for a merry gathering.

SERVES 8 TO 12

Special Equipment
5-gallon pot; meat lacing needle

Suckling Pig
2 gallons water
1½ cups kosher salt
1 cup dark brown sugar
1 garlic head, halved
½ bunch fresh thyme
24 fresh sage leaves
2 fresh rosemary sprigs
1 tablespoon toasted fennel seeds
1 tablespoon whole black peppercorns
1 suckling pig, 10 to 12 pounds, deboned
½ cup extra virgin olive oil
2 large onions, cut into 2-inch pieces
2 large carrots, peeled and cut into 2-inch pieces
3 celery stalks, cut into 2-inch pieces

Stuffing
⅓ cup chopped pistachios
¼ cup pine nuts
1½ teaspoons fennel seeds
4 tablespoons extra virgin olive oil
8 ounces fresh porcini mushrooms, diced
1 tablespoon chopped garlic
Sea salt and freshly ground black pepper
1 cup thinly sliced white onion
10 ounces pancetta, finely diced
2½ pounds ground pork belly
22 ounces hot Italian sausage
15 ounces foie gras, diced
¾ cup fresh parsley, chopped
¼ cup chopped onion
¼ cup fresh sage, chopped
1 tablespoon fresh rosemary, chopped

continued

Brine the pig ➤ Two days before you plan to serve this dish, prepare the brine. Combine the water, salt, sugar, garlic, thyme, sage, rosemary, fennel seeds, and peppercorns in a large pot with a capacity of at least 5 gallons. Bring the mixture to a simmer, stirring until all ingredients are well combined. Remove from the heat and immerse the pot in an ice bath to cool. Once cooled to room temperature, add the pig, ensuring that it is completely submerged. Cover and refrigerate for at least 6 hours or overnight.

Remove the pig from the brine and pat it dry with a kitchen towel. Place the pig on a rack set over a large rimmed baking pan and allow the pig to dry in the refrigerator for 12 hours.

Prepare the stuffing ➤ Toast the pistachios, pine nuts, and fennel seeds in a small sauté pan over medium heat until fragrant, about 2 minutes.

Heat 2 tablespoons of the olive oil in a large sauté pan over medium heat. Add the porcini mushrooms and garlic and sauté until golden brown, about 4 minutes. Season to taste with salt and pepper and set aside to cool.

Heat the remaining 2 tablespoons of olive oil in a clean sauté pan over medium heat. Add the sliced onion and sauté until caramelized, about 10 minutes. Season to taste with salt and pepper and set aside to cool.

Sauté the pancetta in a small sauté pan over medium heat until crispy, about 4 minutes. Using a slotted spoon, remove the pancetta from the pan and place it on a plate lined with paper towels; set aside to cool.

Mix the cooked pancetta with the pork belly, Italian sausage, and foie gras in a large bowl until well combined. Add the toasted nuts and fennel seeds, sautéed porcini mushrooms, caramelized onions, parsley, chopped onion, sage, and rosemary; mix until well combined. Add the cheese, wine, Armagnac, and egg whites and mix until well incorporated. Season to taste with the fleur de sel and black pepper.

Roast the pig ➤ Preheat the oven to 425°F. Pack the stuffing in the cavity of the pig. Using a meat lacing needle, sew the openings of the pig together. Rub the entire pig with the olive oil and wrap the ears and the tail with aluminum foil. Spread the onions, carrots, and celery evenly in a roasting pan. Place the pig, belly side down, on top the vegetables. Roast for 45 minutes and then reduce the oven temperature to 375°F. Continue to roast until a thermometer inserted into the middle of the pig reads 155° to 160°F, about 1 hour and 15 minutes more. Let rest for 30 minutes before serving.

1½ cups grated Meadow Creek Grayson cheese (or another washed-rind, semi-soft, pungent, cow's-milk cheese, similar to a domestic Taleggio)
¾ cup dry white wine
¼ cup Armagnac
2 large egg whites
3 tablespoons fleur de sel
1 tablespoon freshly ground black pepper

To serve ➤ Using an electric serrated knife, slice the stuffed pig vertically into 1-inch-thick slices, beginning behind the shoulder and reserving the head for presentation. Serve immediately.

Wine suggestion ➤ Serve this with a jammy and spicy red wine made from the uniquely American Zinfandel grape variety with notes of jammy raspberries, incense, and spices, such as Zinfandel, Mauritson Family "Rockpile," 2005, Rockpile, California.

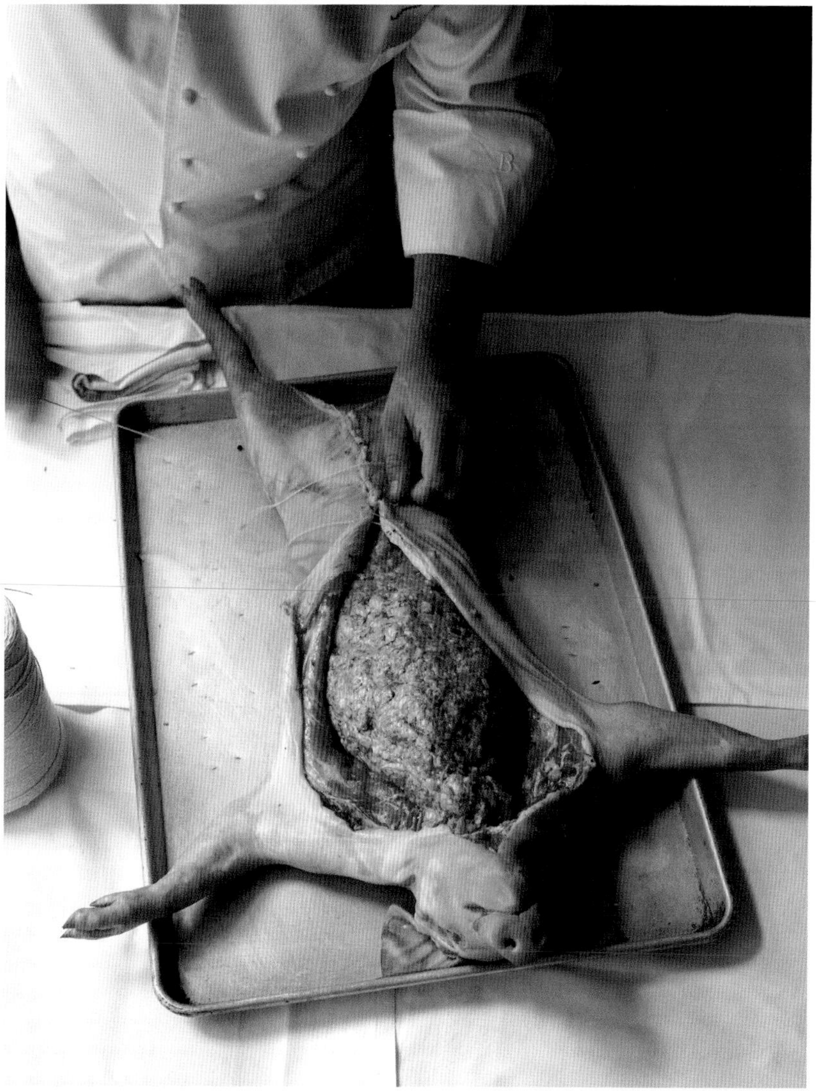

SUCKLING PIGS are generally less than 6 weeks old and are exclusively fed on their mother's milk, so the flesh is very pale and tender. The process of cooking a suckling pig is not a simple one, so it is usually reserved for special occasions. Roasted suckling pigs are part of many European, Russian, Chinese, Filipino, and Latin American celebrations. In Spain, the pigs are stuffed with paella, while in the Philippines and parts of the Caribbean, the pigs are roasted on a spit or in the ground with coals.

Dry-Aged Roasted Prime Rib with Caramelized Onion-Porcini Bread Pudding & Confit Garlic Jus

This prime rib has an added layer of flavor due to the brief smoking period in the beginning. If you don't have a grill, sear the beef in a large roasting pan on your stovetop.

SERVES 6

Caramelized Onion–Porcini Bread Pudding

1 small loaf country bread, crust trimmed and bread cut into ½-inch cubes (about 5 cups)
¼ cup olive oil
6 ounces porcini mushrooms, sliced into ¼-inch-thick slices
2 tablespoons unsalted butter
1 tablespoon chopped garlic
2 teaspoons fresh thyme leaves
1 sweet onion, thinly sliced
Sea salt and freshly ground black pepper
½ cup dry red wine
1½ cups heavy cream
¾ cup grated Sartori Stravecchio cheese (or another domestic Parmesan cheese)
1 large egg
2 large egg yolks
2 tablespoons chopped fresh parsley

Garlic Confit

3 garlic heads
2 tablespoons extra virgin olive oil
1 bay leaf
4 fresh thyme sprigs

Prime Rib

6½- to 7-pound dry-aged bone-in beef prime rib roast, frenched and brought to room temperature
6 tablespoons unsalted butter, softened
2 tablespoons fleur de sel
2 tablespoons coarsely ground black pepper
2 cups hickory wood chips, soaked in water

continued

Make the bread pudding ➤ Preheat the oven to 325°F. Arrange the bread cubes on a baking sheet and toast until dry and lightly browned, about 25 minutes. Leave the oven on to bake the bread pudding and the garlic confit.

Heat 3 tablespoons of the olive oil in a large sauté pan over high heat. Add the mushrooms and sauté until lightly browned, about 3 minutes. Add the butter, garlic, and thyme and cook until the butter is foamy and the garlic is tender. Transfer the mushroom mixture to a large bowl and set aside to cool.

In the same pan, heat the remaining 1 tablespoon of olive oil over medium heat. Add the onion and cook until caramelized, about 10 minutes. Season to taste with salt and pepper. Add the wine and simmer until the wine is completely absorbed, about 7 minutes.

Whisk the cream, ½ cup of the cheese, the egg, egg yolks, and parsley in a medium bowl to blend. Season to taste with salt and pepper. Pour the cream mixture into the bowl with the mushrooms. Stir in the caramelized onions and toasted bread and mix until well combined. Allow the mixture to sit for 30 minutes so the bread can absorb the cream and eggs.

Butter a standard 6-cup muffin pan. Divide the pudding evenly among the cups and bake until browned, about 20 minutes. Cover with aluminum foil and bake until the pudding has set, about 15 minutes. Remove from the oven and sprinkle the remaining ¼ cup of cheese over the tops. The puddings can be baked several hours ahead and reheated in the oven just before serving.

Make the garlic confit ➤ Cut a ¼-inch slice off the top of each head of garlic, leaving the bottom intact. Place the garlic in the middle of a sheet of heavy-duty aluminum foil. Drizzle the olive oil over the garlic heads and season with salt and pepper. Place the bay leaf and thyme over the garlic. Seal the foil and bake in the oven at 325°F until very tender, about 1 hour.

Prepare the prime rib ➤ Increase the oven temperature to 350°F. Heat a charcoal grill until the coals are grey and very hot. Truss the rib roast with kitchen twine. Brush with the softened butter and season well with fleur de sel and coarsely ground black pepper. Remove the wood chips from the water and scatter them over the charcoal. Place the meat on the grill and cover the grill hood to allow the smoky flavors to penetrate the meat. Sear for about 2 minutes on each side. Lay the meat, bone side down, in a large roasting pan. Roast for 1 hour and 15 minutes,

continued

Jus

2 tablespoons grapeseed oil
¾ pound beef chuck, cut into 1½-inch cubes
1 cup thinly sliced shallots
3 garlic cloves, crushed
3 tablespoons unsalted butter
2 cups dry red wine
6 cups Veal Stock (page 303)
4 fresh thyme sprigs
1 tablespoon whole black peppercorns
2 tablespoons fresh thyme leaves, roughly chopped

rotating the pan halfway through. To test for doneness, insert an instant-read thermometer in the center of the meat, without touching the bone. Once the temperature reaches 95°F, remove the meat from the oven. Cover loosely with foil and allow the meat to rest for 25 minutes before slicing. The meat will continue to cook to 125°F for rare doneness. Collect all the pan juices and reserve them for the garlic confit jus.

Make the jus ➤ Heat the grapeseed oil in a medium saucepan over high heat until nearly smoking. Add the beef chuck and sear it on all sides until brown, about 7 minutes. Remove the beef chuck from the pan. Add the shallots, garlic, and butter and reduce the heat to medium-low. Cook until the shallots are tender, about 3 minutes.

Return the beef chuck to the saucepan and increase the heat to medium. Add the wine and simmer until the alcohol has evaporated, about 5 minutes. Add the stock, thyme sprigs, and peppercorns. Simmer until the liquid has thickened slightly, about 30 minutes. Strain the sauce through a fine-mesh sieve into a small saucepan. Discard the solids. Gently squeeze the individual cloves of the garlic confit into the jus, being careful not to include any skin and keeping the cloves intact. Add the chopped thyme and reserved pan juices and season to taste with salt and pepper.

To serve ➤ Carve the prime rib to remove the meat from the bone. Carve the meat into 1-inch-thick slices and arrange them with the bones on a platter. Serve with the garlic confit jus and caramelized onion–porcini bread pudding.

Wine suggestion ➤ Serve this dish with a classic Napa Valley Cabernet Sauvignon with flavors of black currants, spice box, and crushed rocks, such as Cabernet Sauvignon, "One Point Five," Shafer Vineyards, 2005, Napa Valley, California.

DRY-AGING BEEF is a practice of aging meat in a climate-controlled environment for a certain period of time. Large cuts of beef are stored on shelves with plenty of room between them to allow for proper air circulation while the temperature of the room hovers just above freezing. The meat is aged in this environment for ten to twenty-eight days depending upon the cut and size. During the aging process, enzymes break down the muscle fibers and the meat becomes more tender. Flavor is also concentrated as the meat begins to shrink by about 10 to 15 percent due to fiber breakdown and moisture loss. Dry-aging results in an incredibly rich and nutty flavor. This technique can be applied to lamb and pork as well, but it is most commonly used on beef.

Honey Crisp Apple Cakes with Pumpkin Spice Ice Cream

I adapted this cake from my recipe for a classic carrot cake. The result is a spicy apple cake with all the moistness of a traditional carrot cake. This recipe can also be used to make one larger cake by using a 9-inch round cake pan.

SERVES 6

Special Equipment
Six 3-inch ring molds (2 inches high)

Apples
3 tablespoons unsalted butter
⅓ cup dark brown sugar
1 tablespoon ground cinnamon
3 Honey Crisp apples, peeled, cored, and halved

Cake Batter
Nonstick cooking spray
1½ tablespoons turbinado sugar
¾ cup all-purpose flour
¾ cup grated Honey Crisp apple
⅓ cup dark brown sugar
⅓ cup vegetable oil
¼ cup canned crushed pineapple
2 large eggs
2 tablespoons sugar
¾ teaspoon baking soda
½ teaspoon baking powder
½ teaspoon ground cinnamon
½ teaspoon salt
¼ teaspoon ground allspice
¼ teaspoon ground cloves
¼ teaspoon ground nutmeg

Calvados Sauce
1⅓ cups dark brown sugar
1 cup heavy cream
¼ cup Calvados or other apple brandy
4 tablespoons unsalted butter
½ teaspoon salt

Pumpkin Spice Ice Cream (page 310)

Caramelize the apples ➤ Melt the butter in a sauté pan over medium-low heat. Stir in the brown sugar and cinnamon. Place the apples in the pan, cut side up, and cook over very low heat until the apples are tender and nearly cooked through, about 15 minutes. Set aside to cool slightly.

When the apples are cool enough to handle, slice them lengthwise into ¼-inch-thick slices, keeping the top ½-inch of the apple halves intact so that the apple halves stay intact but can be fanned.

Make the cakes ➤ Preheat the oven to 325°F. Line a baking sheet with parchment paper. Wrap the bottom of six 3-inch ring molds (2 inches high) with heavy-duty aluminum foil. Spray the inside of the molds with nonstick cooking spray and sprinkle with the turbinado sugar. Place the ring molds on the lined baking sheet.

Using a stand mixer fitted with the paddle attachment, mix the remaining ingredients in the mixer bowl at low speed until just combined. Make sure not to overmix the batter.

Place the caramelized apple halves, core side up, in the molds, pressing the apples down to fan out the slices. Divide the batter evenly among the ring molds and bake until a knife inserted in the middle of the cakes comes out clean, about 20 minutes. Let the cakes cool to room temperature.

Run a paring knife around the edge of each cake and gently remove the cakes from the molds. Invert the cakes so the apples are facing up.

Make the sauce ➤ Combine the brown sugar, cream, Calvados, butter, and salt in a small saucepan and bring to a boil over medium-low heat. Reduce the heat and simmer until the sauce thickens, about 5 minutes.

To serve ➤ Rewarm the cakes for a few minutes in a 375°F oven, if necessary. Drizzle the warm Calvados sauce over the cakes and serve with a scoop of the ice cream.

Wine suggestion ➤ Serve this with a sweet wine made from the Muscat Alexandria grape variety with notes of apple jelly, honeysuckle, and vanilla, such as Muscat Alexandria, "Jackass Hill," Martinelli, 2004, Russian River Valley, California.

Chestnut Floating Island with Honey Mendiant

This unconventional dessert is gorgeous to look at and to eat! The chestnut crème anglaise is a pale milky bath that the meringues float upon. This dessert delivers intense flavors but is still quite light.

SERVES 6

Special Equipment

8-inch square baking dish; 1½-inch ring cutter (1½ inches high)

Chestnut Crème Anglaise

1½ cups heavy cream
1½ cups whole milk
8 large egg yolks
7 tablespoons sugar
⅔ cup chestnut paste

Meringue

6 large egg whites
½ cup + 2 tablespoons sugar
1½ teaspoons cornstarch
½ teaspoon cream of tartar

Honey Mendiant

1 cup honey
3 tablespoons chopped toasted almonds
3 tablespoons chopped toasted hazelnuts
3 tablespoons chopped toasted pistachios
3 tablespoons finely diced dried apricots
3 tablespoons finely diced dried cranberries
3 tablespoons finely diced dried figs

Make the chestnut crème anglaise ➤ Bring the cream and milk to a simmer in a medium saucepan over medium heat. Whisk the egg yolks and sugar in a large bowl until pale and fluffy. Carefully pour the hot milk over the eggs, whisking constantly to make sure the eggs do not scramble. Transfer the mixture back into the saucepan and simmer over low heat until the mixture thickens enough to coat the back of a wooden spoon, about 4 minutes. Strain the mixture through a fine-mesh strainer into a clean bowl set over a bowl of ice water. While still hot, whisk in the chestnut paste until well combined. Set aside to cool to room temperature.

Make the meringues ➤ Preheat the oven to 325°F. Line a shallow 8-inch square baking dish with wax paper. Using a stand mixer fitted with a whisk attachment, whisk the egg whites, sugar, cornstarch, and cream of tartar in the mixer bowl at high speed until the mixture forms stiff peaks, about 5 minutes.

Pour the meringue into the dish, making sure to spread it evenly. Bake until the meringue no longer looks wet, about 5 minutes. Let the meringue cool to room temperature and then refrigerate for at least 3 hours.

Using a 1½-inch ring cutter (1½ inches high), cut the meringue into 18 small meringues. Dip the cutter in warm water between each cut to ensure a clean cut. The meringues will resemble marshmallows. Once cut, transfer the meringues to a clean plate and refrigerate until ready to serve.

Make the honey mendiant ➤ Combine all of the ingredients in a small saucepan and simmer over low heat, stirring constantly so that the honey does not burn, about 2 minutes.

To serve ➤ Pour the chestnut crème anglaise into a large glass serving bowl. Float the meringues in the crème anglaise and drizzle with the honey mendiant.

Wine suggestion ➤ Serve this with an American cream sherry with notes of butterscotch, pecans, and hazelnuts, such as St. Julian, Solera Cream Sherry, NV, Michigan.

Nougat Glace with Volcano Cookie

If you haven't tried a glace yet, you should. The meringue and the whipped cream create an incredibly light and creamy backdrop for the crunchy sugared almonds. In the winter, I make this dessert with confit orange zest. I named these cookies because when they come out of the oven they look like crackling lava from a volcano.

SERVES 6

Caramelized Almonds

1½ cups almonds
1⅓ cups sugar
1 tablespoon unsalted butter, softened

Glace

2⅓ cups heavy cream
1 cup + 2 tablespoons sugar
½ cup egg whites
1½ cups chestnuts in syrup, drained and roughly chopped (see Sources, page 317)
¼ cup amaretto or other almond liqueur

Caramel-Chestnut Sauce

1 cup sugar
1 cup heavy cream
1 cup whole milk
1¼ cups chestnut paste

Volcano Cookie

⅓ cup + 1½ tablespoons almonds
⅓ cup + 1½ tablespoons hazelnuts
¾ cup + 2 tablespoons sugar
2 large egg whites, lightly beaten
1 teaspoon brewed coffee

Caramelize the almonds ➤ Preheat the oven to 350°F. Line a baking sheet with parchment paper. Scatter the almonds over another baking sheet and toast in the oven until fragrant, about 10 minutes.

While the almonds are toasting, bring the sugar and ¼ cup of water to a boil in a small saucepan over medium-high heat. Cook, swirling the pan often, until a deep amber color develops, about 5 minutes. Remove from the heat and stir in the toasted almonds and butter. Pour the caramelized almonds onto the baking sheet lined with parchment paper and spread evenly using a spatula. Set aside to cool and then roughly chop.

Make the glace ➤ Using a stand mixer fitted with a whisk attachment, whisk the heavy cream in the mixer bowl until it reaches soft peaks. Transfer the whipped cream to a medium bowl and clean the mixer bowl and whisk attachment.

Combine the sugar and ⅓ cup of water in a small saucepan over medium heat. Meanwhile, place the egg whites in the clean mixer bowl and begin beating the egg whites in the stand mixer fitted with the whisk attachment at a low speed until frothy. Once the sugar syrup reaches 240°F, remove it from the heat. With the mixer running, carefully pour the hot sugar syrup into the egg whites. Increase the mixer speed to high and beat until the egg whites are glossy, tripled in volume, and at room temperature.

Using a rubber spatula, fold the caramelized almonds, chestnuts, amaretto, and whipped cream into the egg whites. Transfer to a plastic or metal container and freeze until firm.

Make the sauce ➤ Combine the sugar and 3 tablespoons of water in a medium saucepan over medium-high heat. Simmer the syrup, swirling the pan often, until a deep amber color develops, about 5 minutes. Remove the pan from the heat and whisk in the cream and milk. Simmer over low heat until thickened, about 4 minutes. Remove from the heat and whisk in the chestnut paste until well combined. Strain the sauce through a fine-mesh strainer set over a clean bowl and set aside to cool.

Make the cookies ➤ Preheat the oven to 325°F. Line a baking sheet with parchment paper. Roughly chop the almonds and hazelnuts. Combine the almonds, hazelnuts, sugar, egg whites, and coffee in a medium sauté pan over medium heat. Cook, stirring constantly with a wooden spoon, until the mixture forms a ball and is warm to the touch (about 113°F). Remove from the heat.

Spoon nickel-size pieces of the dough onto the prepared baking sheet. Bake until the cookies are golden brown, about 20 minutes.

To serve ➤ Spoon the glace into glass dessert bowls. Drizzle the caramel sauce over the glace and serve the cookies alongside.

Wine suggestion ➤ Serve with an ice wine–style wine made from Vidal Blanc with aromas of tangerines, peaches, and honey, such as Vidal Blanc Ice Wine, Debonne Vineyards, 2005, Grand River Valley, Ohio.

Grand-Mère Rousseau's Creusois with Dried Fruit Ice Cream

My great-grandmother often made this simple hazelnut cake for our family lunch on Sunday afternoons. Its simplicity will fool you though. The flavor is delicate and intense at the same time and I love the slightly crunchy, sugary crust on the outside.

SERVES 6

Special Equipment
8-inch round cake pan

Cake
3 tablespoons unsalted butter, melted
1 tablespoon + ¾ cup sugar
4 large egg whites
¾ cup hazelnut flour
⅔ cup all-purpose flour

Hazelnut-Caramel Sauce
½ cup sugar
¼ cup heavy cream
¼ cup whole milk
3 tablespoons hazelnut praline

Dried Fruit Ice Cream (page 308)

Make the cake ➤ Preheat the oven to 375°F. Butter the inside of an 8-inch round cake pan with 1 tablespoon of the butter, and then sprinkle the 1 tablespoon of sugar over the inside of the pan, shaking the pan so the sugar is evenly distributed. Tap out any excess sugar.

Using a stand mixer fitted with the whisk attachment, whisk the egg whites and half of the remaining sugar in the mixer bowl until medium peaks form. Whisk the hazelnut flour, all-purpose flour, and the remaining sugar in another large bowl to blend. Using a rubber spatula, fold half of the dry ingredients into the egg whites until nearly combined. Gently fold in the remaining dry ingredients until fully incorporated. Fold in the remaining 2 tablespoons of melted butter and pour the batter into the prepared cake pan. Smooth the top of the cake with an offset spatula. Bake the cake until a cake tester inserted in the middle of the cake comes out clean, about 10 minutes.

Make the sauce ➤ Bring the sugar and 3 tablespoons of water to a boil in a small saucepan over medium-high heat. Simmer the syrup, swirling the pan often, until a deep amber color develops, about 5 minutes. Remove the pan from the heat and whisk in the cream and milk. Simmer over low heat until thickened, about 4 minutes. Remove from the heat and stir in the hazelnut praline until well combined.

To serve ➤ Drizzle the caramel sauce over the bottom of each plate. Place a slice of cake on top of the caramel sauce and serve with a scoop of ice cream.

Wine suggestion ➤ Serve this dish with an American take on the classic wine of Madeira with notes of caramel, hazelnuts, and figs, such as Texas Madeira, Haak Winery, 2003, Gulf Coast, Texas.

Meyer Lemon Curd with Maine Blueberry Compote & Madeleines

The peak time for blueberries is late summer to early fall. Their sweetness is tempered here with a tangy lemon curd lightened with whipped cream. The result is a beautiful and simple dessert.

SERVES 6

Special Equipment
Small madeleine molds

Blueberry Compote
⅓ cup sugar
1 pint Maine blueberries

Meyer Lemon Curd
½ cup freshly squeezed lemon juice
½ cup freshly squeezed Meyer lemon juice
2 tablespoons lemon zest
2 tablespoons Meyer lemon zest
5 large eggs
⅔ cup sugar
5 tablespoons unsalted butter

Madeleines
¼ cup sugar
1 large egg
½ vanilla bean, split lengthwise and seeds scraped
1 teaspoon lemon zest
1 teaspoon orange zest
3½ tablespoons unsalted butter, melted
1½ teaspoons orange blossom water
⅓ cup all-purpose flour
¼ teaspoon baking powder
Confectioners' sugar for dusting

1 cup heavy cream

Make the compote ➤ Bring the sugar and 3 tablespoons of water to a simmer in a small saucepan. Stir in the blueberries, being gentle so as not to burst them. Cook until the blueberries are soft but have not burst, about 2 minutes. Transfer the berries to a bowl. Refrigerate until ready to use.

Make the curd ➤ Combine both of the lemon juices and zests with the eggs, sugar, and butter in a double boiler set over gently simmering water. Cook over medium heat, whisking constantly, until thickened, about 5 minutes. Strain the curd though a fine-mesh strainer into a clean bowl. Press a sheet of plastic wrap directly on the surface of the curd to prevent a skin from forming. Refrigerate until cool.

Make the madeleines ➤ Whisk the sugar, egg, vanilla bean seeds, lemon zest, and orange zest in a medium bowl until pale and fluffy. Stir in the melted butter and orange blossom water. Sift the flour and baking powder over the batter and stir to combine. Let the batter rest for 30 minutes.

Preheat the oven to 400°F. Butter and lightly flour small madeleine molds and divide the batter equally among the molds to make 25 madeleines total. Bake until the madeleines spring back when lightly touched, about 6 minutes. Remove the madeleines from the molds and dust with confectioners' sugar.

To serve ➤ Using a stand mixer fitted with the whisk attachment, whisk the heavy cream in the mixer bowl at medium-high speed until stiff peaks form. Using a rubber spatula, gently fold the lemon curd into the cream until it's fully combined. Divide the blueberries among 6 glass serving bowls, spoon the lemon curd cream over the top and serve the madeleines on the side.

Wine suggestion ➤ Serve a jammy, juicy, and delicious sweet wine made from native New Jersey blueberries, such as Alba Blueberry Wine, Milford, New Jersey.

Granola-Cranberry Tart with Mandarin Sorbet

This tart is perfect for a dinner party because the granola and compote can be made ahead during the day and the tart can easily be assembled just before serving. I love the contrast of the sweet, soft cranberry compote and the crunchy, slightly salty, granola.

SERVES 6

Special Equipment
9-inch tart pan with removable bottom; pie weights or dried beans

Cranberry Compote
2 pounds fresh strawberries, roughly chopped
½ cup sugar
1 tablespoon cornstarch
2 cups dried cranberries
1 tablespoon orange zest

Dough
1⅓ cups all-purpose flour
2 teaspoons sugar
¼ teaspoon salt
4 tablespoons cold unsalted butter, cut into ½-inch pieces
4 tablespoons vegetable shortening
2 tablespoons ice cold water
½ teaspoon white vinegar

1½ cups My Favorite Granola (page 299)
Mandarin Sorbet (page 313)

Make the compote ➤ Combine the strawberries, sugar, and 1 cup of water in a medium saucepan and gently cook over low heat until all the juices from the strawberries are released, about 15 minutes. Pour the compote through a fine-mesh strainer into a clean saucepan and discard the solids. Heat the liquid over low heat and whisk in the cornstarch, stirring constantly until the mixture thickens, about 3 minutes. Pour into a large bowl and stir in the cranberries while the liquid is still hot. Cool to room temperature and then refrigerate overnight or for at least 6 hours.

Make the crust ➤ Preheat the oven to 325°F. Using a stand mixer fitted with the paddle attachment, mix the flour, sugar, and salt in the mixer bowl at medium-low speed. Slowly add the butter and mix until pea-size lumps form. Add the shortening and mix until coarse grains form. Add the water and vinegar and mix until the dough is smooth and uniform. Form the dough into a ball and flatten into a disk. Wrap the dough in plastic wrap and refrigerate for at least 30 minutes before rolling out.

Using a lightly floured rolling pin, roll out the dough on a lightly floured surface to a ⅛-inch-thick round. Fit the dough into a 9-inch round tart pan and trim any excess dough from around the edge of the tart pan. Line the dough with parchment paper and fill with dried beans or pastry weights. Bake until the crust is golden brown and completely cooked through, about 20 minutes.

Assemble the tart ➤ Preheat the oven 325°F. Remove the compote from the refrigerator and set it aside to come to room temperature. Stir the orange zest into the compote. Fill the tart shell with the compote and cover the top evenly with granola. Bake until the compote is bubbling and warm and the granola is crisp, about 15 minutes.

To serve ➤ Serve the tart warm or at room temperature with the sorbet.

Wine suggestion ➤ Serve an ice wine made from Syrah with aromas of cranberries, pomegranate, and strawberry, such as Syrah Ice Wine, Zerba Cellars, 2005, Columbia valley, Oregon.

Panna Cotta with Vermont Crème Fraîche & Crushed Concord Grapes

This recipe is only as good as the crème fraîche you use. In the last 10 years a rash of low-quality crème fraîche has been making its way into larger supermarkets. Seek out a local one that has a thick consistency and pronounced tanginess. I am particularly fond of the Vermont Butter and Cheese Company product, which is available at many local cheese shops or online.

SERVES 6

Panna Cotta

- ¾ cup whole milk
- ⅓ cup + 2 tablespoons sugar
- 1 vanilla bean, split lengthwise and seeds scraped
- 1 cup + 2 tablespoons heavy cream
- ¼ cup + 2 tablespoons buttermilk
- 3 gelatin sheets, soaked for 2 minutes in cold water to soften
- 1 cup + 2 tablespoons Vermont Butter and Cheese Company crème fraîche

Concord Grape Compote

- 3 cups halved Concord grapes
- ⅓ cup light brown sugar
- 1½ tablespoons freshly squeezed lemon juice
- 2 tablespoons Cointreau

Make the panna cotta ➤ Bring the milk, sugar, and vanilla bean seeds to a boil in a small saucepan over medium-high heat. Remove from the heat and add the heavy cream, buttermilk, and gelatin sheets. Stir until the gelatin dissolves, and then strain through a fine-mesh strainer into a large clean bowl. While still warm, stir in the crème fraîche and then ladle the mixture into six 4-ounce ramekins or small glasses. Refrigerate until fully set, at least 4 hours.

Make the Concord grape compote ➤ Combine 1½ cups of the grapes, the brown sugar, lemon juice, and 3 tablespoons of water in a small saucepan over medium-low heat. Simmer until the grapes are tender and beginning to break down, about 4 minutes. Purée the grape mixture in a blender or a food processor fitted with a metal blade until loose, making sure not to break up too many of the seeds. Strain the mixture through a fine-mesh strainer set over a clean mixing bowl. While the liquid is still warm, stir in the remaining 1½ cups of grapes and the Cointreau.

To serve ➤ Run a paring knife around the edge of each panna cotta and unmold onto a cold dessert plate. Spoon the grape compote on top and around the panna cotta.

Wine suggestion ➤ Serve a sweet wine made from the Muscat grape variety with notes of vanilla, apricots, and honey, such as Muscat de Beaulieu, Beaulieu Vineyards, NV, Napa Valley, California.

CONCORD GRAPES were developed in Concord, Massachusetts in the mid–1800s by a scientist who researched upwards of 20,000 grape seedlings before deciding this was the perfect species. Concord grapes have an amazingly sweet and aromatic flavor compared to the ubiquitous green and red grapes that line the produce section at the supermarket. The dark purple skins are somewhat chewy, but once crushed, concord grapes reveal a translucent flesh that has a most concentrated grape flavor. Bite into a concord grape and there is no doubt childhood memories of the grape jelly in those ever present peanut butter and jelly sandwiches will come flooding back.

Warm Chocolate-Hazelnut Cake with Chai Tea Ice Cream

This cake is cooked in a water bath and covered with foil, which results in a texture that is smooth and almost pudding-like. The richness of the chocolate and hazelnuts blends well with the spice of the ice cream. They are perfect together but just as great enjoyed on their own.

SERVES 6

Special Equipment
9-inch springform pan

Cake
9 ounces bittersweet chocolate (66% cocoa), chopped
12 tablespoons unsalted butter
6 large eggs
1 cup light brown sugar
¼ cup Frangelico or other hazelnut liqueur
1 cup finely ground hazelnuts
1 teaspoon kosher salt

Frangelico Whipped Cream
½ cup heavy cream
3 tablespoons Frangelico or other hazelnut liqueur
2 tablespoons confectioners' sugar

Chai Ice Cream (page 307)

Make the cake ➤ Preheat the oven to 350°F. Butter and lightly flour the inside of a 9-inch springform cake pan. Wrap the bottom of the pan with heavy-duty aluminum foil to make sure no water from the water bath leaks into the pan.

Melt the chocolate and butter in a double boiler set over gently simmer water, whisking constantly to ensure a silky consistency. Using a stand mixer fitted with the whisk attachment, whisk the eggs, brown sugar, and liqueur in the mixer bowl at high speed until pale and frothy. Slowly add the melted chocolate mixture, whisking until combined. Fold in the hazelnuts and salt. Pour the batter into the prepared cake pan.

Place the cake pan in a large roasting pan. Pour enough hot water into the roasting pan to come halfway up the sides of the cake pan, being careful not to get any water inside the pan. Cover the roasting pan with aluminum foil and bake until a knife inserted in the middle of the cake comes out clean, about 1 hour and 20 minutes. Remove the cake pan from the water bath and let cool for 5 minutes. Once the cake has cooled slightly, remove the foil, run a paring knife around the edge of the cake, and remove the cake from the pan.

Make the whipped cream ➤ Using a stand mixer fitted with the whisk attachment, whip the cream in the mixer bowl until it forms medium peaks. Add the liqueur and sugar and mix until just combined.

To serve ➤ Slice the cake into wedges while still warm and serve with Frangelico whipped cream and ice cream.

Wine suggestion ➤ Serve this with a late harvest-blend of Zinfandel and Petite Sirah that offers notes of framboise, cassis, and violets, such as T-Vine, "Psychedelic Rooster," Sticky Late Harvest Red, 2006, California.

Bosc Pear Frangipane Tart

The dark and sometimes rough peel of a Bosc pear conceals a firm texture and sweet flesh, making them perfect for poaching. Bosc pears are widely available, but if you are unable able find them, you can substitute Anjou pears.

SERVES 6

Special Equipment
9-inch round ceramic tart pan

Poached Pears
4 cups Simple Syrup (page 314)
½ cup Poire Williams or other pear-flavored eau-de-vie
5 Bosc pears, peeled, halved, and cored

Caramel
¾ cup + 1 tablespoon sugar
2 tablespoons light corn syrup
1½ teaspoons unsalted butter

Frangipane
½ cup confectioners' sugar
½ cup finely ground blanched almonds
4 tablespoons unsalted butter, softened
1 large egg

1 sheet store-bought frozen puff pastry, preferably Dufour brand, thawed

Almond Milk Sorbet (page 311)

Poach the pears ➤ Combine the simple syrup and Poire Williams in a large saucepan over medium heat and bring to a boil. Arrange the pears, cut side down, in the simmering syrup. Reduce the heat to a simmer and poach the pears, partially covered, until tender, about 15 minutes. Allow the pears to cool in the poaching liquid. Once the poaching liquid reaches room temperature, remove the pears from the liquid and slice lengthwise into 1-inch-thick slices.

Make the caramel ➤ Combine the sugar, corn syrup, and 1½ tablespoons of water in a small saucepan over medium-high heat. Bring to a simmer, swirling the pan every so often, until it reaches a deep amber color, about 4 minutes. Remove the pan from the heat and whisk the butter in the caramel. Immediately pour the caramel into the bottom of a 9-inch round ceramic tart pan.

Make the frangipane ➤ Using a stand mixer fitted with the paddle attachment, mix the confectioners' sugar, ground almonds, butter, and egg at medium-high speed until fluffy.

Assemble the tart ➤ Preheat the oven to 350°F. Tightly fan the pear slices over the caramel in a circular pattern. Using a lightly floured rolling pin, roll out the pastry on a lightly floured surface to a ¼-inch thickness. Trim the puff pastry to an 11-inch round. Spread the frangipane over the puff pastry and place, frangipane side down, over the pears. Press the puff pastry so it adheres to the tart pan. Bake until the pastry is golden brown and the caramel is bubbling, about 30 minutes. Cool on a wire rack for 10 minutes.

To serve ➤ Invert the tart, pear side up, onto a serving platter while still warm and serve with the sorbet.

Wine suggestion ➤ Serve with an ice wine made from Semillon that offers aromas of roasted pears, honeysuckle, and pineapple, such as Semillon Ice Wine, "Seven Hills Vineyard," L'Ecole No. 41, 2005, Columbia Valley, Washington.

Mecox Cheese Tricorne

This savory little treat is perfect any time of the day, but I love to serve them for brunch or as an appetizer with a simple green salad. You can also add blanched and finely chopped spinach to the béchamel. Many store-bought brands of puff pastry can be gummy and tasteless, so make sure to use fresh, high-quality puff pastry.

SERVES 6

- 6 bacon slices, diced
- 2 medium portobello mushroom caps, halved and sliced ¼ inch thick
- 2 tablespoons extra virgin olive oil
- 1 teaspoon finely chopped garlic
- ¾ cup grated Mecox Sunrise cheese (see below)
- ½ cup Béchamel Sauce (page 304)
- Sea salt and freshly ground black pepper
- 2 sheets store-bought frozen puff pastry, preferably Dufour brand, thawed
- 1 large egg yolk whisked with 1 tablespoon cold water

Cook the bacon in a large sauté pan over medium heat until the bacon is crisp and all the fat has been rendered, about 6 minutes. Add the mushrooms, olive oil, and garlic and cook until the mushrooms are soft, about 5 minutes. Transfer to a medium bowl. Stir in the cheese and béchamel sauce and season to taste with salt and pepper.

Preheat the oven to 375°F. Line a baking sheet with parchment paper. Using a lightly floured rolling pin, roll out each sheet of pastry on a lightly floured surface to a ⅛-inch thickness. Cut the pastry into 12 triangles that have 6½-inch sides.

Place 2 tablespoons of the mushroom mixture in the center of each pastry triangle and brush the edges with the egg wash. Gather the 3 points of the triangle and bring them together at the top, forming a triangular pouch. Pinch the edges together and seal tightly. Brush the outside of the pouches with the remaining egg wash and place them on the prepared baking sheet.

Bake until the pastry is cooked through and golden brown, about 22 minutes. Serve warm.

MECOX BAY DAIRY is situated on a beautiful piece of land on Long Island near the town of Bridgehampton. The dairy is owned and operated by the Ludlow family, who tend a small herd of Jersey cows. This fourth generation of farmers turned their potato farm into a dairy in 2001 and started making cheese shortly thereafter. The raw milk cheeses are aged for a minimum of sixty-one days and present unique flavors derived from the rich soil and sweet bay and ocean breezes. They are handmade with whole milk in small batches, which makes them characteristic of farmstead artisanal cheeses. Seasonal variations are evident as the cows' diet changes from grasses in the summer to hay in the winter.

Maine Blueberry Pancakes with Orange Blossom Maple Syrup

Upstate New York rivals Vermont in maple syrup production. The climate at Mapleland Farms, located in northeastern New York, provides the ideal amount of sunshine and cold temperatures to produce a deep, amber-colored and perfectly sweet maple syrup.

SERVE 6

Syrup

1 cup Mapleland Farms maple syrup
1 tablespoon orange blossom water

Pancakes

1 cup whole milk
2 large eggs
2 tablespoons vegetable oil
1 stick (4 ounces) unsalted butter, melted and slightly cooled + 3 tablespoons, softened for cooking
1 cup all-purpose flour
2 tablespoons baking powder
4 teaspoons sugar
1 teaspoon salt
1½ cups Maine blueberries

Make the syrup ➤ Whisk the maple syrup and orange blossom water in a small bowl to blend. Place over a small pan of simmering water to warm.

Make the pancakes ➤ Whisk the milk, eggs, and oil in a medium bowl to blend. Slowly whisk in the melted butter, making sure not to cook the eggs. Whisk the flour, baking powder, sugar, and salt in a medium bowl. Whisk the egg mixture into the flour until just combined. Be careful not to overmix or the batter will break.

Heat a griddle or large nonstick pan over medium heat and brush the surface with 1 tablespoon of the softened butter. Using ¼ cup of batter for each pancake, ladle the batter onto the griddle. Cook for 2 minutes. Sprinkle some of the blueberries evenly over the pancakes, then flip the pancakes over. Cook until the pancakes are brown on the bottom and cooked through, about 2 minutes. Repeat with the remaining butter, batter, and blueberries.

To serve ➤ Serve immediately with the warm orange blossom maple syrup on the side.

Gingerbread Brioche Pain Perdu

My chef from the Ritz Carlton and I created this recipe together. Serve with Mapleland Farms maple syrup or The Hamptons honey and fresh berries. I like them with bananas Foster as a decadent way to kick off the weekend.

SERVES 6

Gingerbread Spice

2½ tablespoons sugar
2 teaspoons ground cinnamon
2 teaspoons ground ginger
½ teaspoon ground allspice
½ teaspoon ground cardamom
½ teaspoon ground nutmeg
¼ teaspoon ground cloves

Pain Perdu

2¼ cups heavy cream
1½ cups whole milk
¾ cup sugar
3 large eggs
2 large egg yolks
2½ tablespoons bourbon
2½ tablespoons orange blossom water
2 teaspoons dried orange zest
1½ teaspoons vanilla extract
2 loaves of brioche, sliced into twelve 1½-inch-thick slices

2 tablespoons confectioners' sugar

Make the gingerbread spice ➤ Whisk all the ingredients in a small mixing bowl to blend.

Make the pain perdu ➤ Preheat the oven to 375°F. Whisk the cream, milk, sugar, eggs, egg yolks, bourbon, orange blossom water, orange zest, and vanilla in a large rimmed baking sheet. Soak the brioche in the egg mixture for 30 seconds on each side.

Heat a large nonstick sauté pan over medium heat. Scatter 1 teaspoon of the gingerbread spice over the bottom of the pan. Place 2 slices of brioche in the pan on top of the spices. Cook until golden brown and fragrant, about 2 minutes. Sprinkle 1 teaspoon of the spices on the uncooked side of each slice of brioche and then turn the bread slices over. Cook for an additional 2 minutes. Transfer the brioche to a clean large baking sheet. Repeat the process with the remaining brioche slices.

Bake the pain perdu until the brioche has crisped up ever so slightly, about 10 minutes.

To serve ➤ Sprinkle the brioche with a pinch of the gingerbread spice and dust with the confectioners' sugar.

Coffee Cake with Espresso Glaze & Cardamom Crumble

This rich, buttery breakfast treat is best enjoyed with hot coffee and plenty of milk. I like to dunk a slice of it in my coffee, and then my favorite part is enjoying all the moist bits of cake at the bottom of the cup.

SERVES 6

Cake

Nonstick cooking spray
1 cup sugar
12 tablespoons unsalted butter
2 large eggs
2 teaspoons vanilla extract
2 cups all-purpose flour
1 teaspoon baking powder
½ teaspoon baking soda
¼ teaspoon salt
1 cup sour cream

Glaze

2 tablespoons brewed coffee
1½ teaspoons instant espresso powder
¾ cup confectioners' sugar

Crumble

¼ cup + 1 tablespoon light brown sugar
2 tablespoons sugar
4 tablespoons unsalted butter, melted
¼ teaspoon ground cardamom
Pinch of salt
½ cup + 3 tablespoons all-purpose flour
½ cup roughly chopped toasted pecans

Make the cake ➤ Preheat the oven to 350°F. Spray an 8-inch bundt cake pan with nonstick cooking spray. Using a stand mixer fitted with the paddle attachment, beat the sugar and butter in the mixer bowl at medium-high speed until light and fluffy, about 5 minutes. Add the eggs, 1 at a time and mixing well between each addition, and then add the vanilla.

Sift the flour, baking powder, baking soda, and salt into another large bowl. Add the dry ingredients to the butter mixture in 3 batches and mix until just combined between each addition. Add the sour cream and mix until completely incorporated.

Pour the batter into the bundt pan and bake until a knife inserted near the middle of the cake and comes out clean, about 30 minutes. Let cool on a wire rack for about 15 minutes and then invert the cake onto the rack and allow to cool completely.

Make the glaze ➤ Stir the coffee and espresso powder in a small bowl until the powder has completely dissolved. Stir in the confectioners' sugar. If the glaze is too thick, add a splash of regular brewed coffee or water.

Make the crumble ➤ Preheat the oven to 350°F. Line a baking sheet with parchment paper. Combine both sugars in a medium bowl. Add the butter, cardamom, and salt and mix until well combined. Add the flour and mix to form a pebbly consistency. Stir in the pecans. Scatter the crumble evenly over the lined baking sheet and bake until toasted, about 5 minutes. Remove from the oven and set aside to cool.

To serve ➤ Drizzle the glaze over the top of the cake. While the glaze is still wet, press the crumble into the glaze to set for 10 minutes before serving.

Wine Harvest

MENU

Appetizers

Mecox Cheese Tricorne

or

Venison Bolognese Pappardelle with Kale
and Vermont Shepherd Cheese

or

Roasted Root Vegetable Salad
with Marcona Almonds

Main Courses

Aromatic Stuffed Suckling Pig

or

Roasted Pheasant with Braised Cabbage
and Chestnuts

or

Jamison Farm Rack of Lamb with Salsify and Walnuts
and Jurançon-Chanterelle Jus

COCKTAIL

Concord Spritzer

DESSERTS

Grand-Mère
Rousseau's Creusois
with Dried Fruit Ice Cream

or

Meyer Lemon Curd
with Maine Blueberry Compote
and Madeleines

Thanksgiving

MENU

COCKTAIL

Cranberry-Mint Martini

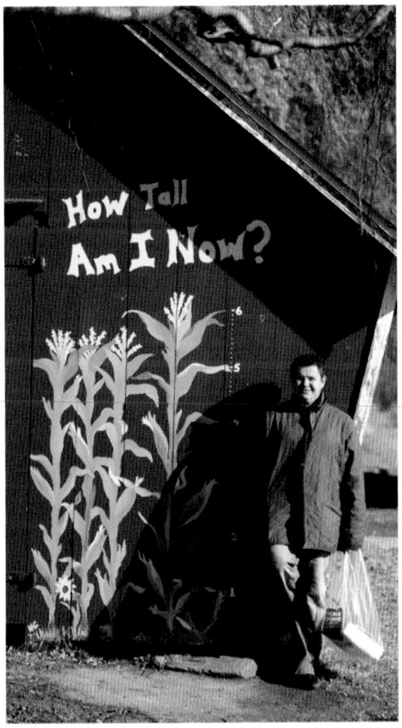

Appetizers

Pigs in a Blanket "Ritz Carlton"

or

Nantucket Bay Scallops with Smoked Fingerling Potato Salad, Endive, and McIntosh Apple

or

Duck Confit and Parsnip Risotto with Sage-Garlic Brown Butter

or

Butternut Squash Soup with Foie Gras and Wild Mushroom Crostini

Main Courses

Roasted Turkey with Chestnut-Sausage Stuffing, Cranberry-Grenadine Relish, and Rosemary Gravy

or

Dry-Aged Roasted Prime Rib with Caramelized Onion-Porcini Bread Pudding and Confit Garlic Jus

or

Pan-Seared East Coast Halibut with Caramelized Cauliflower and Hazelnuts

DESSERTS

Honey Crisp Apple Cakes and Pumpkin Spice Ice Cream

or

Chestnut Floating Island with Honey Mendiant

or

Granola-Cranberry Tart with Mandarin Sorbet

Winter

The chill of winter conjures up memories of time-worn, earthenware pots simmering throughout the day on my grandmother's stove, saturating the whole house with the rich aromas of beef shanks and red wine or my father's favorite, braised game. And, if it wasn't too cold, I would go mushroom hunting with my parents and grandfather on Sunday mornings. These freshly foraged mushrooms, like porcini or the local rosé mushroom, added an earthy and hearty element to whatever dish they made their way into. These comforting, warm, rich meals satisfied my winter cravings.

Cold weather calls for serious stick-to-your-ribs food, and while I may turn to my pantry for more red wine, fragrant spices, grains, and other staples, there is still an abundance of winter produce to be enjoyed. Root vegetables, hearty greens, and heady black and white truffles add so much depth and flavor while pomegranates and a variety of citrus provide brightness and offer a refreshing counterpoint. Comfort foods of winter aren't necessarily always heavy. Winter fruits add a punch of color and levity to any dish, and pairing seafood with earthier winter produce, like mushrooms, creates a balanced dish. Enjoy the longer cooking methods used in these recipes and take a Sunday afternoon nap, one of the most decadent winter pleasures.

The holiday season is also in full swing during the winter months. One-pot meals, like stews, pan roasts, and braised dishes, lend themselves well to entertaining. Appetizers like terrines, pâté, and soups are best made a day or two in advance, so if you are hosting a gathering of two or ten you can still take pleasure in the evening along with your guests. I have assembled a few holiday menus in the following pages that I hope you will enjoy. As a chef, I love cooking long lavish meals that run well into the night, however personalize the menus to your own tastes and appetite.

January

Vegetables
Beet
Brussels Sprout
Cabbage
Cardoon
Celery Root
Collard Green
Endive
Fennel
Fingerling Potato
Kale
Mâche
Parsnip
Rutabaga
Salsify
Turnip

Fungi
Black Truffle
Black Trumpet
Porcini

Seafood
Clam
Dover Sole
Hake
Halibut
Maine Sea Scallop
Mussel
Nantucket Bay Scallop
Rock Shrimp
Skate
Stone Crab

Poultry & Game
Partridge
Venison

Fruit
Banana
Blood Orange
Grapefruit
Kumquat
Meyer Lemon
Passion Fruit
Persimmon
Pineapple
Pomegranate
Quince
Tangerine

February

Vegetables
Beet
Brussels Sprout
Cabbage
Cardoon
Celery Root
Collard Green
Endive
Fingerling Potato
Kale
Mâche
Parsnip
Rutabaga
Salsify
Turnip

Fungi
Porcini
Black Truffle

Seafood
Clam
Dover Sole
Hake
Halibut
Maine Sea Scallops
Mussel
Nantucket Bay Scallop
Skate
Stone Crab

Poultry & Game
Partridge
Venison

Fruit
Banana
Blood Orange
Grapefruit
Kumquat
Meyer Lemon
Passion Fruit
Pineapple
Pomegranate
Tangerine

March

Vegetables
Artichoke
Beet
Cabbage
Cauliflower
Celery Root
Fennel
Fingerling Potato
Kale
Mâche
Salsify
Spring Onion

Fungi
Black Truffle
Morel
Mousseron

Seafood
Cod
Dover Sole
Hake
Maine Sea Scallop
Mussel
Salmon

Meat
Spring Lamb

Fruit
Banana
Blood Orange
Meyer Lemon
Passion Fruit
Pineapple
Rhubarb

Pomegranate Sidecar

Pomegranates are very well suited for cocktails. The juice and seeds add sweet, tart flavor and a vibrant jewel tone.

SERVES 1

Sugar
2 ounces Hennessy VO cognac
1 ounce pomegranate syrup, preferably Monin brand
½ ounce freshly squeezed lemon juice
½ ounce POM Wonderful pomegranate juice
1 tablespoon pomegranate seeds

Moisten the rim of a martini glass with water. Dip the rim of the glass into the sugar to coat it lightly.

Combine the cognac, pomegranate syrup, lemon juice, and pomegranate juice in a cocktail shaker. Add ice and shake. Strain into the martini glass and garnish with the pomegranate seeds floating on top.

Blood Orange Margarita

Blood oranges lend a beautiful color and sweetness to this timeless cocktail. I like to use a silver or white tequila that has not been aged; however, you may substitute an añejo, or aged tequila, for a deeper more caramel flavor.

SERVES 1

2 ounces freshly squeezed blood orange juice
1½ ounces Sauza blanco tequila or other premium white tequila
1 ounce freshly squeezed lime juice
½ ounce Simple Syrup (page 314)
½ ounce triple sec
1 thin blood orange slice
3 to 4 small fresh mint leaves

Combine the blood orange juice, tequila, lime juice, simple syrup, and triple sec in a cocktail shaker. Add ice and shake. Pour into a highball glass and garnish with the slice of blood orange and the mint.

Blood Orange Margarita

Passion Fruit Punch

Passion fruits are deceptively flavorful; their dark exterior gives way to a brilliant orange jelly-like flesh that is incredibly tangy and peppered with little black seeds.

SERVES 1

½ passion fruit
2 ounces Bacardi light rum
1 ounce Kern's guava nectar
1 ounce passion fruit purée
1 ounce Simple Syrup (page 314)
½ ounce freshly squeezed lime juice

Scoop the flesh of the passion fruit into a cocktail shaker. Add the rum, guava nectar, passion fruit purée, simple syrup, and lime juice. Add ice and shake. Pour over fresh ice in a highball glass.

Kumquat Mojito

A mojito is a traditional Cuban highball made by muddling mint, sugar, and lime and topping it off with rum. While I love the traditional preparation, the addition of kumquats adds a lot of color and flavor.

SERVES 1

8 fresh mint leaves
5 kumquats, cut in half
1 ounce Simple Syrup (page 314)
2 ounces Bacardi light rum or other premium light rum
¼ ounce freshly squeezed lime juice
Club soda
1 fresh mint sprig

Muddle the mint leaves and kumquats with the simple syrup in a cocktail shaker. Add the rum and lime juice. Add ice and shake. Pour into a highball glass and top with a splash of soda. Garnish with the mint sprig.

Meyer Lemon 75

This cocktail is classic French 75 with the addition of Meyer lemon juice. The result is a sophisticated but simple cocktail with all the fragrance and flavor of Meyer lemons.

SERVES 1

Juice of 1 Meyer lemon
1 ounce Plymouth gin or other premium gin
1 ounce Simple Syrup (page 314)
Sparkling wine (Prosecco, cava, or Champagne)
Lemon twist

Combine the Meyer lemon juice, gin, and simple syrup in a cocktail shaker. Add ice and shake. Strain into a Champagne glass, top with a splash of sparkling wine, and garnish with the lemon twist.

Cauliflower & Rock Shrimp Risotto with White Truffles

Cauliflower is best in the winter when it's at its sweetest and has a nutty undertone. The silken texture and milky flavor of the cauliflower purée add so much creaminess to the risotto, while the pungent aroma of the truffles adds an earthen depth.

SERVES 6

Cauliflower Purée
2 pounds cauliflower
1 cup heavy cream
1 cup whole milk
2 fresh thyme sprigs
Sea salt and freshly ground black pepper

Truffle Sauce
¼ cup skim milk
1 teaspoon white truffle oil

Mushroom Duxelles
1 tablespoon extra virgin olive oil
1 cup mixed wild mushrooms
1 shallot, diced
1 garlic clove, finely chopped

Risotto
5 cups Chicken Stock (page 303) or Vegetable Stock (page 304)
4 tablespoons extra virgin olive oil
1 small onion, chopped
2 garlic cloves, finely chopped
2 cups Arborio rice
1 cup dry white wine
1 pound rock shrimp, peeled and deveined
½ cup grated Sartori Stravecchio cheese (or another domestic Parmesan cheese)
2 tablespoons finely chopped fresh chives
1 tablespoon white truffle oil

Shaved white truffle (optional)

Prepare the cauliflower purée ➤ Using a paring knife, trim enough of the cauliflower into 1½-inch florets to yield 3 cups of florets; set aside 3 florets for garnish. Reserve the remaining cauliflower.

Bring a small saucepan of salted water to a boil and add the 3 cups of florets. Cook until tender, about 2 minutes. Using a slotted spoon, immediately transfer the cauliflower to a bowl of ice water. Once cool, drain the cauliflower.

Roughly chop the reserved remaining cauliflower, including the stems, and place it in a medium saucepan. Add the heavy cream, milk, and thyme and simmer over low heat until the cauliflower is very tender, about 20 minutes. Remove the thyme and discard. Purée the cauliflower mixture in a blender or food processor fitted with a metal blade until smooth. Season to taste with salt and pepper.

Make the truffle sauce ➤ Combine ¼ cup of the cauliflower purée with the skim milk in a small saucepan over low heat. Add the truffle oil and simmer until slightly thickened, about 2 minutes.

Make the mushroom duxelles ➤ Heat the olive oil in a small sauté pan over medium heat. Add the mushrooms, shallot, and garlic and sauté until the mushrooms are golden brown and soft, about 5 minutes. Remove from the heat and allow the mixture to cool. Finely chop the mushrooms by hand or in a food processor fitted with a metal blade.

Make the risotto ➤ Warm the stock in a small saucepan. Heat 3 tablespoons of the olive oil in a medium saucepan over medium heat. Add the onion and garlic and sauté until the onion is translucent, about 5 minutes. Add the rice and stir to coat with the oil. Add the wine and lower the heat. Simmer until most of the wine has evaporated, about 5 minutes. Add 1 cup of the warm stock to the pan and cook, stirring constantly, until most of the stock is absorbed. Repeat the process with the remaining 4 cups of stock, making sure each addition of stock is fully absorbed before adding more.

Heat the remaining 1 tablespoon of olive oil in a medium sauté pan over medium heat. Add the shrimp and sauté until just pink and firm, about 1 minute. Season to taste with salt and pepper.

Fold the sautéed shrimp into the risotto. Gently stir in the steamed cauliflower florets, the remaining cauliflower purée, mushroom duxelles, cheese, chives, and truffle oil until well combined. Season to taste with salt and pepper.

continued

Sauté the florets ➤ Slice the reserved 3 florets in half. Heat a medium cast-iron pan over high heat. Once the pan is very hot, dry sauté the florets until charred but still firm, about 1 minute per side.

To serve ➤ Divide the risotto evenly among 6 bowls. Using a blender or immersion blender, blend the truffle sauce until it begins to foam. Spoon the sauce over the risotto and garnish with the sautéed florets and shaved truffle, if using. Serve the dish immediately.

Wine suggestion ➤ Serve this dish with a nutty, aromatic white wine made from Roussanne that offers flavors of honeycomb, lime zest, and a touch of hazelnut, such as Roussanne, "James Berry," Copain, 2006, Paso Robles, California.

WHITE TRUFFLES are the most decadent winter ingredient. The best white truffles are found in the countryside of northern Italy around the city of Alba and have sold for nearly $3,500 a pound. These "white diamonds" of food are not much to look at, resembling small lumpy potatoes or some sort of porous rock; however, once cut their fragrance is intoxicating. The flavor of the truffle mostly lies in its aroma, which has been described as mildly garlicky, earthy, and cheesy. The best place to find these prized specimens is buried in the ground amongst the root structure of trees in damp and wooded areas. Truffles were once hunted for by trained pigs; however, now most truffle hunters, or *trifulao*, use dogs instead.

Wild Boar Tagliatelle Carbonara

Wild boar provides an amazingly original alternative to pork. The sweet, rich, and nutty flavor is due to a natural diet of foraged grass, roots, nuts, and acorns. Wild boars are raised on ranches primarily in the southwestern states. We purchase our boar meat from a ranch in Texas, owned and operated solely by women.

SERVES 6

- 12 ounces pancetta, cut into ¼-inch-thick strips
- 6 ounces double-smoked bacon, cut into ¼-inch-thick strips
- 1 pound wild boar shoulder, coarsely ground
- 10 large white mushrooms, cleaned and finely diced
- ½ cup finely diced sweet onion
- 2 tablespoons finely chopped garlic
- Sea salt and freshly ground black pepper
- 1 cup grated Meadow Creek Grayson cheese + more for serving (or another washed-rind, semi-soft, pungent cow's-milk cheese, similar to a domestic Tallegio)
- 1 cup heavy cream
- 2 fresh duck eggs
- 2 pounds fresh tagliatelle pasta
- ½ cup roughly chopped fresh parsley

Heat a large sauté pan over medium heat. Add the pancetta and bacon and cook until the fat has rendered and the pancetta and bacon are crispy, about 5 minutes. Add the boar meat and sauté until golden brown, about 4 minutes. Add the mushrooms, onion, and garlic and sauté until the onion is translucent, about 3 minutes. Season the meat sauce to taste with salt and pepper.

Whisk the 1 cup of cheese with the heavy cream, eggs, and 1 teaspoon of black pepper in a small bowl; set the cream mixture aside until ready to use.

Meanwhile, bring a large pot of salted water to a boil. Add the tagliatelle and cook until al dente.

Drain the pasta and add it to the meat sauce. Next, stir in the cream mixture and the parsley. Fold the pasta into the sauce until well combined. The sauce will begin to thicken as the starch from the pasta is incorporated and the heat begins to cook the eggs and reduce the cream.

Divide the pasta among 6 dishes and serve immediately with additional grated cheese on the side.

Wine suggestion ➤ Serve this dish with a super–Tuscan–inspired red wine with flavors of black cherries, plums, and notes of baking spices, such as Llano Estacado, "Viviano," 2005, Texas Hill Country, Texas.

Pan-Seared Foie Gras & Late Harvest Chardonnay–Grapefruit Reduction

Late harvest wines are made with grapes that stay on the vine longer than usual. The result is a dramatic concentration of the grapes' natural sugars. These sweeter dessert wines complement the rich, buttery foie gras.

SERVES 6

Apple Purée

3 tablespoons unsalted butter
3 Granny Smith apples, peeled, cored, and thinly sliced
¾ cup dry white wine
3 tablespoons quince jelly or quince paste

Foie Gras and Reduction

6 pieces grade A foie gras, 4 ounces each
Sea salt and freshly ground black pepper
1 cup freshly squeezed grapefruit juice
½ cup late harvest Chardonnay
Zest of ½ orange
¼ teaspoon finely chopped fresh rosemary
1½ teaspoons unsalted butter

Brioche Toast

6 slices brioche, ½ inch thick

½ cup mâche (optional)

Make the apple purée ➤ Melt the butter in a medium sauté pan over medium heat. Once the butter begins to foam, add the apples, wine, and jelly. Cook until the apples are tender, about 5 minutes. Transfer the mixture into a blender and purée until smooth.

Sear the foie gras and make the reduction ➤ Place a large sauté pan over high heat. Using a paring a knife, gently score the foie gras slices in a diagonal pattern on 1 side. Season to taste with salt and pepper. Place 3 slices of foie gras in the pan and sear until golden brown, about 2 minutes. Reduce the heat, turn the foie gras over, and cook for an additional 2 minutes. Transfer the foie gras to a clean plate and set aside to rest. Wipe the pan clean and repeat the process with the remaining 3 slices of foie gras.

Pour the excess fat out of the pan, reserving 3 tablespoons of the pan drippings to add to the reduction, and deglaze the pan with the grapefruit juice, scraping up any browned bits with a wooden spoon; simmer to reduce the juice by half, about 2 minutes. Add the Chardonnay, orange zest, rosemary, and the reserved pan drippings and simmer to reduce for 1 minute. Add the butter and whisk until well combined. Season the reduction to taste with salt and pepper.

Toast the brioche ➤ Preheat the broiler. Using a 3-inch round cookie cutter, cut the brioche into rounds and place them on a baking sheet. Toast the brioche rounds under the broiler until golden brown, about 1 minute per side.

To serve ➤ Place the brioche toasts in the center of 6 serving plates. Lay the foie gras slices on top of the brioche. Spoon the apple purée around the foie gras, drizzle with the grapefruit reduction and scatter the mâche leaves over the top.

Wine suggestion ➤ Serve this dish with a Hudson Valley sweet wine made from Seyval that offers aromas of dried peaches and candied citrus, such as Seyval Late Harvest "Romance," Clinton Vineyards, 2006, Hudson Valley, New York.

HUDSON VALLEY FOIE GRAS provides some of the best foie gras in all of the United States and perhaps the world. Located in Ferndale, New York, just a few hours north of Manhattan, Hudson Valley Foie Gras specializes in Moulard duck foie gras. It also so happens to be co-owned and operated by a good friend of mine, Michael Ginor. Michael is a passionate epicure and organizes chef dinners around the globe; we met when I was participating in one several years ago, and we have since collaborated on many more.

Bluefin Tuna & Pickled Beets with Confit Kumquat Vinaigrette & Green Olive Tapenade

Kumquats are a variety of citrus that resemble a small oval orange. The entire fruit is edible, skin and all; however, the seeds can be quite bitter. Kumquats can be eaten raw or candied and are ripe when the skin has turned bright orange and lost any hint of green.

SERVES 6

Green Olive Tapenade
½ cup pitted green olives
1 tablespoon extra virgin olive oil
1 teaspoon freshly squeezed lemon juice
½ teaspoon lemon zest
½ teaspoon lime zest
½ teaspoon orange zest

Kumquat Vinaigrette
1 cup kumquats, thinly sliced and seeded
½ cup sugar
1 tablespoon freshly squeezed lemon juice
1 tablespoon freshly squeezed lime juice
1 tablespoon freshly squeezed orange juice
6 tablespoons extra virgin olive oil
Sea salt and freshly ground black pepper

Pickled Beets
1 cup rice vinegar
½ cup water
¼ cup sugar
1 bay leaf
1 fresh thyme sprig
1 garlic clove, halved
1 teaspoon coriander seeds
1 teaspoon whole black peppercorns
½ teaspoon sea salt
Pinch of dried hot red pepper flakes
1 large beet, peeled and thinly sliced on a mandolin

Tuna
1 pound sushi-grade bluefin tuna
⅓ cup small fresh basil leaves
1 tablespoon chopped fresh chives
1 tablespoon mustard oil

Make the tapenade ➤ Combine all of the ingredients in a food processor fitted with a metal blade and purée until it forms a paste.

Make the kumquat vinaigrette ➤ Bring a small saucepan of water to a boil over high heat. Add the kumquats and simmer for 2 minutes. Using a slotted spoon, transfer the kumquats to a strainer and run cold water over them to stop them from cooking. Repeat the process with the same kumquats 2 more times.

Bring the sugar and ½ cup of fresh water to a boil in another small saucepan. Continue to simmer over high heat until the mixture becomes syrupy, about 3 minutes. Add the kumquats and simmer over low heat until the kumquats begin to candy and their skins turn translucent, about 10 minutes. Pour the mixture into a medium bowl. Once the kumquats are cool enough to handle, remove them from the syrup and finely chop them. Return the chopped kumquats to the mixing bowl with the syrup and whisk in the lemon juice, lime juice, and orange juice. Gradually whisk in the olive oil to blend. Season to taste with salt and pepper.

Pickle the beets ➤ Combine all of the ingredients except the beets in a medium saucepan and bring to a boil over high heat. Continue to simmer for 5 minutes. Strain the liquid into a separate medium saucepan, discarding the solids. Add the sliced beets to the liquid and simmer over low heat until the beets are tender, about 5 minutes. Pour the mixture into a mixing bowl set over a bowl of ice water. Once cool, strain the beets and discard the liquid. Fold the beet slices in half and then in half once again so they form a triangular shape.

Slice and plate the tuna ➤ Cut the tuna into 2 rectangular 8-ounce pieces. Slice each piece of tuna into ¼-inch-thick slices. Arrange 4 to 6 tuna slices on each of 6 plates and season to taste with salt and pepper. Using a teaspoon, spoon the green olive tapenade onto the plates. Place 5 of the folded beets around the tuna and drizzle with the vinaigrette. Garnish with basil leaves, chives, and a drizzle of mustard oil.

Wine suggestion ➤ Serve this dish with a crisp and citrus-laden Pinot Grigio that offers flavors of orange zest and a touch of spice, such as Pinot Grigio, Terlato Family Vineyards, 2007, Russian River Valley.

Turnip Velouté & Roasted Hazelnuts & Shaved Turnips Tossed in Preserved Lemon

Preserved lemons are a mainstay of Moroccan and Middle Eastern cooking. They are basically just lemons that have been pickled in salt and their own juices. They can be chopped up and used in relishes, cooked in stews, or in a salad, as in this recipe.

SERVES 6

Velouté

4 tablespoons unsalted butter
1 medium onion, cut into a large dice
2 celery stalks, sliced ¼ inch thick
1 leek (white and light green parts only), sliced ¼ inch thick
3 garlic cloves, thinly sliced
2 pounds turnips, peeled and roughly chopped
1 bouquet garni (1 dark green leek leaf, 3 fresh thyme sprigs, 1 bay leaf; see page 305)
10 cups Chicken Stock (page 303)
1 teaspoon (about) sugar
Sea salt and freshly ground black pepper
2 cups heavy cream

Turnip Salad

3 tablespoons blanched hazelnuts
6 baby turnips, peeled and thinly sliced
2 tablespoons extra virgin olive oil
1 tablespoon chopped fresh parsley
1 tablespoon freshly squeezed lemon juice
1 teaspoon chopped preserved lemon rind

Make the velouté ➤ Melt the butter in a large saucepan over medium heat. Add the onion, celery, leek, and garlic and sauté until the onion and celery begin to soften, about 5 minutes. Add the turnips and bouquet garni and continue to cook until the turnips begin to release their juices, about 5 minutes. Add the stock and simmer until the turnips are tender, about 30 minutes. Season to taste with the sugar and salt and pepper. Discard the bouquet garni. Working in batches, purée the soup with the cream in a blender or food processor. Strain the velouté through a fine-mesh strainer into a clean medium sauté pan.

Make the baby turnip salad ➤ Preheat the oven to 350°F. Spread the hazelnuts on a baking sheet. Toast the nuts in the oven until light brown and fragrant, turning with a spatula every few minutes, about 10 minutes. When cool enough to handle, roughly chop the nuts.

Toss the sliced baby turnips with the olive oil, parsley, lemon juice, and chopped preserved lemon in a medium bowl. Season to taste with salt and pepper.

To serve ➤ Divide the turnip salad among 6 soup bowls and sprinkle with the toasted hazelnuts. Ladle the velouté over the top and serve.

Wine suggestion ➤ Serve this dish with a crisp and nutty sparkling wine that offers flavors of sweet apples, lemon zest, and roasted almonds, such as Gruet, "Blanc de Blancs," NV, Engle, New Mexico.

Baby Kale Salad with Lemon Fiscalini-Caper Dressing

The mild, almost fleshly, texture of kale is the perfect foil to the briny, bright, and rich dressing. If you are unable to find baby kale, use whole leaf spinach, but not the baby variety, as it will hold up to the dressing better.

SERVES 6

Dressing

1 cup grated Fiscalini San Joaquin Gold cheese (or another firm, nutty, easy-melting, aged cow's-milk cheese similar to an aged cheddar or a young Parmesan)
3 tablespoons freshly squeezed lemon juice
2 salt-packed anchovy fillets, rinsed and chopped
1 teaspoon finely chopped garlic
½ teaspoon dried hot red pepper flakes
⅓ cup extra virgin olive oil
2 tablespoons salt-packed capers, rinsed and chopped
Tabasco
Sea salt

Salad

3 bunches baby kale leaves (about 8 cups)
3 hard-cooked eggs (see page 306), peeled and chopped
2 tablespoons chopped fresh parsley

Make the dressing ➤ Using a spoon, mix the cheese, lemon juice, anchovies, garlic, and red pepper flakes in a medium bowl until smooth. Slowly add the olive oil, whisking with a fork until smooth. Add the capers and a dash of Tabasco. Adjust the seasoning to your taste, adding salt and more Tabasco as necessary.

To assemble and serve the salad ➤ Toss the baby kale with the dressing in a large bowl, making sure all the leaves are evenly dressed. Divide the kale among 6 plates and scatter the chopped egg and parsley over.

Wine suggestion ➤ Serve this dish with a Cal-Ital white wine made from Arneis that offers flavors of stone fruits, citrus, and tingling acidity, such as Arneis, Seghesio Family Vineyards, 2007, Alexander Valley, California.

Baked Gnocchi with Porcini, Gorgonzola, Prosciutto, Walnuts, & Sage

Rogue Creamery, nestled in the Rogue River Valley of Oregon, has ties to some of the oldest cheesemakers in the United States. They are very well known for their blue cheeses, in particular, and have won several international awards. Their Oregonzola is made in the style of a classic Italian Gorgonzola, which produces a cheese with sharp and tangy flavors and a rich buttery texture.

SERVES 6

Gnocchi

2 cups coarse sea salt
2 pounds russet potatoes (about 3 medium potatoes)
1 large egg
1 large egg yolk
2 tablespoons ricotta cheese
1½ cups (about) all-purpose flour
¼ cup grated Sartori Stravecchio cheese (or another domestic Parmesan cheese)
1 teaspoon sea salt + more to taste
¼ teaspoon freshly grated nutmeg
⅛ teaspoon freshly ground white pepper + more to taste

Sauce and Topping

6 tablespoons extra virgin olive oil
6 large fresh porcini mushrooms, quartered
3 tablespoons unsalted butter
2 ounces La Quercia prosciutto, cut into matchstick-size strips
3 tablespoons chopped walnuts
10 fresh sage leaves, thinly sliced
5 tablespoons panko (Japanese breadcrumbs)
2 tablespoons chopped fresh parsley
1 cup crumbled Rogue Creamery Oregonzola cheese (or other Gorgonzola-style cheese)

Make the gnocchi ➤ Preheat the oven to 375°F. Mound the 2 cups of coarse salt in the center of a baking sheet. Place the potatoes on top of the salt and bake until a knife easily pierces the center of the potato, about 1 hour. When cool enough to handle, peel the potatoes and pass them through a ricer or a food mill into a large bowl, or mash them thoroughly with a potato masher. Stir in the egg, egg yolk, and ricotta, then add 1 cup of the flour, the cheese, 1 teaspoon of the salt, the nutmeg, and ⅛ teaspoon of the white pepper. Mix well. If the dough is too sticky, add a little more of the remaining flour until the dough is easy enough to handle.

Divide the dough into 6 pieces. On a lightly floured surface, roll each piece into a ¾-inch-thick rope. Cut each rope into 1-inch pieces.

Oil a large rimmed baking sheet. Bring a large pot of salted water to a boil. Add one third of the gnocchi to the boiling water and cook until they float to the surface, about 2 minutes. Remove the gnocchi with a slotted spoon, draining them well, and spread them on the oiled baking sheet. Repeat cooking the remaining gnocchi. The gnocchi can be made up to 24 hours in advance, covered with plastic wrap, and refrigerated until ready to use.

Make the sauce ➤ Preheat the broiler. Heat 4 tablespoons of the olive oil in a large nonstick sauté pan over medium-high heat. Add the mushrooms and sauté until golden brown, about 3 minutes. Add the butter. Once the butter melts and begins to foam, add the cooked gnocchi, the prosciutto, walnuts, and sage and continue to sauté until the gnocchi begin to caramelize, making sure to stir constantly, about 2 minutes. Season to taste with salt and pepper, and spoon the mixture into a large ovenproof oval gratin dish.

Make the topping ➤ Toss the panko and chopped parsley with the remaining 2 tablespoons of olive oil. Evenly distribute the breadcrumb mixture over the gnocchi and scatter the Oregonzola cheese over the top. Broil until the cheese melts and the breadcrumbs brown, about 1 minute.

To serve ➤ Serve the gnocchi family style, in the center of the table, or spoon it onto individual serving plates while still hot.

Wine suggestion ➤ Serve this dish with a rich Pinot Gris that offers flavors of honeydew melon, citrus, and a touch of nuttiness, such as Pinot Gris Reserve, Chehalem, 2007, Willamette Valley, Oregon.

Diver Sea Scallops with Endive Marmalade & Caramelized Tangerine–Meyer Lemon Vinaigrette

Meyer lemons, a citrus native to China, are thought to be a hybrid of true lemon and Mandarin orange. They are a seasonal, sweet variety of lemons that are usually available from January through early spring.

SERVES 6

Endive Marmalade
1 tablespoon unsalted butter
2 endive heads, cored and thinly sliced
2 tablespoons sugar
1 tablespoon freshly squeezed lemon juice
Pinch of dried red pepper flakes

Scallops
1½ tablespoons unsalted butter
18 diver scallops, muscle removed
Sea salt and freshly ground black pepper
2 ounces paddlefish caviar (optional)

Vinaigrette
2 Meyer lemons, peeled and segmented
⅓ cup freshly squeezed tangerine juice
⅓ cup Sauternes wine
1 tablespoon cold unsalted butter

Make the endive marmalade ➤ Melt the butter in a medium sauté pan over medium heat. Add the endive and sauté until it begins to wilt, about 3 minutes. Add the sugar, lemon juice, and pepper flakes and continue to cook until the endive begins to caramelize, about 5 minutes.

Cook the scallops ➤ Heat ½ tablespoon of the butter in a large sauté pan over medium-high heat. Season the scallops with salt and pepper and place 6 of the scallops in the sauté pan. Sear until they begin to caramelize, about 3 minutes; turn the scallops over and cook for 1 minute more. Transfer the scallops to a warm plate and repeat the process 2 more times with the remaining butter and scallops.

Make the vinaigrette ➤ Add the Meyer lemon segments to the sauté pan that the scallops were seared in and cook until lightly browned, about 2 minutes. Deglaze the pan with the tangerine juice and simmer until reduced and slightly syrupy, about 2 minutes. Deglaze again with the Sauternes wine and simmer until the vinaigrette begins to thicken, about 3 minutes. Slowly whisk in the butter.

To serve ➤ Spoon the endive marmalade in the center of 6 plates. Place 3 scallops on top of the marmalade and drizzle with the vinaigrette. Garnish each scallop with a dollop of caviar, if using. Serve immediately.

Wine suggestion ➤ Serve this dish with an Rkatsiteli that offers flavors of exotic citrus fruit, ripe mangoes, and white flowers, such as Rkatsiteli, Dr. Konstantin Frank, 2006, Finger Lakes, New York.

CAVIAR, like most luxury products, has to fulfill certain requirements in order to brandish the name. Therefore, roe from any fish other than sturgeon has to be noted as such. Due to the massive overfishing of sturgeon, paddlefish, or spoonbill, caviar has been on the rise. Paddlefish is the preeminent variety of American caviar. The fish are generally found in the freshwater rivers of Louisiana and Tennessee. Despite its lower cost, paddlefish has a very buttery texture and fresh-from-the-sea flavor. The eggs are much smaller than sturgeon caviar and tend to range from dark grey to black in color.

Salad Fromage de Tête

The name *fromage de tête*, or head cheese, is misleading because it is in fact not a cheese, but rather a terrine of meat made from the head of a calf or pig or sometimes even a sheep or full-fledged cow. It may also include meat from the feet and is usually served cold or at room temperature and thinly sliced like American luncheon meat. This labor intensive dish is worth the effort, though you can also purchase *fromage de tête* at your local gourmet market and serve it with the salad and bread.

SERVES 6

Special Equipment
12⅔ × 4-inch terrine mold

Brine
1 pig head, ears and tongue intact, about 10 pounds
4 gallons warm water
2 garlic heads, halved
5 tablespoons pink salt
5 tablespoons sugar
2 tablespoons sea salt
2 tablespoons white wine vinegar
2 tablespoons whole black peppercorns
1 tablespoon juniper berries
1 fresh thyme bunch
4 bay leaves
1 teaspoon whole cloves

Head Cheese
1 veal foot, 2 pounds
2 teaspoons pink salt
1 teaspoon sea salt
4 gallons cold water
2 onions
8 whole cloves
3 carrots
3 celery stalks
2 leeks, halved lengthwise
6 fresh thyme sprigs
3 bay leaves
1 tablespoon whole black peppercorns
¼ teaspoon Four-Spice Mix (page 305)

Gelée
1¼ cups dry white wine
Sea salt and freshly ground black pepper
5 tablespoons chopped fresh curly parsley leaves, stems reserved

continued

Brine the pig head ➤ Rinse the head under gently running cold water for 2 hours. Combine all the remaining ingredients for the brine in a large container and bring to room temperature. Add the cleaned head; cover and refrigerate for 16 hours.

Make the head cheese ➤ Remove the head from the brine and place it in a large stock pot. Add the veal foot, pink salt, and sea salt and cover completely with the 4 gallons of cold water. Bring to a boil over medium-low heat, then reduce the heat so that the liquid simmers gently. Meanwhile, stud the onions with the whole cloves.

Using a ladle, skim off the foam that rises to the surface of the cooking liquid. When the water is clear and no more foam is rising to the surface, add the clove-studded onions, carrots, celery, leeks, thyme, bay leaves, black peppercorns, four-spice mix, and the reserved parsley stems (from gelée). Continue to gently simmer over medium-low heat until the meat on the pig head is beginning to pull away from the bone, about 4 hours.

Using a slotted spoon, remove the veal foot and pig head from the cooking liquid. Discard the veal foot. Remove and discard the excess fat from the head. Remove the meat from the head. Slice the meat into ¾-inch-thick slices and place it in a large bowl.

Make the gelée ➤ Place a fine-mesh strainer over a clean large saucepan and strain the cooking liquid into the saucepan. Place the saucepan over medium-high heat and simmer to reduce the liquid by half, about 2 hours. Add the wine and continue to cook until the liquid is reduced to 3 cups, about 1 hour. Season the gelée to taste with salt and pepper. Transfer to a bowl set over another bowl of ice and stir constantly to bring the gelée to room temperature. Once cool, stir in the chopped parsley.

Make the terrine ➤ Line a 12⅔ × 4-inch terrine mold with plastic wrap, allowing the wrap to overhang by 3 inches on each side. Place the picked meat in the terrine. Pour the gelée over the meat, pressing the meat firmly to compress and remove any air bubbles. Fold the ends of the plastic wrap over to seal the terrine and refrigerate until very cold and the gelée has set, about 24 hours.

Make the vinaigrette ➤ Whisk the vinegar and mustard in a small bowl to blend. Slowly whisk in the grapeseed oil until emulsified.

Vinaigrette
3 tablespoons red wine vinegar
2 tablespoons Dijon mustard
2 tablespoons grapeseed oil

Salad
½ onion, thinly sliced
6 cornichons, thinly sliced
3 tablespoons roughly chopped flat leaf parsley

12 slices (¼ inch thick) country bread, toasted

To serve ➤ Using a meat slicer, thinly slice half of the fromage de tête. The remaining half of the fromage de tête can be refrigerated for up to a week. Combine the sliced fromage de tête with the onion, cornichons, and parsley. Season to taste with salt and pepper and gently toss with the vinaigrette. Serve with the toasted country bread.

Wine suggestion ➤ Serve this dish with a dry rosé made from Pinot Noir that offers flavors of fresh strawberries, spice, and violets, such as Rosé of Pinot Noir, Soter, 2007, Willamette Valley, Oregon.

Country Duck Pâté

A pâté is perfect for a party because you can make it several days in advance. The flavors only get better when they have a day or two to mellow.

SERVES 6

Special Equipment
Meat grinder; 12⅔ × 4-inch terrine mold

Duck Marinade
¼ cup ruby port
1 tablespoon cognac
1 fresh thyme sprig
⅛ teaspoon Four-Spice Mix (page 305)
⅛ teaspoon freshly ground black pepper
⅛ teaspoon pink salt
Pinch of ground juniper berries
11 ounces foie gras, cut into 1-inch pieces
10 ounces boneless skinless duck breast, cut into ¼-inch-thick slices

Pork and Veal Marinade
1 pound pork shoulder, cut into 1-inch pieces
1 pound veal neck, cut into 1-inch pieces
¾ cup dry white wine
2 small shallots, thinly sliced
2 bay leaves
2 tablespoons chopped fresh curly parsley
1 tablespoon pink salt
1½ teaspoons cognac
1 teaspoon fresh leaves thyme
¾ teaspoon finely chopped garlic
¼ teaspoon Four-Spice Mix (page 305)
¼ teaspoon freshly ground black pepper

Chicken Livers
1 tablespoon extra virgin olive oil
7 ounces chicken livers
Sea salt and freshly ground black pepper
1 small shallot, finely diced
1 teaspoon fresh thyme leaves
2½ tablespoons cognac

Pâté
l large egg, beaten
5 tablespoons pistachios, toasted
1 tablespoon all-purpose flour
1½ pounds thinly sliced bacon

Accompaniments
Toasted sliced country bread, cornichons, pickled onions, and Dijon mustard

Marinate the duck ➤ The day before proceeding with the recipe, stir the port, cognac, thyme, four-spice mix, black pepper, pink salt, and juniper berries in a large bowl. Add the foie gras and duck to the marinade and refrigerate for at least 12 hours.

Marinate the pork and veal ➤ Combine the pork, veal, wine, shallots, bay leaves, parsley, pink salt, cognac, thyme, garlic, four-spice mix, and pepper in a large bowl. Cover and marinate in the refrigerator for 3 hours.

Prepare the chicken livers ➤ While the meats are marinating, heat the olive oil in a small sauté pan over medium-high heat. Season the chicken livers with salt and pepper and then sear them in the hot oil. Add the shallot and thyme. Deglaze the pan with the cognac and simmer until the livers are medium-rare, about 2 minutes. Scrape the liver mixture onto a large plate and cool completely.

Stir the cooled chicken liver mixture into the marinated veal and pork. Remove the bay leaves. Using a meat grinder fitted with the largest die, grind the meat mixture. Place the ground meat mixture in a large bowl and mix in the beaten egg, pistachios, flour, and salt to taste; mix until well incorporated. Refrigerate until ready to use.

Bake the pâté ➤ Preheat the oven to 350°F. Stir the marinated duck and foie gras into the ground meat mixture.

Line the bottom and the sides of a 12⅔ × 4-inch terrine mold with plastic wrap and then line the mold with the bacon slices, overlapping the edges of the bacon slightly and leaving a 3-inch overhang on the long sides. Gently spread the meat mixture over the bacon in the terrine. Using the plastic wrap, fold the overhanging bacon to cover the top completely. Then cover the terrine with a double layer of foil. Place the terrine in a large roasting pan and add enough hot water to the roasting pan to come halfway up the sides of the terrine. Bake until an instant-read thermometer inserted into the center of the pâté registers 155° to 160°F, about 1 hour. Remove the terrine from the water bath and let it cool completely on a rack. Refrigerate overnight.

To serve ➤ Leaving the pâté in the terrine, cut it into six 1-inch-thick slices and arrange the slices on a serving platter. Serve with the toasted sliced country bread, cornichons, pickled onions, and Dijon mustard. Any leftover pâté can be tightly wrapped and stored in the refrigerator for 1 week.

Wine suggestion ➤ Serve this dish with a French country-inspired dry rosé that offers flavors of fresh picked strawberries, pomegranate, and a hint of earthiness, such as Rosé, "Sanglier," Andrew Murray Vineyards, 2007, Santa Barbara County, California.

Widow's Hole Oyster & Caramelized Onion Pan Roast

Widow's Hole oysters started appearing on menus several years ago when a former computer programmer turned oyster farmer named Mike Osinski began to cultivate them in the Peconic Bay off Greenport in Long Island. They are so incredibly creamy and briny—they are perfect raw with a dash of Tabasco or gently cooked as in this pan roast. This recipe was created by my friend and fellow chef Bobby Flay. I decided to borrow it when we made it together on a television show.

SERVES 6

2 tablespoons extra virgin olive oil
1 tablespoon unsalted butter
3 Spanish onions, thinly sliced
3 garlic cloves, finely chopped
3 tablespoons sugar
2 medium Yukon Gold potatoes, skin on and cut into ½-inch dice
6 cups clam broth
3 dozen Widow's Hole oysters or other East Coast oysters, shucked
½ cup Vermont Butter Company crème fraîche
Sea salt and freshly ground black pepper
2 tablespoons finely chopped fresh tarragon

Heat the olive oil and butter in a medium saucepan over medium heat. Add the onions, garlic, and sugar and cook until onions begin to soften, stirring often and adding 1 tablespoon of water, if necessary, to ensure the onions do not begin to stick to the pan, about 15 minutes, Add 1 cup of water and reduce the heat to low. Cook the onions until they are completely caramelized and dark brown, stirring occasionally, about 45 minutes.

Meanwhile, place the potatoes in a medium saucepan filled with cold salted water. Bring to a boil over high heat and simmer until the potatoes are just cooked through, about 5 minutes. Drain the potatoes.

Add the clam broth to the onions and simmer for 5 minutes. Add the oysters and the potatoes to the onions and continue to simmer just until the oysters have cooked through, about 2 minutes. Carefully whisk in the crème fraîche and season to taste with salt and pepper. Remove from the heat and stir in the tarragon.

To serve ➤ Divide the soup among 6 soup bowls and serve immediately.

Wine suggestion ➤ Serve this dish with a Chardonnay from the North Fork of Long Island that offers classic apple and pear flavors, such as Chardonnay, "Old Vine," Lenz, 2007, North Fork Long Island, New York.

Broccolini Soup & Sartori Stravecchio Cookie

Broccolini is a cross between good old-fashioned broccoli and Chinese broccoli. The result is a unique vegetable that resembles asparagus in appearance, with long stalks topped by elegant buds. The flavor is quite sweet and delicate with only a hint of broccoli-bite. The entire vegetable, both stalk and bud, is edible. This recipe calls for a rather unexpected ingredient: store-bought onion soup mix. I admit, it's one of my guilty little secrets—the saltiness and straightforward onion flavor is hard to trump.

SERVES 6

Cookies

9 tablespoons grated Sartori Stravecchio cheese (or another domestic Parmesan cheese)
9 tablespoons unsalted butter, softened
½ cup all-purpose flour
2½ tablespoons store-bought powdered onion soup mix

Broccolini Soup

2 bunches broccolini
3 tablespoons unsalted butter
1 small onion, thinly sliced
1 leek (white and pale green parts only), thinly sliced
3 garlic cloves
Sea salt and freshly ground black pepper
3 Yukon Gold potatoes, peeled and cut into large dice
1 bouquet garni (1 dark green leek leaf, 4 fresh thyme sprigs, 1 bay leaf; see page 305)
½ cup dry white wine
6 cups Chicken Stock (page 303)
Pinch of freshly ground nutmeg
8 ounces grated Beecher's Flagship Reserve cheese (or another sharp white cheddar)
1 cup heavy cream

Make the cookies ➤ Preheat the oven to 350°F. Line a baking sheet with parchment paper. Combine all the ingredients in a stand mixer fitted with the paddle attachment. Mix at medium-low speed until it comes together to form a dough, about 1 minute. Wrap the dough in plastic wrap and let rest in the refrigerator for 30 minutes.

Using a rolling pin, roll out the dough on a lightly floured surface to a ⅛-inch-thick rectangle that is about 12 × 4 inches. Cut the rectangle into 2-inch squares and place them on the lined baking sheet. Refrigerate for 10 minutes and then bake until golden brown, about 8 minutes.

Make the soup ➤ Meanwhile, bring a large saucepan of salted water to a boil. Add the broccolini and cook until crisp-tender, about 2 minutes. Drain and immediately transfer the broccolini to a bowl of ice water. Once cool, remove the broccolini from the water and pat dry with a kitchen towel. Roughly chop.

Melt the butter in a large heavy saucepan over medium heat. Add the onion, leek, and garlic, Season to taste with salt and sauté the vegetables until translucent, about 3 minutes. Add the potatoes and cook 2 minutes. Add the bouquet garni and wine. Bring to a simmer and cook until the alcohol has evaporated, about 2 minutes. Add the chicken stock and nutmeg and simmer until the potatoes are tender, about 15 minutes. Season to taste with salt and pepper. Add the chopped broccolini and the grated cheese and stir until the cheese is well incorporated. Cook until the broccolini is tender, about 2 minutes. Add the heavy cream. Remove the pan from the heat and discard the bouquet garni. Using a blender and working in batches, blend the soup until smooth.

To serve ➤ Ladle the soup into 6 serving bowls and serve with the cookies on the side.

Wine suggestion ➤ Serve this dish with a sparkling white wine that offers aromas of ripe apples, hazelnuts, and a crisp, clean finish, such as Kluge SP, "Blanc de Blancs," 2004, Albemarle County, Virginia.

Indian Curry Braised Short Ribs with Cardoons & Lemongrass Sticky Rice

I learned to make this curry dish from an Indian chef when I was working in London in the mid-1980s. The flavor of the banana isn't pronounced but instead adds a bit of silken sweetness to the sauce. Cardoons, a winter delight, look like overgrown prickly celery stalks. They are related to artichokes and have a very similar sweet, nutty flavor.

SERVES 6

Short Ribs

6 beef short ribs, about 9 pounds total
Sea salt and freshly ground black pepper
6 tablespoons canola oil
3 tablespoons unsalted butter
2¼ cups diced white onion
2 fresh thyme sprigs
7 tablespoons madras curry powder, preferably Lalah's brand
3 tablespoons tandoori masala powder
3 green cardamom pods, crushed
2¼ cups diced peeled Golden Delicious apples
1½ cups diced tomatoes
1 cup diced peeled mango
½ cup diced banana
½ cup raisins
3 tablespoons purchased mango chutney
7½ cups Chicken Stock (page 303)
3 cups unsweetened coconut milk
2 tablespoons chopped fresh cilantro

Cardoons

1 large bunch cardoons
Juice of 2 lemons
3 tablespoons all-purpose flour
½ cup dry white wine

Lemongrass Sticky Rice

2 cups sushi rice, rinsed
2 cups unsweetened coconut milk
1½ cups water
5 kaffir lime leaves, torn
½ teaspoon salt
¼ teaspoon sugar
1 lemongrass stalk (3 inches), grated with a Microplane grater

Prepare the short ribs ➤ Preheat the oven to 325°F. Cut the short ribs into 2 to 3 pieces, depending on how large they are, and season generously with salt and pepper. Heat the oil in a large sauté pan until nearly smoking. Sear the ribs in the oil until dark brown on all sides, about 15 minutes.

Heat a large Dutch oven over medium heat. Melt the butter in the Dutch oven. Add the onions and thyme and sauté until the onions are translucent, about 8 minutes. Add the curry powder, masala powder, and the cardamom and sauté until fragrant, about 2 minutes. Add the apple, tomatoes, mango, banana, raisins, and mango chutney. Sauté until beginning to soften, about 3 minutes. Add the chicken stock and coconut milk. Bring to a simmer and add the short ribs. Cover with a lid or aluminum foil and place in the oven. Braise the ribs in the oven until the meat is very tender, about 2½ hours.

Cook the cardoons ➤ Cut the cardoons lengthwise to separate into individual stalks and remove all the leaves and any soft, wilted, or hollow stalks. Using a paring knife, pull off the tough strings that run the length of the cardoon. Peel off the tough film on the inside of each stalk. Cut the cardoons into 2-inch pieces and place them in a bowl of cold water; add the lemon juice.

Bring a large saucepan of salted water to boil. Sift the flour into the boiling water and then add the wine. Drain the cardoons from the lemon water and place them in the boiling water. Cook until tender, about 3 minutes. Drain and set aside.

Make the rice ➤ Place all the ingredients in a rice cooker, reserving 1 tablespoon of lemongrass, and cook according to the manufacturer's instructions. Once the rice is cooked, stir in the reserved lemongrass.

Finish the ribs and serve ➤ Using a slotted spoon, remove the ribs from the braising liquid. Place the Dutch oven over medium heat and simmer to reduce the liquid to a sauce-like consistency, skimming off the excess fat as it reduces, about 3 minutes. Return the short ribs to the sauce and nestle the cardoons around the ribs. Sprinkle with the chopped cilantro and serve with the rice.

Wine suggestion ➤ Serve this dish with an exotically aromatic Zinfandel that offers flavors of stewed cherries, violets, and fresh herbs, such as Zinfandel, Elyse, 2005, Howell Mountain, California.

Pistachio-Crusted Venison with Caramelized Quince & Red Cabbage

Some of the best venison comes from farm-raised Red Deer, which are larger than other deer breeds and related to the American elk. The flavor of venison is less assertive than lamb but more distinctive than beef.

SERVES 6

Venison

1 tablespoon fennel seeds
1 tablespoon juniper berries
½ teaspoon whole allspice
½ teaspoon whole black peppercorns
1 fresh rosemary sprig
6 double-cut venison rib chops, 12 ounces each
3 tablespoons canola oil
¼ cup honey
2 cups chopped pistachios

Cabbage

1 small head red cabbage, quartered and cored
1 medium red beet
½ cup red wine vinegar
¼ cup sugar
5 tablespoons butter
1 small onion, thinly sliced
1 bouquet garni (1 dark green leek leaf, 4 fresh thyme sprigs, 2 fresh rosemary sprigs, 1 bay leaf; see page 305)
½ cup freshly squeezed orange juice
½ cup dry red wine, preferably Cabernet Sauvignon
Sea salt and freshly ground black pepper

Caramelized Quince

2 tablespoons canola oil
2 quince, peeled, cored, and cut into 6 wedges each
2 tablespoons sugar
¼ cup brandy

Sauce

1 tablespoon unsalted butter
2 tablespoons finely diced shallots
½ teaspoon chopped fresh rosemary
½ cup dry red wine
¼ cup ruby port
½ cup freshly squeezed orange juice

Season the venison ➤ Combine the fennel seeds, juniper berries, allspice, and peppercorns in a sauté pan over medium heat. Toast the spices until fragrant, about 1 minute, and then transfer to a spice grinder. Add the rosemary and process until fine ly ground. Season the venison chops evenly with the spice blend. Cover with plastic wrap and refrigerate for 2 hours. The venison should be at room temperature when you cook it, so remove it from the refrigerator at least 30 minutes prior to cooking.

Prepare the cabbage ➤ Slice the cabbage into ¼-inch-wide ribbons and place in a large bowl. Peel the beet and grate it on the large holes of a box grater. Add the grated beet, vinegar, and sugar to the cabbage and mix until well combined. Set aside for 30 minutes.

Melt 3 tablespoons of the butter in a large deep sauté pan over medium heat. Add the onion and sauté until golden brown, about 5 minutes. Add the marinated cabbage mixture and bouquet garni and cook for 10 minutes. Add the orange juice and wine and simmer until the cabbage is tender and the liquid has reduced by half, about 15 minutes. Season to taste with salt and pepper and stir in the remaining 2 tablespoons of butter.

Caramelize the quince ➤ Heat the canola oil in a large sauté pan over high heat. Combine the quince and sugar in a medium bowl and toss to coat. Immediately add the quince to the pan and sear for 2 minutes. Reduce the heat to medium and cook until the quince is evenly browned. about 2 minutes. Pour out any excess oil.

With the pan off the heat, deglaze with the brandy, being careful as it might flame. Add 1 tablespoon of water and swirl the pan to evenly glaze the quince.

Cook the venison ➤ Preheat the oven to 350°F. Wrap the venison bones with aluminum foil to keep them from burning and season the meat with salt. Heat the oil in a very large ovenproof sauté pan over high heat. Sear the venison until brown on all sides, about 1 minute per side. Roast the venison in the oven until cooked to medium-rare doneness, about 8 minutes. To test for doneness, insert an instant-read thermometer into the thickest section of the chop. For medium-rare doneness the temperature reading should be 140° to 150°F. Remove the venison from the pan, reserving the pan for later use.

Brush the venison with the honey and roll in the pistachios to coat. Place the venison chops on a platter and tent with aluminum foil to keep warm.

continued

Make the sauce ➤ Melt the butter in the reserved sauté pan over medium heat. Add the shallots and rosemary and cook until the shallots are tender but not brown, about 2 minutes. Deglaze with the wine and port, scraping up any browned bits from the bottom of the pan to incorporate into the sauce, and simmer until the alcohol has evaporated, about 1 minute. Add the orange juice and cook until the sauce begins to thicken, about 2 minutes.

To serve ➤ Spoon the cabbage onto a large platter. Arrange the venison chops over the cabbage and nestle the caramelized quince next to the venison. Spoon the sauce over and serve immediately.

Wine suggestion ➤ Serve this dish with a plumy Merlot that offers flavors red currants, spice, and velvety tannins. Such as Merlot, Bravante, 2005, Howell Mountain, California.

Roasted Guinea Hens with Chestnut, Porcini, Fingerling Potatoes, & Sausage

This recipe is based on one that my great grandmother would make in her hulking charcoal oven. She almost always roasted guinea hens but this recipe is well-suited for poussin, turkey, Amish chickens, pheasant, or whatever type of fowl you fancy.

SERVES 6

Hens and Vegetables

1½ pounds fingerling potatoes, cut into ¼-inch-thick slices
1 small celery root, peeled and cut into large dice
1 small onion, cut into large dice
1 large carrot, cut into large dice
2 medium shallots, cut into large dice
4 garlic cloves
3 bay leaves
2 tablespoons chopped fresh rosemary
2 tablespoons fresh sage leaves
¼ cup extra virgin olive oil
Sea salt and freshly ground black pepper
3 large guinea hens, 2½ to 3 pounds each
3 cups Chestnut-Sausage Stuffing (page 194; half of the recipe)
3 tablespoons unsalted butter
½ pound fresh porcini mushrooms, cut into ½-inch-thick slices

Jus

½ cup dry white wine
1½ cups Chicken Stock (page 303)
2 tablespoons unsalted butter

Prepare the hens and vegetables ➤ Preheat the oven to 425°F. Oil a large roasting pan. Toss the potatoes, celery root, onion, carrot, shallots, garlic, bay leaves, rosemary, and sage with the olive oil in a large bowl. Season with salt and pepper and arrange the vegetables in the center of the prepared pan.

Stuff the cavity of each hen with 1 cup of the stuffing and then truss the hens using kitchen twine. Brush the hens with the 3 tablespoons of butter, season with salt and pepper, and arrange the hens on top of the vegetables.

Roast the hens, basting occasionally with the pan juices and rotating every 15 minutes, until the skin is golden brown and crisp and the juices run clear when the hen is pierced with a knife at the joint of the leg, about 50 minutes. Transfer to a cutting board and cover loosely with foil to keep warm.

Turn the broiler to high. Add the porcini mushrooms to the roasted vegetables in the pan and toss together. Place the pan under the broiler and cook until the vegetables are well browned and tender, stirring and turning the vegetables over once or twice as they broil, about 5 minutes. Using a slotted spoon, transfer the vegetables to a large serving platter.

Make the jus ➤ Spoon any excess fat off the top of the juices in the roasting pan. Place the pan on the stove over medium heat, add the wine, and simmer to reduce the liquid by half. Add the stock and bring to a boil, scraping up browned bits from the bottom of the pan and stirring them into the sauce. Simmer until the sauce is reduced to 1 cup, about 10 minutes. Remove the pan from heat and whisk in the butter. Pour the jus into a gravy bowl.

To serve ➤ Carve the hens into quarters. Remove the stuffing from the cavities and place it in a serving bowl. Arrange the hens on top of the vegetables and serve with the jus and stuffing on the side.

Wine suggestion ➤ Serve this dish with juicy, smoky Grenache that offers flavors of plums, cherry pie, and a touch of cocoa, such as Grenache, Edward Sellers, 2005, Paso Robles, California.

Roasted Berkshire Pork Tenderloin with Caramelized Salsify, Apple, Brussels Sprouts, & Apple Cider Jus

Berkshire pigs are renowned for their tender, flavorful, and juicy meat. The name is derived from Berkshire County in the United Kingdom, where this breed dates back nearly four hundred years. They have been carefully cultivated in America since the late 1800s.

SERVES 6

Caramelized Vegetables and Apples

Juice of 1 lemon
½ pound salsify, peeled and cut into 1½-inch pieces
1 pound Brussels sprouts, trimmed and halved
3 tablespoons unsalted butter
2 Granny Smith apples, peeled, cored, and each cut into 6 wedges
1 teaspoon sugar
1 cup pearl onions, peeled and halved
3 garlic cloves, smashed
3 fresh thyme sprigs
2 cups apple cider
1 tablespoon cider vinegar

Pork

2 tablespoons fennel seeds
2 tablespoons juniper berries
2 tablespoons whole black peppercorns
1 teaspoon whole allspice
1 tablespoon mustard seeds
3 pork tenderloins, 1 pound each, cut in half crosswise
Sea salt and freshly ground black pepper
3 tablespoons grapeseed oil

Prepare the vegetables ➤ Bring a medium saucepan of salted water to a boil and add the lemon juice. Add the salsify and cook until tender, about 5 minutes. Immediately transfer the salsify to a bowl of ice water. Once cool, drain and pat dry.

Bring another saucepan of salted water to a boil and cook the Brussels sprouts until tender, about 3 minutes. Immediately transfer the Brussels sprouts to a bowl of ice water. Once cool, drain and pat dry.

Prepare the pork ➤ Preheat the oven to 350°F. Place the fennel seeds, juniper berries, black peppercorns, allspice, and mustard seeds in a small sauté pan over medium heat and toast until fragrant, about 1 minute. Once toasted, transfer the spices to a spice grinder and coarsely grind.

Season the pork with salt and the spice mixture. Heat the oil in a large cast-iron pan over high heat. Sear the tenderloins on all sides, about 1 minute on each side. Transfer the tenderloins to a plate.

Caramelize the vegetables and apples ➤ Melt 2 tablespoons of the butter in the cast-iron pan over high heat. Add the apples and sugar and cook until the apples begin to caramelize, about 2 minutes. Using a slotted spoon, transfer the apples to a plate.

Melt the remaining 1 tablespoon of butter in the same pan and add the pearl onions, garlic, and thyme and sauté for 1 minute. Add the blanched salsify and Brussels sprouts and cook until lightly browned, about 3 minutes. Deglaze with the apple cider and vinegar, scraping up any brown bits from the bottom of the pan. Return the apples to the pan.

Finish cooking the pork ➤ Arrange the pork on top of the vegetables and apples. Roast until an instant-read thermometer inserted into the pork registers 160°F, about 8 minutes. Allow the pork to rest for 3 to 4 minutes before slicing.

To serve ➤ Divide the vegetables and apples among 6 plates. Slice the tenderloins and arrange them on top. Spoon the pan juices around the pork and serve.

Wine suggestion ➤ Serve this dish with a rich and creamy Chardonnay that offers flavors of golden apples, pain grille, and mouth-watering acidity, such as Chardonnay, Patz and Hall, 2006, Russian River Valley, California.

Breaded Partridge à la Kiev with Sage-Garlic Butter & Swiss Chard

The name *à la Kiev* would generally lead one to believe that this dish comes from the Russian town of Kiev. However it was actually created by a Frenchman in the late eighteenth century. During that era, French food was in demand among the Russian aristocracy so the dish became widely associated with Russians and eventually took on the name Chicken or Partridge à la Kiev. If you are unable to find partridge, make this recipe with small organic chicken breasts instead.

SERVES 6

Partridge

6 Scottish partridges, about 8 to 10 ounces each
2 heads roasted garlic (see page 306)
10 tablespoons unsalted butter, softened
2 tablespoons chopped fresh parsley
1 tablespoon chopped fresh sage
2 teaspoons fresh thyme
1 teaspoon finely diced shallots
Sea salt and freshly ground black pepper
2 cups all-purpose flour
4 large eggs
3 cups panko (Japanese breadcrumbs)
1 tablespoon chopped fresh chives
¼ teaspoon cayenne pepper
1½ cups canola oil
½ lemon
6 fresh sage leaves, for garnish

Swiss Chard

2 bunches Swiss chard, leaves only
2 tablespoons extra virgin olive oil
½ cup diced onion
1 tablespoon finely chopped garlic
1 tablespoon fresh thyme
Pinch of dried hot red pepper flakes
3 tablespoons unsalted butter

Prepare the partridge ➤ Remove the breasts in 2 pieces from the partridge. Save the carcasses for stock or another use. Using a paring knife, carefully make a horizontal incision into the thickest part of each breast, moving the knife gently back and forth to form a small pocket and being careful not to cut entirely through the other side. Cover with plastic wrap and refrigerate.

Squeeze the heads of garlic into a mixing bowl, releasing the cloves, and discard the skin. Mix in the butter, 1 tablespoon of the parsley, the sage, thyme, and shallots until well combined. Transfer to a piping bag fitted with a fine tip.

Preheat the oven to 350°F. Remove the partridge from the refrigerator and season with salt and pepper. Pipe the butter into the opening of each breast, being careful not to overfill. Place the breasts back in the refrigerator for 15 minutes.

Scatter the flour in a large shallow bowl. Beat the eggs in another bowl with 1 tablespoon of water. Place the panko in a food processor and process until finely ground. Transfer the panko to a shallow bowl and stir in the remaining 1 tablespoon of parsley, the chives, and cayenne pepper until well incorporated. Season to taste with salt and pepper.

Working with 1 partridge breast at a time, dredge the partridge breast in the flour, shaking off any excess. Dip the breast in the egg wash and then immediately into the breadcrumb mixture, pressing to ensure the entire breast is well coated. Place the coated breasts on a baking sheet and refrigerate uncovered for 10 minutes to allow the breading to adhere.

Heat a sauté pan over medium-high heat. Add the canola oil and shallow-fry the partridge breasts, 6 at a time, until golden brown, about 1 minute on each side. Transfer the partridge breasts to a baking sheet and bake for 5 minutes. Remove from the oven and place on a baking sheet lined with paper towels to absorb any excess oil.

Cook the Swiss chard ➤ Meanwhile, bring a large saucepan of salted water to a boil. Add the Swiss chard leaves and cook for 2 minutes. Immediately transfer the chard to a bowl of ice water. Once cool, drain the Swiss chard, squeezing any excess water, and roughly chop it.

Heat the olive oil in a sauté pan over medium heat. Add the onion and garlic and cook until tender, about 2 minutes. Add the thyme and red pepper flakes and cook for 1 minute. Add the chard and cook until heated through and all the excess

water has cooked off, about 2 minutes. Add the butter and continue to stir until it has been completely absorbed. Season to taste with salt and pepper.

To serve ➤ Spoon the Swiss chard in the center of a large platter. Arrange the partridge breasts over the Swiss chard. Squeeze the juice of the lemon over the top, garnish with sea salt and the sage leaves.

Wine suggestion ➤ Serve this dish with a Pinot Noir that offers flavors of fraises de bois, raspberries, and a hint of forest floor, such as Pinot Noir, Flowers, 2006, Sonoma Coast, California.

Stuffed Chicken with Mushroom Jus & Grilled Endive

Portobellos are such underrated mushrooms, perhaps because they are generally relegated to some standby vegetarian plate. I love to stuff them with cheese and serve them as a hearty side dish or as here, part of both the stuffing and the jus.

SERVES 6

Mushroom Stuffing

3 small portobello mushroom caps, stemmed and dark gills removed
1 tablespoon unsalted butter
1 small shallot, finely diced
1 teaspoon finely chopped garlic
3 tablespoons Vermont Butter and Cheese Company crème fraîche
Sea salt and freshly ground black pepper
1¼ cups Homemade Boursin (page 30) or store-bought Boursin

Chicken

1 whole organic chicken, 4½ to 5 pounds
2 tablespoons unsalted butter, cut into small pieces
¼ cup dry white wine

Grilled Endive

6 medium Belgian endives, cut in half lengthwise
4 tablespoons extra virgin olive oil
12 pancetta or bacon slices

Make the mushroom stuffing ➤ Using a food processor fitted with the metal blade, finely chop the mushrooms with 1 cup of water. Transfer the mushrooms and water into a strainer lined with cheesecloth and set over a bowl. Squeeze all of the mushroom water into the bowl, reserving the mushrooms and the water separately.

Melt the butter in small sauté pan over medium heat until foaming. Add the shallot and garlic and cook until translucent. Add the chopped mushrooms and cook until they release all of their liquid, about 3 minutes. Add the crème fraîche and bring to a simmer. Season to taste with salt and pepper. Transfer to a medium bowl and refrigerate to cool completely. Once cool, stir in the Boursin.

Roast the chicken ➤ Preheat the oven to 375°F. Place the chicken upside down on a work surface. Make a 2-inch incision in the skin along the backbone running between the thighs. Using the handle of a wooden spoon or the back of a fork, loosen the skin between the thighs and breast. Gently spread the stuffing under the skin of the thighs and breasts. Place the chicken in a roasting pan, breast side up, and season with salt and pepper. Scatter the pieces of butter evenly over the top of the chicken.

Roast the chicken until the skin is golden brown and crisp and the juices run clear when the chicken is pierced with a knife at the joint of the leg, about 1 hour. To check for doneness, insert an instant-read thermometer in the thickest part of the thigh, making sure it does not touch the bone. The temperature reading should be 165° to 175°F. Transfer the chicken to a platter.

Grill the endive ➤ While the chicken is roasting, heat a grill pan over medium heat. Brush the endives with olive oil, season with salt and pepper, and wrap with the pancetta. Grill on all sides until the pancetta is crisp and the endive has softened, about 2 minutes per side.

Make the jus ➤ Pour the juices and pan drippings from the roasting pan into a bowl and reserve. Place the roasting pan over low heat and add the wine. Using a wooden spoon, scrape up any browned bits on the bottom of the pan and stir them into the wine. Simmer until the wine is almost dry, about 1 minute. Add the reserved mushroom water and simmer to reduce the liquid to ½ cup. Whisk in the reserved pan juices and drippings. Transfer to a sauce boat.

To serve ➤ Cut the chicken into 8 pieces by gently pulling the legs away from the body and cutting the leg and the thigh off in 1 piece. Cut the leg and the thigh apart at the joint and repeat the process for the other leg. Cut the breasts away from the

main breast bone, scraping the breast meat away from the bone with the knife. Cut each breast in half. Serve with the jus and grilled endive on the side.

Wine suggestion ➤ Serve this dish with an earthy Marsanne that offers aromas of heirloom apples, quince, and gunflint, such as Marsanne, Qupe, 2005, Santa Ynez Valley, California.

Beef Shank Stew with Celery Root, Turnips, Rutabaga, Parsnips, & Fingerling Potatoes

In the past I have invited friends over to trim the Christmas tree and served this rich warm stew. The shanks can be braised a day or two in advance and the flavors will develop even more during that time. Bring the stew up to simmer and add the cut vegetables an hour before you want to serve.

SERVES 6

Beef Shank Marinade

8 cups dry red wine, preferably Cabernet Sauvignon
2 cups ruby port
2 small onions, thinly sliced
1 garlic head, halved crosswise
3 fresh thyme sprigs
1 bay leaf
1½ teaspoons salt
½ teaspoon whole black peppercorns
2 beef shanks, top and bottoms trimmed, about 8 pounds each

Stew

Sea salt and freshly ground black pepper
¼ cup vegetable oil
4 tablespoons unsalted butter
2 tablespoons all-purpose flour
2 tablespoons tomato paste
8 cups Veal Stock (page 304)
1 bouquet garni (1 dark green leek leaf, 4 fresh sage leaves, 4 fresh thyme sprigs, 2 fresh rosemary sprigs, 2 bay leaves; see page 305)
1 small celery root, peeled and cut into 6 wedges
2 medium turnips, peeled and cut into 12 wedges total
1 rutabaga, peeled and cut into 12 wedges
2 parsnips, peeled and cut into 1½-inch pieces
6 fingerling potatoes, halved on the bias

Caper-Tarragon Brown Butter

3 tablespoons unsalted butter
1 tablespoon finely chopped garlic
1 tablespoon salt-packed capers, rinsed and drained
1 tablespoon chopped fresh tarragon

Marinate the beef shanks ➤ Combine the wine, port, onions, garlic, thyme, bay leaf, salt, and peppercorns in a large nonreactive container. Add the beef shanks, cover, and refrigerate for at least 6 hours or overnight.

Make the stew ➤ Preheat the oven to 350°F. Remove the beef shanks from the marinade and reserve both the solids and liquid from the marinade separately. Blot any excess moisture from the shanks and season with salt and pepper. Heat the oil in a large Dutch oven over medium-high heat. Once the oil is nearly smoking, sear the beef shanks evenly on all sides, about 6 minutes per side. Transfer the beef shanks to a plate. Drain the excess fat from the Dutch oven. Add the butter and the reserved solids from the marinade and cook until lightly caramelized, about 3 minutes. Add the flour and tomato paste and cook until the paste has browned, about 2 minutes. Add the reserved liquid from the marinade and bring to a boil. Simmer for 5 minutes. Add the veal stock and bouquet garni and bring back to a boil. Place the shanks in the simmering liquid.

Cover the Dutch oven loosely with foil and place it in the oven. Braise until the beef is very tender, about 3½ hours. Add the celery root, turnips, rutabaga, parsnips, and potatoes. Cook until the vegetables are tender and easily pierced with a fork, about 45 minutes.

Gently remove the beef shanks and vegetables from the Dutch oven. By this point the meat will be just falling off the bone. Strain the braising liquid through a fine-mesh strainer into a clean large saucepan. Bring the liquid to a simmer. Skim the fat from the surface and simmer until the sauce is thick, rich, and glossy, about 15 minutes. Season the sauce to taste with salt and pepper. Return the meat and vegetables to the sauce, basting with the sauce to reheat.

Make the caper-tarragon brown butter ➤ Heat the butter and garlic in a small saucepan over medium heat, swirling the pan until the garlic is golden and the butter is just beginning to brown, about 2 minutes. Add the capers and cook 2 minutes, making sure the butter does not burn. Remove from the heat and stir in the tarragon.

To serve ➤ Transfer the stew to a large serving bowl and drizzle the caper-tarragon brown butter over the stew. Serve immediately.

Wine suggestion ➤ Serve this dish with a rustic Cabernet Sauvignon that offers flavors of crème de cassis, pencil shavings, and cedar, such as Cabernet Sauvignon, Forman, 2005, Napa Valley, California.

Hachis Parmentier of Braised Oxtail with Cabernet Franc

The name of this incredibly rich dish comes from a famous French army pharmacist by the name of Antoine-Augustin Parmentier, who lobbied in the early 1800s for acceptance of the potato as suitable for human consumption; until that point, the potato was widely regarded as poisonous.

SERVES 6

Oxtail

¼ cup grapeseed oil
8 pounds oxtail, cut into 3-inch-thick pieces, each piece tied with kitchen string
Sea salt and freshly ground black pepper
8 ounces double-smoked bacon, cut into ¼-inch-thick pieces
1 large sweet onion, roughly chopped
3 cups roughly chopped peeled celery root
2 carrots, roughly chopped
12 white mushrooms, quartered
7 garlic cloves
3 tablespoons tomato paste
1 cup red wine vinegar
1 bottle (750 ml) Cabernet Franc
8 cups Chicken Stock (page 303)
4 cups Veal Stock (page 304)
10 fresh thyme sprigs
3 fresh rosemary sprigs
2 bay leaves
1 tablespoon whole black peppercorns

Roasted Garlic Potatoes

2 pounds russet potatoes, scrubbed
1 head roasted garlic (see page 306)
6 tablespoons unsalted butter, cold + 1 tablespoon melted butter
1 cup grated Sartori Stravecchio cheese (or another domestic Parmesan cheese)
¾ cup warm whole milk
2 large eggs
2 tablespoons chopped fresh chives

Vegetables

¼ pound bacon, cut into ¼-inch-wide pieces
1 cup white pearl onions, peeled and halved
8 white mushrooms, quartered
3 tablespoons sliced garlic
1 carrot, cut into ½-inch dice
2 cups ½-inch-thick slices of celery root

Prepare the oxtail ➤ Preheat the oven to 300°F. Heat the grapeseed oil in a roasting pan over medium-high heat. While the oil is heating, season the oxtail generously with salt and pepper. Once the oil is nearly smoking, sear the oxtail until golden brown on all sides, about 4 minutes on each side. Remove the oxtail from the pan and discard the oil, wiping the pan clean with paper towels.

Place the roasting pan over medium heat. Add the bacon and cook until crisp, about 5 minutes. Add the onion, celery root, carrots, mushrooms, and garlic and sauté until caramelized, about 2 minutes. Add the tomato paste and continue to cook for 3 minutes. Deglaze the pan with the red wine vinegar, scraping up any browned bits and stirring them into the vegetables. Simmer until the liquid has completely evaporated, about 3 minutes. Once the vinegar has cooked off, add the wine and simmer to reduce by half, about 10 minutes. Add the chicken stock, veal stock, thyme, rosemary, bay leaves, and peppercorns and stir until well combined. Add the seared oxtail and bring to a boil. Cover the pan with aluminum foil and braise in the oven until fork tender, about 4 hours.

Remove the oxtail from the roasting pan and set it aside until cool enough to handle. Strain the braising liquid through a fine-mesh strainer into a clean saucepan. Simmer the liquid over medium heat until reduced by half, skimming the fat off the surface with a ladle, about 10 minutes. Remove the pan from the heat. Using your hands, remove the meat from the oxtail bones and add it to the sauce.

Make the roasted garlic potatoes ➤ Increase the temperature of the oven to 375°F. Bake the potatoes until tender when pierced with a fork, about 1 hour. Once cool enough to handle, peel the potatoes. Pass the potatoes through a ricer. Add the roasted garlic cloves and cold butter and mash to combine. Stir in the cheese, warm milk, eggs, and chives. Season to taste with salt and pepper. Maintain the oven temperature.

Cook the vegetables ➤ Render the bacon in a large saucepan over medium heat until crisp, about 5 minutes. Add the onions and cook until caramelized, about 5 minutes. Add the mushrooms and sliced garlic and continue to sauté until fragrant, about 1 minute. Add the carrot and celery root and cook until the mushrooms have released their liquid, about 2 minutes. Add the braising liquid and meat to the vegetables and simmer until the all the vegetables are tender, about 4 minutes. Season to taste with salt and pepper and transfer to a 5-quart baking dish.

To serve ➤ Using a pastry bag fitted with a star tip, pipe the mashed potatoes over the top of the oxtail mixture. Brush the potatoes with the melted butter and bake until golden brown, about 15 minutes, and serve.

Wine suggestion ➤ Serve this dish with a smoky Cabernet Franc that offers aromas of red currants, blackberries, and cloves, such as Cabernet Franc, Tamarack Cellars, 2005, Columbia Valley, Washington.

Crispy Red Snapper with Braised Cabbage & Orange Polenta

The trick to getting a nice crispy skin on the fish is to make sure your oil is good and hot before placing the fish in the pan. I like to serve this dish with a salad of shaved fennel, simply dressed with lemon juice and olive oil, on the side.

SERVES 6

Cabbage

1 small head Savoy cabbage, quartered and cored
4 tablespoons unsalted butter
1 onion, cut into medium dice
2 celery stalks, cut into small dice
1 carrot, cut into medium dice
¼ cup Chicken Stock (page 303)
Sea salt and freshly ground black pepper

Tomato Emulsion

4 cups freshly squeezed orange juice
1 cup fresh or canned tomato juice
½ cup heavy cream
3 tablespoons extra virgin olive oil

Orange Polenta

5 cups whole milk
2 cups instant polenta
2 tablespoons grated Sartori Stravecchio cheese (or another domestic Parmesan cheese)
1 tablespoon mascarpone cheese
Zest of 1 orange
Good-quality extra virgin olive oil, for garnish

Fish

6 red snapper fillets, skin on, 6 ounces each
4 tablespoons extra virgin olive oil

Braise the cabbage ➤ Slice the cabbage into ½-inch-thick ribbons. You should have about 8 cups of cabbage. Melt the butter in a large saucepan over medium heat. Add the onion, celery, and carrot and sauté until the vegetables just begin to soften, about 3 minutes. Add the cabbage and chicken stock and reduce the heat. Cover the saucepan and simmer until the cabbage is tender, about 15 minutes. Season to taste with salt and pepper.

Make the tomato emulsion ➤ Combine the orange juice and tomato juice in a saucepan over medium heat and simmer to reduce the juices by two-thirds, stirring occasionally, about 10 minutes. Strain the reduction through a fine-mesh strainer set over a clean small saucepan. Stir in the cream and season to taste with salt and pepper. Using an immersion blender or a whisk, blend in the oil until smooth and completely emulsified.

Make the orange polenta ➤ Combine the milk and 2 cups of water in a medium saucepan over medium heat and bring to a boil. Reduce the heat to low and whisk in the polenta. Season with salt and pepper and continue to cook, whisking often, about 10 minutes. Remove the pan from the heat. Stir in the grated cheese, mascarpone, and orange zest. Press a sheet of plastic wrap onto the surface of the polenta to prevent a skin from forming.

Cook the fish ➤ Score the skin side of the fish with very shallow 1-inch-long slits. This will keep the fish from curling up in the pan and cooking unevenly. Season the fish with salt and pepper. Heat 2 tablespoons of the olive oil in a large sauté pan over high heat. Once the oil is very hot, place 3 fish fillets, skin side down, in the pan and cook until the skin is crisp, pressing down on the fillets so that they brown evenly, about 4 minutes. Turn the fish over and cook until opaque, about 1 minute. Transfer the fish to a warm plate and repeat the process with the remaining 2 tablespoons of oil and 3 fish fillets.

To serve ➤ Spoon the cabbage into the center of 6 warm bowls. Arrange the fish over the cabbage and drizzle with the tomato emulsion. Drizzle the polenta with the good-quality olive oil and serve on the side.

Wine suggestion ➤ Serve this dish with a crisp and aromatic Sauvignon Blanc that offers flavors of pear, spicy citrus, and herbs, such as Sauvignon Blanc, Cliff Lede, 2007, Napa Valley, California.

Nantucket Bay Scallops & Farfalle with Tarragon, Buddha's Hand, & Lemon Beurre Blanc

Dried fennel pollen has an intense fennel flavor as well as a hint of spice. The exotic Buddha's hand citron can be found at many Asian markets or ordered online. If you are unable to find it, you can use Meyer lemons instead.

SERVES 6

Beurre Blanc

½ cup dry white wine
3 medium shallots, finely diced
2 tablespoons white wine vinegar
1 fresh thyme sprig
1 teaspoon whole black peppercorns
½ cup heavy cream
8 tablespoons cold unsalted butter, diced
1 medium fennel bulb, thinly sliced

Farfalle and Scallops

10 ounces fresh farfalle pasta
1 tablespoon grapeseed oil
1 pound Nantucket bay scallops, muscle removed
Sea salt and freshly ground black pepper
1 tablespoon unsalted butter
2 tablespoons chopped fresh tarragon
1 tablespoon freshly squeezed lemon juice
1 tablespoon grated Buddha's hand zest
½ teaspoon fennel pollen

Make the beurre blanc ➤ Combine the wine, shallots, vinegar, thyme, and peppercorns in a medium saucepan over medium-high heat. Simmer until the liquid has almost evaporated, about 10 minutes. Add the heavy cream and continue to cook until the cream has reduced by half, about 10 minutes. Strain the sauce through a fine-mesh strainer set over a large sauté pan. Warm the sauce over very low heat and slowly whisk in the cold butter 1 piece at a time.

Bring a saucepan of salted water to a boil. Add the fennel and cook until tender, about 2 minutes. Remove the fennel with a slotted spoon and immediately transfer it to a bowl of ice water. Once cool, strain, pat dry, and add the fennel to the beurre blanc.

Cook the farfalle ➤ Bring a large pot of salted water to a boil. Add the farfalle and cook until al dente, about 3 minutes. Drain and add the pasta to the beurre blanc.

Cook the scallops ➤ While the pasta is cooking, heat the grapeseed oil in a medium nonstick pan over medium heat. Dry the scallops with paper towels and season with salt and pepper. Sear the scallops on 1 side until golden brown, about 2 minutes. Add the butter. Once the butter starts to brown, begin swirling the pan in a circular motion until all sides of the scallops are caramelized. Using a slotted spoon, transfer the scallops to a plate lined with paper towels.

To serve ➤ Gently reheat the beurre blanc and pasta over low heat. Add the tarragon, lemon juice, and Buddha's hand zest to the pasta mixture and toss to coat the pasta and incorporate well. Transfer the pasta to a large platter and arrange the scallops on top. Garnish with the fennel pollen.

Wine suggestion ➤ Serve this dish with a rich Sauvignon Blanc that offers flavors of key limes, fresh-cut herbs, and zesty acidity, such as Sauvignon Blanc, "Hyde Vineyard," Selene, 2006, Carneros, California.

BUDDHA'S HAND is an odd-looking and incredibly fragrant type of citrus. It is bright yellow and may have anywhere from 5 to 20 "fingers." Native to Southern India, the Buddha's hand grows on small thorny shrubs and is commonly found as an offering at Buddhist temples. The Buddha's hand is thought to be one of oldest citrus varieties, and unlike other citrus there is no bitter pith. The zest is very flavorful and strongly scented and is used in ice creams and candies, as well as perfumes.

Braised Dover Sole with Mousserons, Sunchokes, & Riesling Nage

Mousseron mushrooms are delicious, small, wild mushrooms regularly found in French cuisine. This versatile mushroom has a full-bodied flavor with a soft and chewy texture. The aroma and distinctive taste of the mousseron is somewhat reminiscent of a porcini mushroom.

SERVES 6

Sole

2 teaspoons unsalted butter
3 Dover sole, 1 pound each, skin and head removed
Sea salt and freshly ground black pepper
½ cup dry Riesling
¼ cup fish stock
¼ cup white vermouth
6 large sunchokes, peeled and thinly sliced
½ cup mousseron mushrooms, cleaned and stemmed
2 tablespoons finely diced shallots

Nage

3 tablespoons dry Riesling
2 tablespoons heavy cream
2 tablespoons unsalted butter
1½ tablespoons chopped fresh chives
1 teaspoon freshly squeezed lemon juice

Braise the sole ➤ Preheat the oven to 350°F. Spread the butter over the inside of a large roasting pan to coat. Season the sole with salt and pepper and arrange in the pan in 1 even layer. Pour the Riesling, fish stock, and vermouth around the fish. Scatter the sunchokes, mousserons, and shallots around the fish, making sure they don't cover the top of fish or it will cook unevenly. Cover the pan with aluminum foil and place on the stovetop over medium heat just until the liquids come to a simmer, about 2 minutes. Transfer the pan to the oven and braise until the fish is white and flaky and just beginning to pull away from the bones, about 6 minutes. Remove from the oven and carefully uncover the pan, taking care not to get a steam burn.

Make the nage ➤ Transfer the sole to a plate. Pour the braising liquid from the roasting pan into a medium saucepan and simmer over medium heat until the sunchokes are tender, about 2 minutes. Whisk in the Riesling, heavy cream, butter, chives, and lemon juice. Gently simmer for 1 to 2 more minutes, making sure not to break the nage.

To serve ➤ Remove the sole fillet from the bones. Arrange 2 fillets on each of 6 plates. Spoon the nage over the fillets and serve.

Wine suggestion ➤ Serve this dish with a dry Riesling that offers flavors of kaffir lime, white peaches, and racy minerality, such as Riesling, Claiborne & Churchill, 2006, Central Coast, California.

DOVER SOLE are flatfish found in the eastern Atlantic Ocean and prized for their mild and buttery flavor. Don't be fooled by the "Pacific Sole," which is actually flounder.

Flatfish are simple to fillet and usually yield two fillets per side. Lay the fish on the counter with its tail pointing toward you. Cut down the backbone along the center of the fish, holding the knife at an angle. Lift the fillet away from the back-bone with one hand while gently scraping the knife downward with small strokes, using the bone structure to guide the knife. Using this technique, cut away the second fillet from the first side. Turn the fish over and repeat the process for the remaining two fillets.

My Dad's Hare Civet with Tourtou

My father has been making this recipe for as long as I can remember. The secret to a rich sauce is a two-step braising process and the addition of the liver and reserved blood. Tourtou, thick buckwheat pancakes from the Corrèze region of France, are the perfect accompaniment to dip into the sauce.

SERVES 6

Marinade

1 young hare, 2½ to 3 pounds, liver and blood reserved
2 teaspoons fresh thyme leaves
2 bay leaves, finely crushed
Sea salt and freshly ground black pepper
1 small onion, thinly sliced
2 tablespoons extra virgin olive oil
1½ tablespoons Armagnac or cognac

Braise

¼ pound fatback, cut into ¼-inch-thick slices
3½ tablespoons unsalted butter
24 small pearl onions, peeled
¼ pound white mushrooms
1 medium onion, cut into ½-inch-thick slices
2 carrots, cut into 1-inch pieces
2 tablespoons all-purpose flour
1 bottle (750 ml) Burgundy or similar red wine
2 garlic cloves, crushed
1 bouquet garni (1 dark green leek leaf, 2 fresh thyme sprigs, 1 bay leaf, 10 whole black peppercorns; see page 305)
¼ cup crème fraîche
1½ tablespoons Armagnac or cognac
3 tablespoons chopped fresh parsley

Tourtou (recipe follows)

Marinate the hare ➤ Cut the hare into 8 pieces and season with the thyme, crushed bay leaves, and salt and pepper. Place the hare in 1 layer in a shallow nonreative baking dish along with the onion, olive oil, and Armagnac. Marinate for 4 hours, turning the hare from time to time.

Braise the hare ➤ Soak the fatback in cold water in a small saucepan for 10 minutes. Place the saucepan over high heat and bring to a boil. Simmer for 5 minutes. Using a slotted spoon, remove the fatback from the saucepan and set it on a plate lined with paper towels. Pat the fatback dry.

Melt the butter in a large heavy skillet or Dutch oven. When the butter is hot, add the fatback to the pan and cook just until the fatback begins to brown, about 2 minutes. Add the pearl onions and cook until they are golden, about 8 minutes. Add the mushrooms, season to taste with salt, and sauté until the mushrooms are just beginning to brown, about 7 minutes. Using a slotted spoon, transfer the mixture to a plate, leaving as much fat in the pan as possible.

In the same pan, sauté the onion slices and carrots over medium heat until lightly caramelized, about 5 minutes. Sprinkle the flour over and stir to coat. Stir continuously with a wooden spoon over low heat until the flour takes on a dark gold color, about 2 minutes.

Preheat the oven to 300°F. Remove the hare from the marinade, pat dry, and season with salt and pepper. Sear the hare in the same pan over medium heat, making sure the roux does not burn. Add the wine and garlic and mix well, scraping up any browned bits from the bottom of the pan and stirring them into the sauce. Bring to a boil, stirring often, so that the roux is incorporated and the sauce is thick and perfectly smooth. Season to taste with salt and pepper and add the bouquet garni. Place the pot in the oven for 45 minutes.

Remove the pot from the oven and raise the temperature to 325°F. Using a slotted spoon, transfer the pieces of hare to another large pot. Arrange the sautéed fatback, pearl onions, and mushrooms on top of the hare. Pour the braising liquid from the first pot through a fine-mesh strainer over the hare, pressing the solids from the sauce through the sieve to thicken the sauce. Bring the sauce to a boil and cover. Braise in the oven for another 45 minutes.

Make the sauce ➤ Pass the reserved liver through a fine-mesh sieve into a bowl. Add the reserved blood, crème fraîche, and Armagnac.

Remove the pot from the oven and place it on the stovetop over very low heat. Slowly add the braising liquid to the liver mixture 1 ladleful at a time, whisking

continued

constantly so the liver cooks very slowly and the sauce does not become lumpy. Strain the sauce through a fine-mesh sieve over the hare while swirling the pot so that the hare is evenly coated. Swirl the pan over low heat until it shows the first signs of boiling. Remove the pot from the heat. The sauce should be perfectly thickened, smooth, and black in color, looking almost burned.

To serve ➤ Pour the stew into a large shallow serving dish and sprinkle with the parsley. Serve with the tourtou on the side.

Wine suggestion ➤ Serve this dish with a deep and rich Petite Sirah that offers aromas of black cherries, violets, and minerals, such as Petite Sirah, "Madrone Spring Vineyard," Rockpile Winery, 2005, Rockpile Winery, California.

Tourtou

- ½ ounce fresh yeast
- 1⅔ cups warm water
- 1¼ cups buckwheat flour
- 1 cup whole wheat flour
- 1 teaspoon sea salt
- ⅔ cup whole milk
- 1½ tablespoons (about) salted butter

Dissolve the yeast in a small bowl with 1½ tablespoons of the warm water. Whisk the buckwheat flour, whole wheat flour, and sea salt in a medium bowl to blend. Using your hands, make a well in the center of the flour mixture. Using a wooden spoon, slowly mix the remaining warm water into the flour mixture. Add the yeast mixture and milk and stir until smooth, making sure not to overmix the batter. Cover with plastic wrap and let rest at room temperature for 2 hours.

Melt 1 teaspoon of the butter in a small nonstick sauté pan over medium heat. Spoon ¼ cup of the batter into the center of pan then tilt the pan quickly to form a 6-inch pancake. Cook for 2 minutes then turn the tourtou over. Cook until lightly browned and cooked through, about 2 minutes. Repeat with the remaining batter, adding more butter as needed.

To serve ➤ Stack the tourtou on a platter and serve warm with salted butter on the side.

Pineapple Fritter & Piña Colada Sorbet

Frying fruit is one of the quickest ways to bring out its sweetness. This recipe is fairly simple and is always a crowd pleaser. The combination of tropical flavors is great year-round, but I especially enjoy this in the winter when pineapples are at their peak of ripeness and I need a little fantasy island vacation—if only for an hour or so.

SERVES 6

½ pineapple, peeled and cored
¾ cup all-purpose flour
2 large eggs
¾ cup panko (Japanese breadcrumbs)
Canola oil for frying
Confectioners' sugar for dusting

Piña Colada Sorbet (page 313)

Cut the pineapple crosswise in half then slice it into 18 sticks that are about 2 inches long and ½ inch thick.

Place the flour in a shallow bowl or pie plate. Beat the eggs in another shallow bowl to blend, and place the panko in a third bowl. Roll each pineapple stick in the flour to coat, then in the eggs to moisten, making sure it is entirely coated with egg, and lastly, coat them with the panko. Place the coated pineapple sticks on a baking sheet.

Heat 4 inches of oil in large heavy pot to 375°F. Add the coated pineapple sticks, a few a time, and fry until light brown in color, about 2 minutes. Using a slotted spoon, transfer the fried pineapple sticks to a plate lined with paper towels and dust with confectioners' sugar. Repeat until all the coated pineapple sticks have been fried.

Scoop the sorbet into serving bowls, arrange 3 pineapple fritters on the side, and serve.

Wine suggestion ➤ Serve this dish with a late harvest Viognier that offers aromas of candied tropical fruits, honeyed apricots, and peaches, such as Viognier Late Harvest, "Ripken Ranch," Rosenblum Cellars, NV, Lodi, California.

Chocolate-Coconut Marquise with Rum Ice Cream

I pilfered this recipe from a good friend of mine, the talented pastry chef François Payard. It's almost like a Mounds candy bar but better. This dessert is so rich that I usually think I can only eat one slice but I am always compelled to go back for another.

SERVES 10

Special Equipment
12⅔ × 4-inch terrine or loaf pan

Ganache
10½ ounces Valrhona semisweet chocolate (66% cocoa), chopped
3½ ounces Valrhona milk chocolate (40% cocoa), chopped
1⅔ cups heavy cream

Syrup
1 cup Simple Syrup (page 314)
3 tablespoons Malibu rum or other coconut-flavored rum

Cake
Nonstick cooking spray
1½ cups sugar
5 large eggs
3⅔ cups shredded unsweetened coconut
1 cup toasted unsweetened coconut flakes

Rum Ice Cream (page 310)

Make the ganache ➤ Place the semisweet chocolate and milk chocolate in a medium bowl. Bring the heavy cream to a boil in a small saucepan over medium-high heat. Pour the boiling cream over the chocolate and mix until smooth, well combined, and glossy. Cool to room temperate. Press a sheet of plastic wrap onto the surface of the ganache to ensure a film does not form on top of the ganache.

Make the syrup ➤ Combine the simple syrup and rum in a small bowl.

Make the cake ➤ Preheat the oven to 350°F. Line an 18 × 13-inch rimmed baking sheet with parchment paper and spray with nonstick cooking spray. Whisk the sugar and eggs in a double boiler set over simmering water until warm to the touch, about 3 minutes. Transfer the mixture to the bowl of a stand mixer fitted with a whisk attachment. Whip at high speed until the mixture has tripled in volume, about 5 minutes. Gently fold in the 3⅔ cups of shredded coconut.

Using an offset spatula, spread the batter evenly in the baking sheet. Bake until golden brown, about 12 minutes. Let the cake cool for 15 minutes. Invert the pan onto a large cutting board and remove the parchment paper from the cake.

Assemble the marquise ➤ Using a pastry brush, brush the cake with just enough syrup to moisten it slightly. Cover and freeze for 30 minutes (this will make it easier to slice the cake).

Line a 12⅔ × 4-inch terrine or loaf pan with plastic wrap, allowing the plastic to hang over the edges of the terrine. Slice the cake into 4 rectangles so that they fit inside the terrine. Place 1 rectangle in the mold. Spread a layer of the ganache, about ¼ inch thick, over the cake. Repeat the layering with the remaining 3 rectangles of cake and ganache, finishing with the cake layer on the top and reserving the leftover ganache. Wrap the terrine with plastic wrap and refrigerate for at least 1 hour.

Unwrap the plastic wrap and carefully invert the cake onto a serving platter and remove the plastic wrap. Spread the reserved ganache over the entire exterior of the cake to cover completely. Decoratively sprinkle with the toasted coconut. Loosely cover with plastic wrap and refrigerate until the ganache has set completely, about 1 hour.

To serve ➤ Cut the marquise into 1½-inch-thick slices and serve at room temperature with the ice cream.

Wine suggestion ➤ Serve this dish with a port-style sweet wine that offers aromas of brown sugar, molasses, and candied figs, such as Del Dotto, "Zinfandel-Syrah Port CharDotto," NV, Napa Valley, California.

Banana Split Bombe Glace with Chocolate Sauce

This is an eye-catching and fun dessert. I strongly recommend that you make your own ice cream, but if you are short on time, use high-quality store-bought ice cream instead.

SERVES 6

Special Equipment
6¼-inch bombe mold or
6¼-inch metal bowl

Bombe
2½ cups Vanilla Ice Cream (page 311)
⅓ cup maraschino cherries, chopped + 1 whole cherry for garnish
1½ cups Chocolate Ice Cream (page 308)
1 cup Banana Ice Cream (page 307)

Chocolate Sauce
½ cup + 3 tablespoons sugar
½ cup unsweetened cocoa powder
½ cup heavy cream

Make the bombe ➤ Place a 6¼-inch bombe mold or 6¼-inch metal bowl in the freezer for 20 minutes. Using a rubber spatula, spread the vanilla ice cream evenly over the bottom and sides of the mold to create a uniform ½-inch-thick layer. Place the mold into the freezer until the ice cream begins to harden, about 20 minutes. Remove the mold from the freezer and spread the chopped maraschino cherries evenly over the vanilla ice cream and freeze for an additional 20 minutes. Repeat the process with the chocolate ice cream and then with the banana ice cream. Freeze until all the ice creams harden completely, at least 4 hours.

Make the chocolate sauce ➤ Bring the sugar and 6 tablespoons of water to a boil in a medium saucepan. Slowly whisk in the cocoa powder until the mixture reaches a smooth consistency. Bring the mixture back to a boil. Stir in the cream. Reduce the heat and simmer until the sauce thickens, about 40 minutes.

To serve ➤ Fill a large bowl with warm water. Dip the bombe mold into the water for 30 seconds so that it the ice cream loosens from the sides of the mold. Unmold the bombe by inverting it onto a serving plate, then remove the mold and garnish with the whole maraschino cherry.

Rinse a knife with warm water and slice the bombe into 6 wedges, rinsing the knife after each cut to ensure it slices evenly. Serve with the hot chocolate sauce on the side or drizzled over the top.

Wine suggestion ➤ Serve this dish with a late harvest Zinfandel that offers aromas of plum pie, raspberries, and hints of chocolate, such as Zinfandel Late Harvest, Opolo, 2005, Paso Robles, California.

Hamptons Honey Tart with Candied Tangerine Sorbet

The Hamptons Honey Company bottles some of the finest raw, unfiltered, and unpasteurized honey. They work with local beekeepers and small apiaries to produce small-batch varieties that maintain the unique aroma, flavor, and texture native to that region and its flora. Seek out a local clover-style honey producer at your own farmers' markets if you don't live in the New York area.

SERVES 6

Special Equipment
Six 3½-inch ring molds (¾-inch high); kitchen torch

Dough
13 tablespoons unsalted butter, at room temperature
⅓ cup confectioners' sugar
1½ cups all-purpose flour
⅔ cup almond flour
Pinch of salt
1 large egg

Honey Cream
3 gelatin sheets
1½ cups heavy cream
½ cup whole milk
⅓ cup clover blossom honey, preferably from The Hamptons Honey Company
5 large eggs

Tangerines
¼ cup clover blossom honey, preferably from The Hamptons Honey Company
Zest of 2 limes + zest of 1 lime for garnish
6 tangerines, peeled and segmented
2 tablespoons turbinado sugar

Candied Tangerine Sorbet (page 312)

Make the dough ➤ Using a stand mixer fitted with the paddle attachment, mix the butter and sugar in the mixer bowl at medium speed until well combined. Add the all-purpose flour, almond flour, and salt and continue to mix until the dough reaches a pebbly consistency. Add the egg and mix until just combined, making sure not to overmix. Wrap the dough in plastic wrap and refrigerate for 1 hour.

Line a baking sheet with parchment paper. Using a lightly floured rolling pin, roll out the dough on a lightly floured surface to a ⅛-inch thickness. Cut the dough into six 5-inch rounds and fit them into six 3½-inch ring molds (¾ inch high), trimming off any excess dough. Place the molds on the lined baking sheet and freeze for at least 1 hour.

Preheat the oven to 325°F. Bake the dough until it is light golden brown and cooked through, about 20 minutes.

Make the honey cream ➤ Soak the gelatin sheets in 2 cups of cold water to soften. Combine the heavy cream, milk, and honey in a small saucepan over medium heat and bring to a boil. Whisk the eggs in a medium mixing bowl. Slowly whisk the hot cream mixture into the eggs making sure not to cook the eggs.

Transfer the mixture back to the saucepan and cook over low heat until the mixture is thick enough to coat the back of a wooden spoon, about 3 minutes. Strain the honey cream through a fine-mesh strainer into a clean mixing bowl. Remove the gelatin sheets from the water, squeezing to ensure all the excess water is removed, and add it to the honey cream. Mix until well combined and then immediately set the bowl over a bowl of ice water. Once cool, whisk until smooth.

Cook the tangerines ➤ Combine the honey and the zest of 2 limes in a medium sauté pan over low heat, stirring frequently so the honey doesn't burn, about 2 minutes. Add the tangerine segments and cook, stirring frequently and making sure the segments don't burn or break, until the segments are soft but still intact, about 2 minutes. Cool to room temperature.

Assemble the tarts ➤ Transfer the honey cream to a pastry bag and pipe it into the prepared tart shells. Refrigerate for 3 hours.

continued

To serve ➤ Remove the tangerines from the honey-lime syrup and place them on a baking sheet. Scatter the turbinado sugar over the tangerines. Using a kitchen torch, caramelize the sugar on each segment, waving the torch for about 30 seconds over each tangerine segment. Arrange the tangerine segments over the honey cream. Drizzle 2 teaspoons of the honey-lime syrup over each tart, sprinkle with the remaining lime zest, and serve immediately with the sorbet.

Wine suggestion ➤ Serve a sweet white wine made from orange Muscat that offers flavors of candied oranges, lychee, and white flowers, such as Orange Muscat, Renwood, 2006, Amador County, California.

Blood Orange Soufflés

This is a great traditional soufflé recipe that can easily be adapted for other types of citrus, like Meyer lemon or grapefruit. Be very careful when making the reduction, as too high a heat will scorch the juice and result in a burnt and bitter flavor. Serve this along with a crème anglaise or a scoop of sorbet.

SERVES 6

Special Equipment
Six 10-ounce soufflé dishes or ramekins

Blood Orange Reduction
2¼ cups freshly squeezed blood orange juice
3 tablespoons Grand Marnier
2 teaspoons blood orange zest

Soufflés
Unsalted butter to coat the soufflé dishes + 2 tablespoons, softened
Sugar to coat the soufflé dishes + 2½ tablespoons
5 large egg yolks
½ cup sugar
1 cup whole milk
¼ cup unsalted butter
⅓ cup + 1 tablespoon all-purpose flour
6 large egg whites
2 tablespoons confectioners' sugar

Make the blood orange reduction ➤ Simmer the orange juice in a small saucepan over low heat until reduced to 3 tablespoons, about 1 hour. Using a spoon, remove the skin that forms over the surface of the reduction. Place the saucepan in a bowl of ice water and let cool. (The reduction can be made up to this point 1 day in advance; cover and refrigerate.) Stir in the Grand Marnier and the zest.

Make the soufflés ➤ Preheat the oven to 375°F. Brush the inside of six 10-ounce soufflé dishes or ramekins with butter and sprinkle with sugar. Using a stand mixer fitted with a whisk attachment, whisk the egg yolks and ¼ cup of the sugar in the mixer bowl at high speed until the eggs are light and fluffy, about 3 minutes.

While the eggs are whisking, bring the milk and the ¼ cup of butter to a boil in a small saucepan over medium-low heat. Once the eggs have reached the proper consistency, reduce the speed to low and add the flour. Continue to mix at high speed for 3 minutes. Once the milk mixture has come to a boil, remove it from the heat. Reduce the mixer speed to low and carefully pour the hot milk mixture into the egg mixture, beating until well blended.

Transfer the mixture to a clean medium saucepan and whisk constantly over low heat until the mixture thickens, about 4 minutes. Transfer to a medium bowl and stir in the blood orange reduction.

Using the stand mixer fitted with a clean whisk attachment, whisk the egg whites and the 2½ tablespoons of sugar in a clean mixer bowl at high speed until medium peaks begin to form, about 3 minutes. Using a large rubber spatula, fold half of the egg whites into the soufflé batter until well combined and lightened. Gently fold in the remaining egg whites until fully incorporated.

Divide the soufflé batter among the prepared soufflé dishes and smooth the top with an offset spatula to ensure that it is even. Place the ramekins on a baking sheet and bake until the meringue sets in the center, turning them halfway through, about 8 minutes.

To serve ➤ Remove the soufflés from the oven and dust with the confectioners' sugar. Serve immediately.

Wine suggestion ➤ Serve this dish with an ice wine made from Riesling that offers flavors of citrus marmalade, honey, and golden pineapple, such as Riesling Late Harvest, "Cluster Select," 2006, Anderson Valley, California.

Bittersweet Chocolate Pudding with Salted Caramel Chantilly

I created this recipe because of my love for salted caramel. Chocolate, caramel, and salt make a perfect triumvirate, playing off each other in perfect harmony.

SERVES 6

Pudding

6 cups half-and-half
1 cup light brown sugar
½ cup sugar
Pinch of salt
6 large egg yolks
⅔ cup cornstarch
⅓ cup unsweetened cocoa powder
4 ounces Valrhona bittersweet chocolate (66% cocoa), chopped
4 tablespoons unsalted butter, softened
1 teaspoon vanilla extract

Salted Caramel Chantilly

½ cup sugar
Pinch of cream of tartar
1 tablespoon unsalted butter
½ teaspoon Maldon sea salt
⅓ cup + 1½ cups heavy cream

Caramel Rice Crispy

⅓ cup + 2 tablespoons sugar
3 tablespoons light corn syrup
2 teaspoons unsalted butter, softened
¼ teaspoon vanilla extract
Pinch of salt
1¾ cups crisp rice cereal

Chocolate sauce (see page 283)

Make the pudding ➤ Combine 4 cups of the half-and-half, the brown sugar, sugar, and salt in a large saucepan over medium heat and bring to a boil. Whisk the remaining 2 cups of half-and-half with the egg yolks, cornstarch, and cocoa powder in a medium bowl until well blended. Slowly pour the hot half-and-half mixture into the cocoa mixture, whisking constantly. Pour the mixture back into the saucepan and bring to a boil over medium heat, whisking constantly, until a thick, smooth, pudding-like consistently forms, about 5 minutes.

Remove the saucepan from the heat and whisk in the chocolate, butter, and vanilla. Pass the pudding through a fine-mesh strainer set over a rimmed baking sheet or a large metal roasting pan. Spread the pudding evenly and press a sheet of plastic wrap onto the surface of the pudding so that a skin does not begin to form. Refrigerate until completely cool, about 3 hours.

Make the salted caramel chantilly ➤ Combine the sugar, cream of tartar, and 3 tablespoons of water in a small saucepan over high heat. Cook the sugar, swirling the pan, until it reaches a deep amber color, about 5 minutes. Remove from the heat and whisk in the butter and salt until well combined. Place the pan back over the heat and whisk in the ⅓ cup of heavy cream. Simmer until the caramel is thick and glossy, about 30 seconds. Remove from the heat and cool to room temperature.

Using a stand mixer fitted with the whisk attachment, whisk the remaining 1½ cups of heavy cream and ⅓ cup of the cooled salted caramel in the mixer bowl until the cream reaches firm peaks, about 3 minutes. Cover and refrigerate until ready to serve.

Make the caramel rice crispy ➤ Line a baking sheet with parchment paper. Combine the sugar, corn syrup, and 2 tablespoons of water in a large saucepan over high heat and cook, swirling the pan, until it reaches a medium amber color. Reduce the heat to medium-low and stir in the butter, vanilla, and salt. Using a silicone spatula, stir in the rice cereal to coat completely. Spread the mixture evenly over the lined baking sheet and set aside to cool. Once cool, break it into 6 pieces.

To serve ➤ Remove the pudding from the refrigerator. If you find that the texture is too dense, transfer it to the bowl of a stand mixer and whisk at medium speed until smooth. Transfer the pudding to a pastry bag and pipe it into six 7-ounce glasses. Spoon chocolate sauce around the top. Transfer the salted chantilly to a pastry bag fitted with a fluted tip and pipe it over the pudding. Place a drop of chocolate sauce on top and serve with a piece of the caramel rice crispy on the side.

Wine suggestion ➤ Serve this dish with a nutty tawny port–style sweet wine that offers aromas of caramel, hazelnut, and a creamy finish, such as Prager Winery and Port Works Tawny Port, "Noble Companion," NV, Napa Valley, California.

Banana–Passion Fruit Vacherin

A vacherin is composed of crisp layers of meringue and sweetened whipped cream. I have transformed the traditional presentation by replacing the whipped cream with a layer of ice cream. The sweet and mellow banana is heightened when contrasted with musky and tart passion fruit.

SERVES 10

Special Equipment
Kitchen torch

Meringue
½ cup confectioners' sugar
⅓ cup sugar
¼ cup egg whites

Passion Fruit Sauce
1 tablespoon cornstarch
1 cup store-bought passion fruit purée (see Chef's note)
3 tablespoons sugar
¼ cup unsalted butter
1 tablespoon freshly squeezed lime juice

Banana–Passion Fruit Sorbet (page 312)
Vermont Double Cream Ice Cream (page 311)

Make the meringue ➤ Preheat the oven to 200°F. Line an 18 × 13-inch rimmed baking sheet with parchment paper. Combine the sugars and egg whites in a small saucepan over medium heat, stirring until the sugars are completely dissolved. Pour the mixture into the bowl of a stand mixer fitted with the whisk attachment. Whisk at high speed until the mixture is fluffy and glossy, about 5 minutes.

Using an offset spatula, spread the meringue evenly over the parchment paper to a ⅛-inch thickness. Bake for 10 minutes. Using a 2-inch round cutter, cut the meringue into 20 rounds and discard the meringue trimmings. Bake the meringue rounds until cooked through, about 20 minutes, making sure they do not brown. Alternatively, pipe the meringue onto a parchment-lined baking sheet forming 2-inch rounds that are ⅛-inch thick, and bake for 30 minutes.

Make the passion fruit sauce ➤ Heat 1 cup of water in a medium saucepan and whisk in the cornstarch. Once the cornstarch is fully dissolved, add the passion fruit purée, sugar, butter, and lime juice and bring to a simmer over medium heat. Whisk until well combined. Let cool to room temperature.

To serve ➤ Using a kitchen torch, caramelize the top of 10 meringues until golden brown. Spoon ¼ cup of the passion fruit sauce into each of 10 shallow bowls. Set 1 meringue atop the passion fruit sauce in the center of each bowl. Place a scoop of the ice cream and the sorbet on top of each meringue. Top with the caramelized meringues. Drizzle with remaining passion fruit sauce and serve immediately.

Chef's note ➤ To make your own passion fruit purée, simply halve passion fruits, scoop out the flesh, and strain through a fine-mesh strainer. Discard the solids and reserve the juice.

Wine suggestion ➤ Serve this dish with a late harvest Sauvignon Blanc that offers aromas of candied citrus peels, tropical fruits, and a touch of honey, such as Sauvignon Blanc Late Harvest, "Vin d'Or," 2005, Eola Hills, Amity–Eola Hills, Oregon.

Steamed Date Pudding with Banana-Kumquat Syrup

I like to serve this riff on a classic baba with a dollop of sweetened whipped cream or a scoop of vanilla ice cream. You can make the puddings earlier in the day and heat them through in the microwave right before serving.

SERVES 6

Special Equipment
Six 2¾-inch ring molds (1¾ inches high)

Steamed Puddings
Salt
9 kumquats, cut into ⅛-inch-thick slices, seeds discarded
¾ cup sugar
Nonstick cooking spray
18 whole Medjool dates, pitted
⅔ cup light brown sugar
4½ tablespoons unsalted butter, room temperature
2 large eggs
½ cup self-rising cake flour, preferably by Presto
1 teaspoon baking soda
3 large ripe bananas, mashed

Sauce and Syrup
1 cup dark rum
½ cup sugar
5 tablespoons unsalted butter
3 ripe bananas, cut into ⅛-inch-thick rounds

Make the steamed puddings ➤ Bring 2 cups of water and a pinch of salt to a boil in a medium saucepan. Add the sliced kumquats and cook until the water is brought back to a boil, about 1 minute. Using a slotted spoon, transfer the kumquats to a strainer and rinse under cold water. Repeat the process 2 more times, using fresh water and a pinch of salt each time.

Once the kumquats have been blanched 3 times, combine 2 cups of water and the sugar in a medium saucepan and bring to a boil over medium heat. Add the kumquats and bring back to a boil. Pour into a medium bowl and refrigerate until cold, about 3 hours.

Preheat the oven to 325°F. Wrap the bottom of six 2¾-inch ring molds (1¾ inches high) with aluminum foil, making sure the foil comes up the sides and nearly reaches the top rims of the molds, and then place the molds in a large roasting pan. Lightly spray the inside of each mold with nonstick cooking spray. Arrange 3 dates in each ring mold.

Using a stand mixer fitted with the paddle attachment, beat the brown sugar and butter in the mixer bowl at medium-high speed until light and fluffy, about 10 minutes. Reduce the speed to low and add the eggs 1 at a time, making sure the egg is fully incorporated before adding another. Add the flour and the baking soda and continue to mix until well blended. Finally add the mashed bananas, scraping the sides of the bowl, and mix until well blended.

Divide the batter evenly among the ring molds. Pour enough hot water into the roasting pan to come one-fourth of the way up the side of the molds. Cover the roasting pan with aluminum foil. Bake until a toothpick inserted in the puddings comes out clean, turning the pan around halfway through, about 25 minutes. Remove the molds from the roasting pan and place on a wire rack to cool.

Carefully remove the aluminum foil and invert the puddings onto a platter so that the dates are on top. Cover with plastic wrap and refrigerate until ready to serve.

Make the rum sauce ➤ Combine the rum, sugar, butter, and ½ cup of water in a saucepan over medium-high heat and simmer until the sauce has reduced to 1 cup, about 10 minutes. Reserve 6 tablespoons of the sauce in a small bowl.

Make the banana-kumquat syrup ➤ Place the saucepan of rum sauce over medium heat and boil until the sauce has reduced by half, about 3 minutes. Add the sliced bananas and gently stir until well coated. Cook for 30 seconds. Strain the candied kumquats from their liquid and very gently stir them into the syrup.

To serve ➤ Warm the puddings in the microwave until just heated through and then arrange them on 6 serving plates. Spoon 1 tablespoon of the reserved rum sauce over the top of each pudding. Spoon the banana-kumquat syrup around the puddings and serve immediately.

Wine suggestion ➤ Serve this dish with a sweet white wine made from Chardonnay that offers flavors of dried apricots, figs, and candied citrus, such as Chardonnay, "Bouche d'Or" Bouchaine, 2007, Carneros, California.

Warm Banana-Almond Milk with Honey

Rum-soaked raisins are a great addition to this recipe. Just soak ¼ cup of dark raisins in 3 tablespoons of dark rum for about 1 hour. Add the raisins with the bananas at the end and you are guaranteed the real breakfast of champions!

SERVES 6

2 cups whole milk
1 cinnamon stick
Pinch of salt
1 cup almond flour
5 ripe bananas, peeled
6 tablespoons elderflower honey
Ground cinnamon

Bring the milk, cinnamon stick, and salt to a boil in a small saucepan. Remove the pan from the heat and whisk in the almond flour. Cover and let the milk infuse for 10 minutes.

While the milk is infusing, purée 4 of the bananas in a blender until smooth. Slice the 1 remaining banana into thin rounds for garnish.

Once the milk has infused, remove the cinnamon stick and stir in the banana purée. Divide the milk among 6 bowls and top with the sliced banana. Drizzle with honey and sprinkle each with a pinch of ground cinnamon.

Buckwheat Crêpe with Melted Hooligan, Black Forest Ham, & Farm Eggs

I like to eat this with a generous dash of Tabasco, a spoonful of crème fraîche, and sometimes, even a frosty pint of lager-style beer if enjoying it later in the day. The crêpe batter is very light but also has a lot of flavor due to the buckwheat. I make many variations of this dish, depending upon what I have in the refrigerator, sometimes herbs and cream cheese, or last night's creamed spinach.

SERVES 6

Crêpes

1¼ cups all-purpose flour
¾ cup buckwheat flour
3 large eggs
Sea salt and freshly ground black pepper
1¼ cups whole milk
2 tablespoons extra virgin olive oil
2 tablespoons unsalted butter, melted

Filling

¼ pound Hooligan cheese, sliced
¼ pound Black Forest ham, sliced
6 large farm fresh eggs

Make the crêpe batter ➤ Whisk both flours in a large bowl to blend. Whisk the eggs in another large bowl until light and frothy, and season with salt and pepper. Pour the eggs into the flours and stir until well blended. Add the milk, 1½ cups of water, and the olive oil and whisk until smooth. Let the batter rest for 2 hours.

Once the batter has rested, whisk in ¼ cup of water to lighten the batter. The batter should have the consistency of heavy cream.

Make and fill the crêpes ➤ Preheat the oven to 200°F. Heat a 12-inch nonstick pan over medium heat and brush with some of the melted butter. Once the pan is hot, ladle ⅓ cup of the batter into the center of the pan and swirl to evenly distribute the batter. Cook until the crêpe has set and is lightly brown, about 1 minute. Flip the crêpe over. Arrange some of the cheese and ham in the center of the crêpe. Once the cheese begins to melt, break an egg over the cheese and season with salt and pepper. Once the white of the egg begins to set, fold the edges of the crêpe over the egg to form a square package, and then turn the crêpe over. Cook until the egg white is fully set but the yolk is still runny, about 3 minutes. Transfer the crêpe to a baking sheet and keep warm in the oven while making the remaining crêpes.

Repeat the process to make 6 crêpes total, brushing the pan with more melted butter as needed. Serve warm.

Creamy White Mushroom Scrambled Eggs

The art of making the perfect scrambled egg is not easy to master. A few simple tips, like whisking plenty of air into the eggs before cooking, will result in very fluffy scrambled eggs. Also, don't cook the eggs in a pan that is too large or they will cook too quickly and dry out. Make sure to remove the eggs from the heat when they are still quite moist, as the carryover heat will continue to cook them through. I like to enjoy these scrambled eggs with toast and crispy bacon.

SERVES 6

Mushrooms

2 pounds white mushrooms, cleaned
2 tablespoons unsalted butter
½ small white onion, finely chopped
1 teaspoon finely chopped garlic
½ cup heavy cream
Pinch of freshly grated nutmeg
Sea salt and freshly ground black pepper

Scrambled Eggs

12 large farm fresh eggs
2 tablespoons unsalted butter
1 cup grated New York sharp cheddar cheese
1 cup heavy cream
2 tablespoons chopped fresh chives
3 tablespoons walnut oil or truffle oil

Prepare the mushrooms ➤ Combine the mushrooms and 1 cup of water in a food processor fitted with a metal blade and process until the mushrooms are puréed. Transfer the mushrooms to a strainer lined with cheesecloth and set over a bowl. Cover and refrigerate for at least 4 hours or overnight.

Squeeze any remaining water from the mushrooms. Transfer all the accumulated liquid to a small saucepan and simmer over medium heat until reduced to a glaze consistency, about 5 minutes.

Melt the butter in a large sauté pan over medium heat. Add the onion and garlic and sauté until translucent, about 4 minutes. Add the chopped mushrooms and cook until soft, about 4 minutes. Add the heavy cream and nutmeg and bring to a boil, stirring often so the mushrooms don't burn. Season to taste with salt and pepper.

Scramble the eggs ➤ Crack the eggs into a large bowl and whisk vigorously for 2 minutes until the whites and yolks are well blended and a lot of air has been incorporated into the eggs. Season with salt and pepper.

Melt the butter in a medium sauté pan over medium heat. Pour the beaten eggs into the pan. Cook the eggs, whisking until they just begin to set. As soon as the eggs begin to firm up, use a wooden spoon or spatula to fold the eggs away from the sides of the pan and into the middle. Continually fold the eggs away from the sides of pan, taking care not to burn the underside of the eggs or allow them to stick to the bottom of the pan. Break up any large pieces of egg as you are folding, and cook just until any runny liquid has disappeared but the eggs are still moist, about 4 minutes.

To assemble and serve ➤ Remove the pan from the heat and stir in the cheese, heavy cream, and 1 to 2 tablespoons of the mushroom reduction and season to taste with salt and pepper.

Divide the scrambled eggs among 6 small bowls. Top with a spoonful of the sautéed mushrooms and sprinkle with the chives. Drizzle with the walnut oil or truffle oil and serve.

Bartlett Pear & Cranberry Muffins with Cinnamon-Walnut Topping

This moist muffin recipe can be easily adapted to any season. I like to make a filling in the summer with lemon zest and blueberries and top the muffins with a sugary almond crumble. In the fall, simply substitute apples for the pears, or in the winter, use mashed ripe bananas and confit kumquats in place of the pears.

YIELDS 16 MUFFINS

Cinnamon-Walnut Topping
½ cup coarsely chopped walnuts
½ cup sugar
2 teaspoons ground cinnamon
2 teaspoons vanilla extract

Pear Filling
2 cups finely diced peeled Bartlett pears
2 tablespoons melted unsalted butter
2 tablespoons sugar
2 teaspoons ground cinnamon

Muffins
Unsalted butter for coating the pans
+ 8 tablespoons (1 stick), at room temperature
All-purpose flour for dusting the pans
+ 2 cups
1 teaspoon baking powder
1 teaspoon baking soda
½ teaspoon salt
1 cup sugar
2 large eggs
1 cup sour cream
1 cup dried cranberries

Make the topping ➤ Stir all of the ingredients in a small bowl.

Make the filling ➤ Mix all of the ingredients in a medium bowl until well combined.

Make the muffins ➤ Preheat the oven to 350°F. Butter and flour 16 muffin cups in 2 standard-size muffin pans. Whisk the 2 cups of flour with the baking powder, baking soda, and salt in a medium bowl to blend.

Using a stand mixer fitted with the paddle attachment, beat the 8 tablespoons of butter with the sugar and eggs in the mixer bowl until smooth. Add the flour mixture alternately with the sour cream, beginning and ending with the flour mixture and beating until the batter is well blended. Using a silicone spatula, gently fold in the pear filling and the dried cranberries.

Divide the batter evenly among the prepared muffin cups. Spoon the topping evenly over the muffins and bake until a toothpick comes out clean, about 20 minutes. Cool on a rack.

My Favorite Granola

This really is the best granola recipe. I tried different versions with all kinds of nuts and dried fruit, but in the end simplicity won out. I like to eat this in a bowl with warm milk and a generous spoonful of bittersweet orange marmalade stirred in.

SERVES 6

2 cups corn flake cereal
2 cups old-fashioned oats
1 cup sliced almonds
1 cup steel-cut oats
1½ teaspoons salt
1 teaspoon ground cinnamon
½ cup canola oil
½ cup honey
½ cup Mapleland Farms maple syrup
Zest of 2 oranges
2 vanilla beans, split lengthwise and seeds scraped

Preheat the oven to 325°F. Line a rimmed baking sheet with parchment paper. Mix the corn flakes, old-fashioned oats, almonds, steel-cut oats, salt, and cinnamon in a large bowl. Bring the oil, honey, maple syrup, orange zest, and vanilla beans and seeds to a boil in a small saucepan over medium heat. Simmer for 1 minute. Remove the vanilla bean and pour the hot liquid over the oat mixture. Using a silicone spatula, mix well.

Pour the oat mixture onto the lined baking sheet and spread the granola evenly using a offset spatula. Bake until golden brown and evenly toasted, tossing the granola halfway through, about 10 minutes.

Place the baking sheet on a rack and cool the granola to room temperature. Break the granola into smaller bite-size pieces. Store the cool granola in an airtight container for up to 1 week.

Christmas Eve

MENU

COCKTAIL

Pomegranate Sidecar

Appetizers

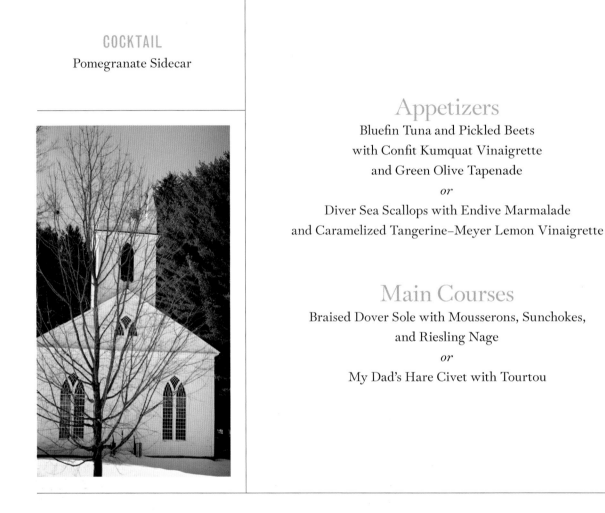

Bluefin Tuna and Pickled Beets
with Confit Kumquat Vinaigrette
and Green Olive Tapenade

or

Diver Sea Scallops with Endive Marmalade
and Caramelized Tangerine–Meyer Lemon Vinaigrette

Main Courses

Braised Dover Sole with Mousserons, Sunchokes,
and Riesling Nage

or

My Dad's Hare Civet with Tourtou

DESSERT

Banana Split Bombe Glace with Chocolate Sauce

New Year's Eve

MENU

Appetizers

Cauliflower and Rock Shrimp Risotto with White Truffles

Pan-Seared Foie Gras and Late Harvest Chardonnay-Grapefruit Reduction

Main Courses

Crispy Red Snapper with Braised Cabbage and Orange Polenta

or

Pistachio-Crusted Venison with Caramelized Quince and Red Cabbage

COCKTAIL

Meyer Lemon 75

DESSERT

Chocolate-Coconut Marquise with Rum Ice Cream

Supplementary Recipes & Charts

Chicken Stock

Using homemade chicken stock makes all the difference in the world. I like to make a batch every couple of weeks to keep on hand. This tried and true stock is the perfect balance of chicken, vegetables, and herbs and is a great building block for many recipes.

YIELDS 10 CUPS

3 pounds chicken bones, preferably backs, fat and skin removed
3 onions, cut into 1-inch pieces
3 medium carrots, cut into 1-inch pieces
4 celery stalks, cut into 1-inch pieces
1 head of garlic, halved
1 bouquet garni (1 dark green leek leaf, 10 parsley stems, 5 fresh thyme sprigs, and 1 bay leaf; see page 305)
10 whole black peppercorns

Place the chicken bones in a large heavy stockpot and cover with 12 cups of cold water. Slowly bring to a boil over medium-high heat. Using a ladle or spoon, skim any fat or coagulated proteins from the top of the liquid and simmer for 30 minutes. Add the onions, carrots, celery, garlic, bouquet garni, and peppercorns and simmer until the liquid is clear, skimming the top as necessary, about 35 minutes.

Strain the stock through a fine-mesh strainer into a clean bowl and cool over ice. Discard the solids. Once the stock has cooled, transfer it to an airtight container. The stock will keep in the refrigerator for 3 to 4 days or several weeks in the freezer.

Fish Stock

YIELDS 8 CUPS

3 pounds bones and heads from white-fleshed fish, gills removed
1 teaspoon canola oil
1 yellow onion, sliced
1 leek (white and pale green parts only), sliced
2 celery stalks, sliced
1 head of garlic, halved crosswise
1 bunch parsley stems
1 bay leaf
2 fresh thyme sprigs
1 tablespoon whole white peppercorns
1 cup dry white wine
Sea salt

Rinse the fish bones and heads well under cold water. Using a large knife or cleaver, chop the fish bones into 3-inch pieces and place them in a large stockpot. Cover the bones with 2 inches of cold water. Bring the water to a boil over high heat. As soon as the stock boils, remove it from the heat and gently strain. Reserve the bones and discard the liquid.

Heat the oil in the same stockpot over medium heat. Add the onion, leek, celery, and garlic and cook until the leeks and onions are translucent, about 8 minutes. Add the parsley stems, bay leaf, thyme, peppercorns, and blanched fish bones and heads to the stockpot and pour the wine over. Bring the wine to a boil and cook until the wine has mostly evaporated, about 5 minutes. Cover the mixture with 10 cups of fresh cold water. Bring the stock to a boil and then reduce the heat and simmer gently, uncovered, until the stock develops a rich fish flavor, about 40 minutes. Using a ladle, push the foam from the center of the surface of the stock toward the side of the pot where it is easy to remove, and skim the impurities from the surface. Remove the pot from the stove, stir the stock again, and allow it to steep for 10 minutes.

Strain the stock through a fine-mesh strainer into a clean bowl and season lightly with salt. Chill the stock over ice. Discard the solids. Once the stock has cooled, transfer it to an airtight container. The stock will keep in the refrigerator for up to 3 days or several weeks in the freezer.

Veal Stock

YIELDS 10 CUPS

4 pounds veal bones, preferably from the legs
5 tablespoons canola oil
4 onions, halved (skins intact)
4 carrots, halved crosswise
4 celery stalks, halved crosswise
1 head of garlic, halved
¼ cup tomato paste
½ cup dry red wine
1 bouquet garni (1 dark green leek leaf, 10 parsley stems, 5 fresh thyme sprigs, 1 bay leaf; see page 305)
10 whole black peppercorns

Preheat the oven to 375°F. Place the veal bones in a large roasting pan and drizzle with 2 tablespoons of the canola oil. Roast the bones until they begin to brown, about 20 minutes. Turn the veal bones over and roast for an additional 10 minutes. Using a slotted spoon or tongs, transfer the bones to a heavy stockpot.

Cover the bones with 16 cups of cold water and bring to a boil over medium-high heat. Once the liquid begins to boil, reduce the heat to medium-low. Using a ladle or spoon, skim any fat or coagulated proteins from the top of the liquid.

While the veal bones are simmering, discard the fat from the roasting pan and place on the stovetop over high heat. Add the onions, cut side down, and sear until well charred, about 8 minutes. Add the remaining 3 tablespoons of oil, the carrots, celery, and garlic and cook until the vegetables begin to caramelize, about 5 minutes. Add the tomato paste and stir to combine. Once the tomato paste begins to darken, after about 2 minutes, add the wine and simmer for 1 more minute. Transfer the vegetables, along with the bouquet garni and peppercorns, to the pot with the simmering veal bones. Gently simmer for 2 hours, skimming the top as necessary. Strain the stock through a fine-mesh strainer into a clean bowl and cool over ice. Discard the solids.

Once the stock has cooled, transfer it to an airtight container. The stock will keep in the refrigerator for 3 to 4 days or several weeks in the freezer.

Vegetable Stock

YIELDS 5 CUPS

1 onion, thinly sliced
3 celery stalks, thinly sliced
½ fennel bulb, thinly sliced
5 fresh thyme sprigs
1 bunch parsley stems
1 teaspoon whole black peppercorns

Combine the onion, celery, fennel, thyme, parsley stems, and peppercorns in a medium pot along with 2 tablespoons water and place over medium heat. Sweat the vegetables just until they begin to wilt, making sure they do not develop any color. Add 6 cups of cold water and simmer for 30 minutes, skimming the top as necessary with a ladle or spoon.

Strain the stock through a fine-mesh strainer into a clean bowl set over a bowl of ice water to cool. Discard the solids. Once the stock has cooled, transfer it to an airtight container. The stock will keep in the refrigerator for 3 to 4 days or several weeks in the freezer.

Béchamel Sauce

YIELDS ABOUT 1½ CUPS

1½ cups whole milk
4 tablespoons unsalted butter
¼ cup all-purpose flour
Pinch of freshly grated nutmeg
Sea salt and freshly ground black pepper

Heat the milk in a small saucepan until small bubbles form around the edge.

Melt the butter in another small saucepan over medium heat until foamy. Add the flour and stir constantly with a wooden spoon until smooth and pale gold in color, about 2 minutes.

Slowly whisk the warm milk into the flour mixture until smooth. Simmer until thick and creamy, whisking constantly, about 3 minutes. Add the nutmeg and season to taste with salt and pepper. Transfer the sauce to a bowl. Press a sheet of plastic wrap directly onto the surface of the sauce to prevent a skin from forming. Cool completely. This can be stored in an airtight container in the refrigerator for up to 3 days.

Blanc

Blanc de Cuisson, or cooking in a white solution, is used abundantly in French cuisine when cooking white offal and certain vegetables. It allows the items being cooked to retain their color and prevents discoloration.

1 cup dry white wine
½ small onion, roughly chopped
4 garlic cloves, smashed
3 fresh thyme sprigs
1 bay leaf
1 tablespoon whole black peppercorns
⅓ cup all-purpose flour

Combine 8 cups of cold water with the wine, onion, garlic, thyme, bay leaf, and peppercorns in an 8-quart saucepan. Sift the flour into the liquid. Stir to combine and bring to a boil over medium-high heat. Remove the saucepan from the heat. Strain the liquid into a large clean saucepan and discard the solids. Bring the liquid to a boil before adding the desired vegetables to be cooked.

Bouquet Garni

Bouquet garni are simply bundles of herbs and aromatics wrapped with a 5-inch-long dark green leek leaf and tied together with kitchen string. To make the bouquet, spread the leek leaf open and place the herbs and aromatics in the middle. Fold the leaf tightly around the herbs, then wrap a piece of kitchen string around the leaf multiple times and tie to secure.

Clarified Butter

Clarified butter is melted butter with the milk solids removed. There are various ways to clarify butter, ranging from slowly cooking out the solids in a large wide pan set over low heat to melting the butter in the microwave and skimming the clarified butter off the top.

I prefer the second method. Place 2 sticks of butter in a glass measuring cup and melt the butter in the microwave. Allow the melted butter to sit for a minute or two and then skim the layer of foam off the top. Spoon the clear yellow liquid, or clarified butter, that is floating above the milky liquid at the bottom into a clean container. Discard the milky liquid. Clarified butter will keep for up to 1 week in the refrigerator.

Four-Spice Mix

Four-spice mix, or quatre épices, is a European blend of spices that can be found at many specialty markets. If you would like to make your own, the recipe is: 1 teaspoon ground white pepper; ½ teaspoon ground cloves; ½ teaspoon ground cinnamon; ¼ teaspoon freshly grated nutmeg.

Hard-Cooked Eggs

Place the eggs in a small saucepan and fill with enough cold water to cover the eggs. Add 1 teaspoon of white vinegar and a pinch of salt. Bring the water to a rapid boil, remove the pan immediately from the heat, and place a tightly fitting lid on top. After 11 minutes, remove the eggs from the pan and place them under cold running water until they are completely cool.

Roasted Garlic

Preheat the oven to 350°F. Trim ¼ inch off a head of garlic. Place the garlic in the center of a piece of aluminum foil and drizzle with 1 tablespoon of olive oil. Place 1 sprig of thyme and 1 bay leaf over the top of the garlic and wrap tightly in foil. Roast until the garlic is tender and golden brown, about 1 hour. When the garlic is cool enough to handle, squeeze the individual cloves from the skins.

Banana Ice Cream

The creamy mellow flavor of the banana is wonderfully offset by the tart crème frîache. For the ultimate late night snack I like to eat this ice cream with a drizzle of chocolate syrup and sprinkle of candied peanuts.

YIELDS ABOUT 2 CUPS

- 1 cup heavy cream
- 1 cup whole milk
- ½ vanilla bean, split lengthwise and seeds scraped
- ⅓ cup sugar
- 4 large egg yolks
- 2 ripe bananas, mashed
- 3 tablespoons crème fraîche or sour cream
- 1 tablespoon freshly squeezed lemon juice

Combine the heavy cream, milk, and scraped vanilla bean seeds in a medium saucepan and bring to a boil over medium heat. Whisk the sugar and egg yolks in a medium bowl to blend. Slowly and carefully pour the hot milk mixture into the egg mixture, stirring constantly to make sure the eggs do not cook.

Transfer the mixture back to the saucepan. Stir over low heat until the mixture thickens enough to coat the back of a wooden spoon or until the temperature reaches 180°F. Pour the custard into a clean large bowl set over an ice bath until cold.

Add the banana, crème fraîche, and lemon juice. Using a handheld immersion blender, mix until smooth. Strain through a fine-mesh strainer. Freeze in an ice cream machine according to the manufacturer's instructions.

Chai Ice Cream

YIELDS ABOUT 3½ CUPS

- 2 cups heavy cream
- 2 cups whole milk
- ¾ cup sugar
- 3 chai tea bags
- 8 large egg yolks

Bring the heavy cream, milk, and half of the sugar to a boil in a medium saucepan over medium heat. Remove the saucepan from the heat and add the tea bags. Allow the tea to steep for 20 minutes. Remove the tea bags and bring the mixture back to a boil.

Whisk the egg yolks and the remaining sugar in a medium bowl until pale and fluffy. Carefully pour the hot milk mixture into the egg mixture, whisking constantly to make sure the eggs do not cook.

Transfer the mixture back to the saucepan and cook over low heat, stirring constantly, until it is thick enough to coat the back of a wooden spoon or until the temperature reaches 180°F. Strain the mixture through a fine-mesh strainer into a clean mixing bowl set over an ice bath. Once cold, freeze the custard in an ice cream machine according to the manufacturer's instructions.

Chocolate Ice Cream

YIELDS 1½ CUPS

¾ cup + 3 tablespoons whole milk
3 tablespoons powdered milk
2 tablespoons sugar
1 tablespoon light corn syrup
3½ ounces milk chocolate (40% cocoa), chopped
1 ounce Vahlrona semisweet chocolate (66% cocoa), chopped
⅓ cup heavy cream
1 large egg

Bring the milk, powdered milk, sugar, and light corn syrup to a boil in a saucepan over medium heat, stirring constantly so that it does not begin to burn. Add both chocolates and continue to stir until the chocolates have completely melted. Whisk the cream and egg in a large bowl to blend. Pour the hot milk mixture over the egg mixture, stirring constantly to make sure the egg does not cook.

Transfer the mixture back into the saucepan and cook over low heat, stirring constantly, until it is thick enough to coat the back of a wooden spoon or until the temperature reaches 180°F. Strain the mixture through a fine-mesh strainer into a clean bowl set over an ice bath. Once cold, freeze the custard in an ice cream machine according to the manufacturer's instructions.

Coffee-Cointreau Crème Glace

YIELDS ABOUT 3½ CUPS

2 cups whole milk
1 cup heavy cream
½ cup + 1 tablespoon sugar
1 tablespoon powdered milk
1 tablespoon roughly chopped coffee beans
2 teaspoons Cointreau

Bring the milk, heavy cream, sugar, and powdered milk to a boil in a small saucepan over medium heat. Remove the pan from the heat and stir in the coffee beans. Cool and then cover with plastic wrap. Allow to infuse overnight in the refrigerator.

Strain and discard the beans. Stir the Cointreau into the milk mixture and freeze in an ice cream machine according to the manufacturer's instructions.

Dried Fruit Ice Cream

YIELDS ABOUT 4 CUPS

4 cups whole milk
⅔ cup honey
¼ cup light corn syrup
9 large egg yolks
¼ cup sugar
¼ cup dark rum
2 tablespoons chopped toasted walnuts
2 tablespoons finely diced dried apricots
2 tablespoons finely diced cherries or cranberries
2 tablespoons finely diced figs
2 tablespoons finely diced golden raisins

Bring the milk, honey, and corn syrup to a boil in a medium saucepan. Whisk the egg yolks and the sugar in a large bowl until pale and fluffy. Carefully pour the hot milk mixture into the eggs, whisking constantly to make sure the eggs do not cook.

Transfer the mixture back to the saucepan and cook over low heat, stirring constantly, until it is thick enough to coat the back of a wooden spoon or until the temperature reaches 180°F. Strain the mixture through a fine-mesh strainer into a clean bowl set it over an ice bath. Once cold, freeze the custard in an ice cream machine according to the manufacturer's instructions. Once the ice cream has properly churned, remove it from the machine and immediately fold in the walnuts and dry fruits.

Hazelnut Ice Cream

YIELDS 3 CUPS

1¼ cups heavy cream
1¼ cups whole milk
1½ vanilla beans, split lengthwise and seeds scraped
7 large egg yolks
½ cup sugar
⅓ cup hazelnut praline

Combine the heavy cream, milk, and vanilla bean seeds in a small saucepan and bring to a boil over medium heat. Whisk the egg yolks and sugar in a medium bowl until pale and fluffy. Carefully pour the hot milk mixture into the eggs, whisking constantly to make sure the eggs do not cook.

Transfer the mixture back to the saucepan and cook over low heat, stirring constantly, until it is thick enough to coat the back of a wooden spoon or until the temperature reaches 180°F. Strain the mixture through a fine-mesh strainer into a clean bowl set over an ice bath. Whisk in the hazelnut praline until fully combined. Once cold, freeze the custard in an ice cream machine according to the manufacturer's instructions.

Lime–Cottage Cheese Ice Cream

YIELDS 2 CUPS

¾ cup water
½ cup sugar
2 cups cottage cheese
Zest and juice of 1 lime

Combine the water and sugar in a medium saucepan and bring to a boil over medium heat. Simmer for 2 minutes. Remove the pan from the heat and stir in the cottage cheese and lime juice. Allow the mixture to cool slightly and then transfer to a blender and process until smooth. Strain through a fine-mesh strainer into a clean bowl. Fold in the lime zest and set the bowl over an ice bath. Once cold, freeze the mixture in an ice cream machine according to the manufacturer's instructions.

Milk Chocolate Ice Cream

YIELDS 3 CUPS

8 ounces milk chocolate (40% cocoa), chopped
2 cups whole milk
1 cup heavy cream
1 cup sugar
⅓ cup corn syrup

Place the chocolate in a medium bowl. Combine the, milk, heavy cream, sugar, and corn syrup in a medium saucepan and bring to a simmer over medium heat. Pour the warm milk mixture over the chocolate and stir until the chocolate melts and the mixture is well blended. Strain through a fine-mesh strainer into a clean bowl and set the bowl over an ice bath. Once cool, freeze the mixture in an ice cream machine according to the manufacturer's instructions.

Pumpkin Spice Ice Cream

YIELDS ABOUT 3 CUPS

2 cups heavy cream
2 cups whole milk
1 vanilla bean, split lengthwise and seeds scraped
2 tablespoons pumpkin pie spice
10 large egg yolks
¾ cup sugar

Combine the heavy cream, milk, scraped vanilla bean seeds, and pumpkin pie spice in a small saucepan and bring to a boil over medium heat. Whisk the egg yolks and the sugar in a medium bowl until pale and fluffy. Carefully pour the hot milk mixture into the egg mixture, whisking constantly to make sure the eggs do not cook.

Transfer the mixture back to the saucepan and cook over low heat, stirring constantly, until it is thick enough to coat the back of a wooden spoon or until the temperature reaches 180°F. Strain the mixture through a fine-mesh strainer into a clean bowl set over an ice bath. Once cold, freeze the custard in an ice cream machine according to the manufacturer's instructions.

Rum Ice Cream

YIELDS ABOUT 3 CUPS

2 cups heavy cream
2 cups whole milk
1 vanilla bean, split lengthwise and seeds scraped
10 large egg yolks
⅔ cup sugar
¼ cup dark rum

Combine the heavy cream, milk, and scraped vanilla bean seeds in a small saucepan and bring to a boil over medium heat. Whisk the egg yolks and sugar in a medium bowl until pale and fluffy. Carefully pour the hot milk mixture into the egg mixture, whisking constantly to make sure the eggs do not cook.

Transfer the mixture back to the saucepan and cook over low heat, stirring constantly, until it is thick enough to coat the back of a wooden spoon or until the temperature reaches 180°F. Strain the mixture through a fine-mesh strainer into a clean bowl set over an ice bath. Once cold, stir in the rum and freeze the custard in an ice cream machine according to the manufacturer's instructions.

Vanilla Ice Cream

YIELDS 2½ CUPS

1 cup heavy cream
1 cup whole milk
1 vanilla bean, split lengthwise and seeds scraped
5 large egg yolks
⅓ cup sugar

Combine the heavy cream, milk, and scraped vanilla bean seeds in a saucepan and bring to a boil over medium heat. Whisk the egg yolks and sugar in a medium bowl until pale and fluffy. Carefully pour the hot milk mixture into the egg mixture, whisking constantly to make sure the eggs do not cook.

Transfer the mixture back to the saucepan and cook over low heat, stirring constantly, until it is thick enough to coat the back of a wooden spoon or until the temperature reaches 180°F. Strain the mixture through a fine-mesh strainer into a clean bowl set over an ice bath. Once cold, freeze the custard in an ice cream machine according to the manufacturer's instructions.

Vermont Double Cream Ice Cream

YIELDS ABOUT 2½ CUPS

1¼ cups heavy cream
1¼ cups whole milk
1½ vanilla beans, split lengthwise and seeds scraped
7 large egg yolks
½ cup sugar
¾ cup Vermont Butter and Cheese Company crème fraîche

Combine the heavy cream, milk, and scraped vanilla bean seeds in a small saucepan and bring to a boil over medium heat. Whisk the egg yolks and sugar in a medium bowl until pale and fluffy. Carefully pour the hot milk mixture into the egg mixture, whisking constantly to make sure the eggs do not cook.

Transfer the mixture back to the saucepan and cook over low heat, stirring constantly, until it is thick enough to coat the back of a wooden spoon or until the temperature reaches 180°F. Strain the mixture through a fine-mesh strainer into a clean bowl set over an ice bath and whisk in the crème fraîche. Once cold, freeze the custard in an ice cream machine according to the manufacturer's instructions.

Almond Milk Sorbet

If I had to choose a favorite nut it would be the almond. It's sweet and rich and so versatile. By steeping ground almonds you capture all of the flavor while still creating a silky smooth sorbet.

YIELDS ABOUT 3 CUPS

3 cups whole milk
⅓ cup honey
1½ tablespoons light corn syrup
¼ cup finely ground blanched almonds
½ teaspoon almond extract

Bring the milk, honey, and corn syrup to a simmer in a medium saucepan over medium-high heat. Remove from the heat. Stir in the almonds. Allow the mixture to sit for 1 hour to infuse the flavors. Strain through a fine-mesh strainer; discard the solids. Stir the almond extract into the almond milk. Freeze in an ice cream machine according to the manufacturer's instructions.

Banana–Passion Fruit Sorbet

YIELDS ABOUT 3 CUPS

1½ cups + 2 tablespoons sugar
1½ cups water
1 cup store-bought passion fruit purée (see Chef's note)
1½ bananas, mashed with fork
2 tablespoons light corn syrup

Stir the sugar, water, purée, bananas, and corn syrup in a medium saucepan over medium heat until the sugar has melted, about 5 minutes. Strain the mixture through a fine-mesh strainer set over a clean bowl. Allow the mixture to cool. Freeze in an ice cream machine according to the manufacturer's instructions.

Chef's note ➤ To make your own passion fruit purée cut the passion fruits in half and scoop out the flesh. Strain the flesh through a fine-mesh strainer. Discard the solids and reserve the juice.

Candied Tangerine Sorbet

YIELDS ABOUT 2¾ CUPS

Candied Tangerine
5 tangerines, peeled, skins reserved
Pinch of salt
1½ cups Simple Syrup (page 314)

Tangerine Sorbet
1½ cups freshly squeezed tangerine juice
¾ cup Simple Syrup (page 314)
½ cup light corn syrup

Make the candied tangerine ➤ Thinly slice the tangerine peel into ⅛-inch-thick strips. Bring 1½ cups of water and a pinch of salt to a boil in a small saucepan over medium heat. Once the water reaches a boil, add the sliced tangerine peel and slowly bring back to a boil. Once the mixture is boiling, cook the peel for 1 minute more. Drain the tangerine slices and immediately rinse with cold water. Repeat this process 3 more times to ensure that any bitterness is removed from the peel.

Combine the simple syrup and blanched tangerine peel in a small saucepan and simmer over medium-low heat until the peel begins to look translucent, about 4 minutes. Transfer the candied tangerine to a clean bowl and refrigerate for at least 5 hours or overnight.

Make the tangerine sorbet ➤ Whisk the tangerine juice, simple syrup, and corn syrup in a large bowl until smooth. Freeze in an ice cream machine according to the manufacturer's instructions.

Drain the tangerine peel from the syrup. Roughly chop the peel and fold it into the frozen sorbet.

Chamomile Sorbet

YIELDS ABOUT 3½ CUPS

6 bags chamomile tea
2 cups Lemon Syrup (page 314)
¼ cup light corn syrup

Bring 2 cups of water to a boil in a small saucepan over high heat. Remove the pan from the heat and submerge the tea bags in the water. Allow to cool and then steep overnight in the refrigerator. Remove the tea bags and discard. Whisk the lemon syrup and corn syrup into the tea. Freeze in an ice cream machine according to the manufacturer's instructions.

Cherry Sorbet

YIELDS ABOUT 3 CUPS

2 cups store-bought cherry purée
1½ cups water
1 cup sugar
2 tablespoons freshly squeezed orange juice
1 tablespoon light corn syrup

Combine the cherry purée, water, sugar, orange juice, and corn syrup in a blender and process until smooth. Freeze in an ice cream machine according to the manufacturer's instructions.

Lemon Verbena Sorbet

YIELDS ABOUT 2½ CUPS

1½ cups water
1 cup Lemon Verbena Syrup (page 314)
½ cup light corn syrup

Whisk the water, lemon verbena syrup, and corn syrup in a large bowl to blend. Freeze in an ice cream machine according to the manufacturer's instructions.

Mandarin Sorbet

YIELDS ABOUT 4 CUPS

3 cups freshly squeezed mandarin orange juice
1½ cups light corn syrup
1½ cups Simple Syrup (page 314)
¼ cup freshly squeezed lemon juice

Whisk the orange juice, corn syrup, simple syrup, and lemon juice in a large bowl to blend. Freeze in an ice cream machine according to the manufacturer's instructions.

Piña Colada Sorbet

YIELDS ABOUT 2 CUPS

¾ cup pineapple juice
¾ cup unsweetened coconut milk
¼ cup sugar
2 tablespoons Bacardi light rum
2 tablespoons light corn syrup

Whisk the pineapple juice, coconut milk, sugar, rum, and corn syrup in a large bowl to blend. Strain the mixture through a fine-mesh strainer and freeze in an ice cream machine according to the manufacturer's instructions.

Simple Syrup

Simple syrup can be made in any quantity from a gallon to a thimbleful. It's all about the ratio of water and sugar. You can flavor your syrup with aromatics like herbs and dried spices by stirring them in after you take the pan off the heat. Allow the flavor to infuse the syrup and then strain before storing.

YIELDS 2 CUPS

1½ cups sugar
1½ cups water

Combine the sugar and water in a medium saucepan over medium-high heat. Bring to a simmer, stirring until the sugar fully dissolves. Remove the pan from the heat and allow to cool. The syrup will keep up to 2 weeks in an airtight container in the refrigerator.

Lemon Syrup

YIELDS 2 CUPS

2 cups Simple Syrup (see recipe above)
2 tablespoons lemon zest
1 vanilla bean, split lengthwise and seeds scraped

Combine the simple syrup, lemon zest, and vanilla bean and seeds in a medium saucepan over medium-high heat and bring to a boil. Remove the pan from the heat and allow to cool. Refrigerate overnight. Strain the syrup through a fine-mesh strainer and discard the solids. The syrup will keep up to 1 week in an airtight container in the refrigerator.

Lemon Verbena Syrup

YIELDS 1½ CUPS

1½ cups Simple Syrup (see recipe above)
1 vanilla bean, split lengthwise and seeds scraped
Zest of 1 lemon
30 lemon verbena leaves

Combine the simple syrup, vanilla bean and seeds, and lemon zest in a medium saucepan over medium-high heat and bring to a boil. Remove the pan from the heat and stir in the verbena leaves. Cover and allow to infuse overnight. Strain the syrup through a fine-mesh strainer and discard the solids. The syrup will keep up to 1 week in an airtight container in the refrigerator.

Ginger Syrup

YIELDS 1 CUP

1 cup sugar
1 cup water
1 piece (3 inches) fresh ginger, peeled and chopped

Combine the sugar and water in a medium saucepan over medium-high heat. Bring to a boil, stirring until the sugar fully dissolves. Add the ginger and remove the pan from the heat. Steep for 1 hour. Strain the syrup into a clean container and discard the solids. The syrup will keep up to 1 week in an airtight container in the refrigerator.

METHODS FOR COOKING VEGETABLES IN WATER

	Bring a large pot of salted water to a rolling boil. Add the vegetables and cook uncovered until tender. Remove the vegetables and plunge them into cold water.	Start the vegetables in cold water. Bring to a rapid boil and add salt. Cook the vegetables until tender. Remove them from the water and allow to cool.	Cook in the Blanc style (see page 305)
ARTICHOKE HEARTS			✖
ARTICHOKES	✖		
ASPARAGUS	✖		
BEETS		✖	
BELGIAN ENDIVE			✖
BOK CHOY	✖		
BROCCOLI	✖		
BRUSSELS SPROUTS	✖		
CABBAGE	✖		
CARDOONS			✖
CARROTS	✖	✖	
CAULIFLOWER	✖		
CELERY ROOT			✖
CORN	✖		
FAVA BEANS	✖		
FENNEL			✖
FIDDLEHEAD FERNS	✖		
FRESH SHELLING BEANS		✖	
GARLIC		✖	
GREEN BEANS	✖		
LEEK	✖		
PARSNIPS	✖	✖	
PEAS	✖		
POTATOES		✖	
RAMPS	✖		
RUTABAGA		✖	
SALSIFY	✖		
SNOW PEAS	✖		
SPINACH	✖		
SUNCHOKES		✖	
SWISS CHARD LEAVES	✖		
SWISS CHARD STALKS			✖
TURNIPS	✖	✖	
WINTER SQUASH	✖		

MEAT COOKING CHART

MEAT	FAHRENHEIT	CELSIUS
BEEF		
RARE	120°–125°	45°–50°
MEDIUM-RARE	130°–135°	55°–60°
MEDIUM	140°–145°	60°–65°
MEDIUM-WELL	150°–155°	65°–70°
WELL	160°	70°+
LAMB & VEAL		
RARE	135°	60°
MEDIUM-RARE	140°–150°	60°–65°
MEDIUM	160°	70°
WELL	165°+	75°+
PORK	160°–170°	65°–70°
CHICKEN & TURKEY	165°–175°	75°–80°

CONVERSIONS

LIQUID MEASURES	SOLID MEASURES
½ FLUID OUNCE = 3 TEASPOONS = 1 TABLESPOON	16 OUNCES = 1 POUND
1 FLUID OUNCE = 2 TABLESPOONS	20 OUNCES = 1¼ POUNDS
2 FLUID OUNCES = 4 TABLESPOONS = ¼ CUP	24 OUNCES = 1½ POUNDS
4 FLUID OUNCES = 8 TABLESPOONS = ½ CUP	28 OUNCES = 1¾ POUNDS
6 FLUID OUNCES = ¾ CUP	32 OUNCES = 2 POUNDS
8 FLUID OUNCES = 1 CUP	36 OUNCES = 2¼ POUNDS
10 FLUID OUNCES = 1¼ CUPS	40 OUNCES = 2½ POUNDS
12 FLUID OUNCES = 1½ CUPS	48 OUNCES = 3 POUNDS
16 FLUID OUNCES = 2 CUPS = 1 PINT	
24 FLUID OUNCES = 3 CUPS = 1½ PINTS	
32 FLUID OUNCES = 4 CUPS = 2 PINTS = 1 QUART	

SOURCES

PRODUCE

Lucky's Real Tomatoes

www.luckytomatoes.com

212-752-4775

A Brooklyn-owned and operated company that sells local farm-raised and hothouse beefsteak tomatoes year-round.

Satur Farms

www.saturfarms.com

631-734-4219

Located on the North Fork of Long Island, Satur Farms specializes in natural, pesticide-free salad greens, root vegetables, herbs, and heirloom tomatoes.

Melissa's

www.melissas.com

Melissa's is a distributor of exotic fruits and vegetables from around the globe.

MEAT

De Bragga and Spitler

www.debragga.com

A New York City company that sells high-quality meat, including American Wagyu beef, and poultry, lamb and sausages.

Jamison Farm

www.jamisonfarm.com

800-237-5262

The Jamison's picturesque 210-acre farm produces some 5,000 lambs annually, which are destined for great cooks at home and the finest chefs and restaurants in the world.

FOIE GRAS & GAME

D'Artagnan

www.dartagnan.com

800-327-8246

World-renowned purveyor of foie gras, duck, and game.

Hudson Valley Foie Gras

www.hudsonvalleyfoiegras.com

845-292-2500

Specializes in American foie gras, duck confit, and other duck products.

FISH

The Lobster Place

www.lobsterplace.com

212-255-5672

Offers a complete line of incredibly fresh finfish, shellfish, and shrimp, as well as specialty items, like caviar and smoked fish. Will ship overnight to any location in the continental United States.

Widow's Hole Oyster Company

www.widowsholeoysters.com

631-477-3442

Family-owned and operated oyster farm. Will ship fresh-from-the-bay oysters anywhere in the continental United States.

BREAD

Sullivan Street Bakery

www.sullivanstreetbakery.com

212-265-5580

Bakers of some of the finest artisan bread in New York with several stores throughout the city. Also available at many gourmet markets.

CHEESE & CURED MEAT

Murray's Cheese

www.murrayscheese.com

(888) MY CHEEZ or 888-692-4339

Murray's Cheese shops are breathtaking and delightfully stinky. Their website and online store provides great information about cheese and cheese makers and helps you find exactly what you are looking for as well as introduce you to hundreds of different cheeses.

La Quercia

www.laquercia.us

515-981-1625

A premier site for learning about and purchasing American artisanal cured meats.

Salumeria Biellese

www.salumeriabiellese.com

212-736-7376

Specializes in old world Italian-style sausages and salumi.

SPICES

Kalustyan's

800-352-3451

www.kalustyans.com

A New York City landmark for international foods and spices with a focus on Asian products and an extensive online catalog.

TRUFFLES

Plantin America

www.plantin.com

888-595-6214

This French-based company was founded in 1930. Their American outpost sells seasonal truffles and all types of truffle products online.

Urbani Truffles and Caviar

www.urbanitruffles.com

215-699-8780

Italian truffle, exotic mushroom, and caviar purveyor.

BAKING NEEDS

The Hamptons Honey Company

www.hamptonshoney.com

888-365-2325

Leading provider of local, raw, artisanal honey located in Long Island, NY.

Mapleland Farms Syrup

www.maplelandfarms.com

518-854-7669

Upstate New York producer of award-winning maple syrup and other maple confections.

JB Prince

www.jbprince.com

800-473-0577

Retailer of a great selection of professional kitchen tools and equipment.

New York Cake and Baking Distributors

www.nycake.com

212-675-2253

Specializes in all your baking needs from cake pans to candied flowers.

Paris Gourmet

www.parisgourmet.com

800-727-8791

Online store sells a wide range of products like fruit purées, chocolate, and nut products.

DISHES & PROPS

Elephant Props

www.elephantprops.com

212-488-6030

A full-service prop house located in the Chelsea neighborhood of Manhattan. They provide a wide range of beautiful rental props for print and film.

Prop Company, Maxine Kaplan and Associates

212-691-7767

Many of the beautiful dishes and props in the photos were provided by these two companies. They have an amazing array of wares to choose from.

RECIPE INDEX

Spring

Cocktails

Appetizers

Main Courses

Desserts

Breakfast

Summer

Cocktails

Appetizers

Main Courses

Desserts

Breakfast

Fall

Cocktails

Appetizers

Main Courses

Desserts

Breakfast

Winter

Cocktails

Appetizers

Main Courses

Desserts

Breakfast

SUBJECT INDEX

Pages with illustrations are indicated in italics.

N

O

P

T

V

W

Z